Mikhael Ramadan

IN THE
SHADOW
OF SADDAM

Translated into English by Jalel al-Qedenni
Revised and dramatised by John O'Toole

GreeNZone

AUCKLAND   LONDON

A GreeNZone Publication

First published in New Zealand 1999

ISBN 0 473 05305 5

Printed and bound in Great Britain by
Caledonian International Book Manufacturing

Typeset in Sabon by Kestrel Data, Exeter

Jacket photograph by Rex Features
Author photograph by Jallah al-Qedenni

GreeNZone Publishing – a division of GreeNZone Ltd

To my wife, Amna, my children, Nadia and Salih, my father, Ramadan, and my mother, Naziha. Memories of you all will burn within my heart until Allah grants that we be reunited once again. Rest in peace.

To Abdul Yunis, my very good friend, who I left behind.

To Latif and those who remain in Iraq fighting for freedom and whom I hope one day to rejoin.

To my family and friends who are still in Iraq and burdened by the cancer that destroys our beloved country.

To Ahmed for his invaluable assistance in preparing and writing this book, and Jalel for the painstaking translation, which I cannot vouch for but which I am sure is impeccable.

To John, who edited and revised the original manuscript so that a wider audience may fully understand the realities of life in Iraq under Saddam.

And, above all, to Sophie to perhaps compensate in some small measure for the suffering she has endured at the hands of my fellow countrymen.

Preface

Over the past five months, I have dictated this story to my friend, whom I shall refer to as Ahmad Mohammed, which is not his real name. It is Ahmed who has patiently listened to my ramblings, recorded them and prepared the typescript. The first draft, in Arabic, came to more than 250,000 words. It was Ahmad who compressed it to a more manageable 100,000.

This was then given to Jalel al-Qedenni, another good friend, who translated the work into English and, once the final draft was prepared, back into Arabic for my alterations, amendments and final approval.

I am also grateful to John O'Toole, who sadly I may never meet. He worked tirelessly to help bring the book up to the required standard for publication.

With regard to the book's contents, not all the names included are necessarily genuine. Some have been changed to protect the identity of those still vulnerable to the evils of Saddam's regime. Others I have simply forgotten with the sands of time. Place and dates, too, may occasionally suffer for the same reason. Where such instances occur, the responsibility is mine.

None of this detracts from the fact that all that has been included in these pages is to the best of my knowledge true. To this effect, I have sworn in Affidavit before a US attorney-at-law.

Mikhael Ramadan
November 1998

Statement

Al-Qedenni is not my real name, but has been used for the purposes of anonymity in the course of translating Mikhael Ramadan's book. I was raised in the United States by my Iraqi mother, who left her home country in 1952. I am bi-lingual Arabic-English and am employed professionally as an interpreter. For my part, the translation for this book was derived from the original text recorded by Ahmad Mohammed. The only alterations I made were to eliminate repetition and grammatical errors.

Jalel al-Qedenni
November 1998

Statement

For dramatic effect, and to avoid lengthy passages of narrative, I have in the course of re-writing Mikhael Ramadan's manuscript made extensive use of direct speech. Mikhael's own recollections of conversations that took place up to twenty years ago are obviously subject to any person's ability to recall in detail what was said so long ago. In such cases, the dialogue is merely as Mikhael remembers it, and in content is a reflection of the exchanges as they took place.

My own reconstruction of dialogue occurs where the original manuscript clearly indicates a conversation took place and where, in my opinion, the reader is best served by the use of direct speech.

This published version of Mikhael's testimony was translated back into Arabic by Jalel al-Qedenni and personally read, edited and approved by Mikhael himself.

John O'Toole
December 1998

In The Shadow of Saddam

Prologue

As the first and most prominent of a number of operational 'doubles' utilised by Saddam Hussein, I was many times a witness to the instruments of terror with which he and his family govern Iraq. For the best part of two decades, I watched as Saddam imposed his absolute authority on his people, brutally eradicating those who dared to oppose him. The written word cannot properly convey the real horror of my experience, but nothing I have recorded here is the product of my imagination, nothing is exaggerated. Indeed, I have found it difficult to fully describe the depths of perverse oppression to which so many Iraqis are subjected.

The decision to reveal such horrors was not taken lightly. I deliberated at length on the possibility that my story could seriously endanger the lives of those people who continue to work against Saddam. Even former revolutionaries and dissidents in exile like myself enjoy only a relative freedom. The overseas activities of Saddam's general intelligence department, al-Mukhabarat, are well documented and have been sufficiently successful to allow few of us to sleep easily in our beds. I have, therefore, avoided implicating those who are not already dead and, to this end, some minor particulars have been altered to disguise the true identity of those involved.

During the course of my service inside the presidential palace, I was in regular personal contact with Saddam and on familiar terms with senior members of his administration and the ruling Ba'ath Socialist Party. Later, I became involved with those disaffected elements of Iraqi society who conspire to overthrow the regime. Although it is impossible for me to recall word for word what was said as long as twenty years ago, I have recorded my encounters with them all as I remember them. The dialogue here is to all intents and purposes an accurate reflection of those exchanges as they occurred. Where there are errors, they are due to lapses of my own memory, but I have endeavoured to reveal the true nature of Saddam's power base and its destructive effect on Iraqi people of all religious and political persuasions as accurately as I can.

This is, however, not my principal purpose.

Despite my many fears and reservations, there are solemn reasons that compel me to tell my story. A few months before my duplicity was exposed and I was forced to flee Iraq, I became aware of the means by which Saddam intends to defeat the nations who stand against him. What I am able to reveal will both help to explain Iraq's recent determination to confront Britain and the United States and declare in the strongest terms the potent threat Saddam represents to millions of people across the Western world.

Throughout the period it has taken me to put my testimony together, I have been careful to confide in only a handful of people, but in order that my evidence be taken seriously, I have decided to be candid about my own complicity. I am aware that I frequently leave myself open to criticism and ridicule. My actions and attitudes were often inconsistent and contradictory and I was not always as courageous as I would like to have been. My naivety in the early years of my association with Saddam embarrasses me now, but a public declaration of my own ineptitude is a small price to pay if it means the world will listen.

For listen it must.

I arrived in North America in early December, 1997. After a few days I was moved to a 'safe' house, if indeed any house can be truly safe from the long reach of Saddam. How long I will be able to stay here is subject to conditions entirely beyond my control.

As an ordinary Arab, devoid of any personal ambition, it is sometimes difficult for me to comprehend how I became embroiled in the terrifying power struggle that constantly pervades the life of Saddam. I was a man who wished for nothing more than to live out his life quietly and in peace. For no other reason than my striking resemblance to the Iraqi President, this has been forever denied me. The only hope I have for the future is that one day Saddam's power structure will collapse and I will be able to return home.

I do not hold my breath awaiting this day.

My full name is Mikhaelef Ramadan Abu Salih al-Kadhimi, the only son of Ramadan Salih and Naziha al-Bahu. I was born in 1944 in the city of Karbala, 100 kilometres south-west of Baghdad, where the tension between the two Islamic factions of Shi'a and Sunni Moslems has in many ways exemplified the religious divide that has burdened Iraq since its conception in the wake of the first world war.

The population of Iraq is almost entirely Moslem, although this is broken down into the three quite separate ethnic-religious factions of Arab Shi'a, Arab Sunni and Kurds. The Kurds, too, are Moslems, most of whom are Sunni. Of the three groups, the Arab Sunni are just the smallest, but it is they who hold the political ascendancy; Saddam, his family and most of those holding positions of authority are Sunni Moslems. Although Karbala is a predominantly Shi'a city, my family, too, are also Sunni.

The theological schism between the Sunni and Shi'a goes back to the 7th century when Ali Ibn-Abi-Talib, cousin and son-in-law of the Prophet Mohammed, was successfully challenged for the position of head (or Caliph) of the Islamic movement by Mu'awiya Ibn-Abi-Sufiyan, governor of Syria, from the Umayyad clan of Makkah (Mecca). As Mu'awiya was supported by rich merchants, Ali became the champion of the underprivileged and remains to this day a potent icon of revolt against wealth and privilege for the Shi'atu Ali, the followers of Ali. Located in Karbala, Iraq is the tomb of Hussein, the most sacred site of pilgrimage for all Shi'a Moslems. Grandson of the Prophet Mohammed and second son of Ali, Hussein was killed in battle in 680AD by the Umayyad on the plains of Karbala and *al-ashura*, his day of martyrdom on the tenth day of the Hijrah calendar month of Muharram, is passionately celebrated each year by Shi'a Moslems.

My father was a schoolteacher, as I was myself until 1979. He was born and raised in Kadhimia, just a few kilometres to the north-west of Baghdad along the Nahr al-Dijlah (River Tigris), where he met and married my mother, Naziha al-Bahu, who was also his second cousin. After my sister, Wahab, was born in 1939, the family moved to Karbala when my father was offered a post as deputy head teacher of a school in a residential Sunni district of the city.

Before the Iranian Revolution fo the Shi'a in 1979, the Ayatollah Khomeini lived in exile for more than a decade in either Karbala or al-Najaf, eighty kilometres to the south where the Imam (head of the Shi'a) Ali is buried. Khomeini frequently irritated the Iraqi government with his claims that the Shi'a shrines of both cities were not subject to Iraqi sovereignty. In 1977, he accused the government of being responsible for the death of his son, Mustapha, who was killed in a car accident in Karbala in what were widely reported as being 'suspicious circumstances'. Thus, Saddam and Khomeini became implacable enemies long before they both came to power – coincidentally, in the same year.

Saddam was already well known in the corridors of

power when he first came to the attention of the Iraqi public in late 1969. Formally elected as a member of the Revolutionary Command Council (RCC), Iraq's governing body, he was immediately elevated to Vice-President to the Premier, Ahmad Hassan al-Bakr, a distant cousin of his mother. In practical terms, Saddam had occupied those positions for more than a year, but he was ever mindful of how swiftly the only previous Ba'athist government had been overthrown; not until the new regime's most dangerous opponents were removed would he become publicly associated with it.

It was in the spring of 1970 when a fellow teacher jokingly congratulated me on being given the honour of escorting President al-Bakr to a Pan-Arabian summit meeting in Baghdad. In his hand was a copy of the official organ of the Ba'ath Socialist Party, *al-Thawra* ('The Revolution'), and spread across the front page was a photograph of the President in the company of Saddam Hussein. It was the first time I had seen the man's face and the similarity between us startled me. As Saddam's notoriety spread, so did the frequency with which I was mistaken for him.

My father, Ramadan, died in 1975 after a long illness, and as Wahab, my only sibling, was already married and living in Baghdad, I lived alone with my mother in an apartment close to the city centre of Karbala. I had never seriously considered marriage, although, in the Arab tradition, I was offered an array of cousins who were willing to be my wife. It had been my father's dearest wish that I should present him with a grandson, but it was not until six months after his death that I met Amna Pasha al-Rabaka, a new teacher at my school and some ten years younger than myself. We could never be described as a passionate couple, but developed a deep fondness for each other and were soon engaged to be married. With two modest but reasonable salaries, we would have an income sufficient to meet our moderate needs.

Amna's father, Pasha Latif al-Rabaka, had in his

younger days been an active member of the Iraqi Communist Party (ICP), and he nearly choked when Amna took me to meet him for the first time. The ICP had some years earlier formed a Socialist alliance with the Ba'athists, but it soon became clear that radical, left-wing policies were never to be a part of Saddam's political agenda. In consequence, it had become increasingly less 'fashionable' to be associated with known ICP activists. Over the years, the Ba'athist movement had gradually drifted to the right of the political spectrum to become a cult of personality in a way remarkably similar to Adolf Hitler and the Nazi Party in the 1930s. What remained of the Ba'athist spirit of *al-ishtirakiya* (socialism) with which it was born in 1947, had long since disappeared.

Pasha's hatred for Saddam was no secret within the family and as I stood before him for the first time, the image of his most despised enemy, it was several moments before he could speak.

'You are very like Saddam,' he said finally, spitting out the Vice-President's name. 'Are you related?'

'Not even remotely,' I replied. 'Both my parents were born in Kadhimia. We have no connections with the al-Takritis.'

Pasha nodded, but remained stern-faced. 'I do not envy you your looks,' he added, before returning to the book he held in his hands.

Once he became used to me, I found him to be an engaging man who was passionate in his beliefs. In those days I had no interest in political theory, but Pasha argued that while Iraqis continued to define themselves as Arab or Kurdish and Shi'a or Sunni, there would be no peace in our country. Only when we realised that, as a proletarian class, we were all exploited by imperial and capital interests sustained by a self-serving Iraqi elite, could we hope to ever liberate ourselves.

Pasha died during the Islamic month of Jumaada al-Thany, in the year my story begins, but his spirit lived on in his children. With her three brothers, Latif, Rafik and

Abdullah, Amna was totally opposed to the despotic law of Saddam, though she accepted my indifference and enjoyed teasing her Communist friends whenever I was introduced to them. On one occasion I was in the bathroom of her parents' home when a cousin called, carrying a copy of the Communist Party newspaper, *Tariq al-Sha'b* ('Road of the People') and generally calling Saddam fit to burn. She raised a finger to her lips.

'Be quiet, Azzam, we have a visitor who would be most interested in your indiscretions!' At that moment, I re-entered the lounge and the blood drained from Azzam's face as he set eyes on me. Amna fell to the floor in a fit of laughter. Even after I had revealed to him my real identity, it was some time before he could enjoy the joke.

More and more frequently I was mistaken for Saddam and stopped in the street by people wishing to shake my hand. Once, on a school visit to Baghdad, I was mobbed by a group of Saddam's supporters in Zowrah Park. It was a nuisance and an intrusion, and I was not flattered. But I learned to live with it.

Chapter One

1979
Safar 1399 – Safar 1400

The early months of 1979, which began with the second Islamic month of Safar in the Hijrah year of 1399, saw a significant increase in the activities of the Mukhabarat, the government's general intelligence department led by Saddam's half-brother, Barzan Ibrahim al-Takriti. The towns and cities were cleared of known or suspected political opposition and thousands of people, many of whom had only the most obscure connections with dissident elements, were arrested. Hundreds of students were snatched from their colleges and an incalculable number of apparently innocent people disappeared forever. In my opinion, the rumours of torture inflicted on those arrested were exaggerated and I chose to dismiss them. I was forced to confront the truth when I walked into the school staff room one afternoon and found Amna comforting Aeshah, one of the older teachers, who was sobbing at her desk.

The woman's husband, also a teacher, had disappeared three days earlier. Her twenty-two-year-old son had arrived at the school to break the news that his father was dead. The son, clearly distressed himself, pulled me to one side and told me what had happened. A government official had called at the house to inform his mother that her husband's body was in the city mortuary and was to be collected at the earliest opportunity. The son, deeply shocked and hoping it was a case of mistaken identity, rushed off to the mortuary to collect his father's body and had very nearly been arrested himself.

'When I arrived there,' he said in a subdued tone, 'and told them the reason for my visit, they refused at first to let me see my father. Only my mother, they said, was permitted to view his body. When I insisted they threatened me with arrest, but one of the officials took pity on me. I was shown the body, which was indeed my father's, and told to make immediate arrangements to have it collected.'

With some difficulty, the young man described the condition of his father's tortured remains.

'His shoulders and legs were full of small holes, as if he had been pierced by some kind of a skewer. His fingernails had been ripped away and there was the remains of a plastic cable melted onto his finger tips from where he had been electrocuted. They finished him off with a bullet to the brain.'

He was mystified as to why his father had been arrested. 'He is . . . was a schoolteacher. He has never so much as spoken out against the regime. Perhaps a member of the Mukhabarat is a former pupil of his, who holds a grudge. I have heard that personal vendettas are carried out in such purges.'

Now he too broke down and began to weep.

Never before had I heard an eye-witness account of such an atrocity. I did not doubt the young man's integrity, but felt sure he must have exaggerated his father's injuries. What would be the point of torturing a schoolteacher?

Such was my innocence. It was not to last.

Saddam was still officially Vice-President, but had for a number of years been the real 'power behind the throne'.

He saw his former allies in the ICP as a threat to his position and in April the offices of the *Tariq al-Sha'b* were closed down and their presses confiscated.

After so much repressive activity, it was no coincidence when a few weeks later Ahmad Hassan al-Bakr was persuaded to stand down as President on the grounds of failing health and his office, without even the most limited democratic process taking place, was passed to Saddam. Almost immediately, the Central Committee of the ICP declared their total opposition to the move and called for the formation of a Democratic Patriotic Front to establish an open democracy in Iraq. Saddam reacted swiftly and many prominent Communists were executed. Even the generally acknowledged moderate, Tariq Aziz, a familiar figure to Westerners since the Gulf War, showed no sympathy. He believed Communists had no place in the new Iraq and said as much on national television.

'If they wish to be martyrs,' he declared with dispassion, 'we will oblige them.'

The occasions on which I was now mistaken for Saddam increased tenfold. Apart from the fact that his photograph now appeared daily in the newspapers, he had ordered giant posters of himself to be erected across every town and city in Iraq. In Karbala, I was confronted by scores of giant images of myself all over the city, some of them ten metres high.

Instead of staring at me inquisitively, people were now startled when I appeared. I would walk into shops and a deathly hush would descend. Shopkeepers served me without delay and with excessive respect. I found it harder to adjust to how some of my old acquaintances began to treat me differently. The head teacher at my school embarrassed me with his deference.

At the end of July Saddam 'uncovered' a conspiracy to assassinate him. Despite the ease with which he had assumed the presidency, he was not without enemies inside the RCC. Muhie Abdullah Mashadi, the Secretary-General, had demanded a vote on al-Bakr's replacement and, as it

3

was essential to Saddam's survival that this early challenge be thwarted, Muhie was arrested and tortured. At a meeting of Ba'ath party leaders, a broken Muhie was forced to admit his part in a plot to overthrow Saddam and to name his co-conspirators. As a result, sixty-eight civilian and military leaders of the Ba'ath party were arrested, five of whom were members of the RCC. All of those accused were actual or potential opponents of Saddam. Following a court of inquiry, orchestrated throughout by Saddam, sixteen of the conspirators, including the five RCC ministers, were shot or hanged.

I know now that this represented only the more publicised elements of Saddam's first purge as President. In fact, more than 500 senior ranking Ba'athists were murdered on Saddam's direct orders. The families of more than one third of all members of the RCC and the Ba'ath party's National and Regional Commands were held hostage while the officials were forced to sign papers condemning their former colleagues. When the death sentences were carried out, the same men were forced to take part in the executions, thus binding themselves to Saddam with their enforced complicity. It is a technique Saddam uses to this day.

In all, tens of thousands of Iraqis are implicated in the evils of Saddam's regime. Apart from the enormous number, like myself, who have ignored the murder or disappearance of friends and neighbours, most Iraqi men have endured long terms of service in the army and been party to the brutalization of both conscripts and ordinary citizens. Many others, whether willingly or coerced, have provided the security services with information that has led to the arrest and killing of countless innocent people. Within the security services, many thousands have taken part in the rape, torture and murder of hundreds of thousands of Iraqis. The river runs deep and many of my countrymen have bathed in its waters.

Clearly, Saddam's immediate priority on becoming President was to consolidate his position. He had cleverly manipulated the Iraqi media during the entire pogrom and there were mass demonstrations in Baghdad in support of the death sentences passed on the 'conspirators'. The plot, it was announced, was a Syrian conspiracy to undermine the new regime and was supported by 'US imperialism in the interests of Zionism and the forces of darkness.' Amna's brother, Latif, wondered aloud why Syria would be remotely concerned with the 'interests of Zionism', but the mood of the masses was in the hands of Saddam.

In Syria, where the allegations were vehemently denied, the Ba'ath party was also in power, but their relations with Iraq had never been easy. In October 1978, Hafez al-Assad, the Syrian President, came to Baghdad and announced his desire to negotiate a political and economic alliance between the two countries. Saddam saw it as a dissolution of Iraqi influence in the Arab world and Syria's conciliatory overtures were firmly rejected.

One of the more consistent features of Saddam's reign has been his determination to dominate the Arab nations. 'The glory of the Arabs,' he declared, 'will grow from the glory of Iraq.' The discovery and public condemnation of the conspirators had enabled Saddam to kill two political birds with the one stone; any support for an alliance with the Syrians disappeared, as did the most potent of his political enemies.

As their father's connections with the ICP were well known to the authorities, the late months of 1979 were tense times for Amna and her three brothers. Although I was sure they had never personally been active themselves, mere association would have been justification enough for her brothers to be arrested. The only solution was to stay out of the way. Her two youngest brothers, Rafik and Abdullah went to stay with friends of their mother's family in al-Mawsil in the north, while the eldest, Latif was moved in with a cousin in al-Hillah some forty kilometres away. The danger for Amna, in a society where a woman's opinion was usually deemed irrelevant, was not so great, but even she had to maintain the lowest of profiles and be most careful not to be seen associating with known dissenters. I heard of many women who disappeared at this time and accounts of entire families being dragged from their homes by the Mukhabarat were commonplace.

In contrast, my brother-in-law, Akram Salem al-Gailani, saw the whole episode as a glorious cleansing of all the disparate elements from Iraqi society. With my sister, Wahab, in full support, he would rejoice in the removal of those who sought to negate the political crusade upon which Saddam had embarked. He is a man limited in his ability to reason and much of what he espoused was lifted directly, *ad verbum*, from the pages of *al-Thawra*. A couple of years earlier, Wahab had persuaded him to join the Ba'ath Socialist Party for no other reason than to further his civil service career. Saddam had announced that all Iraqis, whether they wished it or not, were Ba'athists. Keen to avoid any ambiguity, Akram had signed up notwithstanding.

Though I seldom saw them, neither Akram nor Wahab were easy company, but I was careful to hold my tongue in their presence. They were precarious times and I did not entirely trust Akram to favour the family over the party. Frequently tempted though she was to put him straight, Amna, too, was shrewd enough not to challenge his sometimes outrageous political assertions.

Like most people in Iraq, I did not have a telephone and had to make use of a communal phone located near the entrance to my apartment block. I had just returned home from school one Thalathah (Tuesday) in October when a shout from the stairwell announced that my sister, Wahab, was on the line from Baghdad. When I picked up the receiver, she was in such a state I could barely understand her.

'Mikhaelef! Mikhaelef! You have to come to Baghdad! You will not believe it! You have to come at once!'

I held the receiver away from my ear and frowned. This was so typical of Wahab. Whenever she wanted something, we were all expected to drop everything and rush to her side.

'Please, Wahab, be calm. Are you unwell? What has happened?'

Her voice exploded in reply. 'What has happened? Everything has happened! Akram has just come home from work. He has a message for you!'

'A message for me? Who from?' I could think of nobody in Baghdad who might wish to contact me.

'Who from? Who from? Are you an idiot? From the President!'

'The president of what, Wahab?' I truly had no idea to whom she was referring.

She screamed with exasperation. 'The President of Iraq, you fool! Saddam! Saddam Hussein wants to see you!'

Had I thought Wahab possessed anything resembling a sense of humour, I would have suspected she was playing some sort of practical joke on me.

'Wahab, what is this about?'

She took great delight in telling me.

Her husband, Akram, had been employed for a number of years as an insignificant but self-important official at the Baghdad city hall. Apparently, he had mentioned to his immediate superior how his brother-in-law in Karbala was the image of the new President, no doubt believing in some obscure way that this meaningless fact would reflect well on him. For once, he was right. Word filtered through to the presidential palace and that morning Akram had been called into the office of Khairallah al-Talfah, the mayor of Baghdad and Saddam's uncle, a man previously unaware of his existence. He told my incredulous brother-in-law that the President had been informed of my looks and was curious enough to want to see for himself. To my utter astonishment, I was summoned to meet Saddam the following day.

Amna was troubled by the news. She did not trust Saddam or any member of his nepotic circle and was worried the whole thing might be some kind of a trap. My own view was scarcely less sanguine, yet to set her mind at rest I made light of her fears.

7

'What kind of trap?' I asked her scornfully. 'If Saddam wants to put me in prison, he has only to click his fingers. I am a schoolteacher. What could I do?'

'Then what does he want with you?'

'You are like your father, Amna. Your head is full of plot and intrigue. The President has been told I am like his twin and he would like to see me. For his entertainment, perhaps. It matters little, anyway. I can hardly refuse to go.' For all my bravado, I was quaking inside.

The following morning I was collected by car and taken to my sister's apartment on Umal Street in the al-Ishbiliya district of Baghdad, some two hours drive away. Akram had somehow managed to have himself appointed as my escort and Wahab fluttered about us like a bathing sparrow. She is an incredibly irritating woman at the best of times, but on this morning she was impossible. The very idea that her husband and brother had been granted a personal audience with the 'wonderful' Saddam was beyond the most extravagant of her dreams.

At precisely eleven o'clock, two officers of the Republican Guard, Saddam's own personal security unit, arrived at the apartment and ushered Akram and myself into a bedroom. We were both ordered to undress. I hesitated, exchanging an anxious glance with Akram, but one of the guards quickly stepped forward.

'Why do you have a problem with this?' he said, smiling. 'We are taking you to see the most important man in the Arab world. A man who has enemies. Nobody is permitted to be in the presence of the President unless we have first ensured they carry no weapons. It is simply routine, but there are no exceptions. Please, Saddam awaits you.'

The search was completed within a few minutes, following which we were immediately led from the apartment and loaded into a waiting black BMW. The car pulled away at speed and we left Wahab waving and sobbing happily behind us. Crossing over the Qanaht al-Jaish (Army Canal), we drove along Thawra Street, before turning north and passing the Bab al-Wastani (the Middle

Gate), the only surviving gate of Baghdad's ancient city wall, built nearly 900 years ago. Shortly, we entered the exclusive residential district of Cairo, in the north-west area of the city, and within minutes arrived outside an elegant two-storey mansion, which I correctly assumed to be one of Saddam's several private residences.

We were escorted into the house and taken along a poorly lit hallway, passing several smartly-uniformed guards. A door to the right was opened and we were shown into a vast, superbly decorated room. In contrast to the hallway, here there was an impressive blend of light and splendour, quite breathtaking in its simplicity. The walls and ceiling were an immaculate white plaster, highlighted with ornate panels of gold leaf. Around the room were many ancient relics and works of art that I was unable to identify, but felt sure were a reflection of Saddam's obsession with the ancient civilisations of Mesopotamia, referred to in the Middle East as *Rafidain*, the 'land of the two rivers'. On the banks of the Dijlah and the Nahr al-Furat (River Euphrates), where the great walled city of Babylon had once stood, archaeologists have uncovered treasures dating back more than six thousand years. I did not doubt that many had become the personal possessions of the new President.

In the centre of the room was a magnificent, burgundy-coloured rug bearing the official Iraqi seal, the cost of which no doubt exceeded the value of everything I owned. On it and facing each other were two pairs of straight-back chairs, fashioned in a style borrowed from the age of King Nebuchadnezzar.

Several men were standing about the room. I assumed them to be senior government ministers or hand-picked members of the Republican Guard, but I recognised only one. Taha Yasin Ramadan al-Jazrawi, a short, fat, unpleasant-looking man, and Commander-in-Chief of the Popular Army, the armed militia of the Ba'ath party. He had recently been promoted to First Deputy Prime Minister, but had been a member of the RCC for more than ten years. Though we shared the name Ramadan, I am pleased to report we were not related.

Arab names cause Europeans and Americans no end of trouble and we are frequently amused by attempts to 'Westernise' them. It is the tradition for Arab children to be given their father's first name as their own second. In my own case, Ramadan is my father's forename. Thus, calling me Mr Ramadan is like referring to John F Kennedy as Mr Fitzgerald.

Arab surnames, too, differ from those of the West in that they simply refer to a direct connection with an established family, an ancestral tribe or a place of birth. It is not uncommon for members of the same family to choose different surnames or for individuals to change them at particular stages of their lives. In fact, in an attempt to have the population perceive themselves as Iraqis rather than a product of a particular ethnic or religious group, Saddam banned the use of such names in 1970. This is taken more seriously by some than others and Saddam has not tried to enforce the legislation with any degree of dogma.

Another Arab tradition is to add the name of your eldest son to your own name. Hence, 'Abu Salih', in my case, refers to my being the 'father of Salih'. My family name is al-Kadhimi, meaning simply 'of Kadhimia', which I take out of respect for my father and his extended family.

One of the guards told Akram and myself to sit down. Within a minute we were on our feet again as Saddam entered the room in the company of his fifteen-year-old son, Udai, already the same height as his father. Saddam smiled broadly at us both and opened his arms to embrace me. By kissing both my cheeks in the Arab fashion, Saddam was showing me respect, treating me as an Arab brother. Taking a step back, he raised an open palm towards my face.

'Ha! Am I looking in a mirror?' He smiled broadly at those gathered around the room, then beckoned us to be seated. 'Please, take the weight from your feet. Sit down, sit down.'

I cannot recall ever being so nervous or overawed as I was that morning, though Saddam was hospitality personified. He is not by nature the most charismatic of men, it is his reputation that gives him such enormous presence in a room. I was scared to say anything in case I made a fool of myself. Akram was frozen rigid.

'Where is your mother from, Mikhaelef?' Saddam asked me, a mischievous smile breaking across his face.

'My mother was born and raised in Kadhimia, Your Excellency,' I answered.

Saddam responded playfully. 'I wonder if many years ago my father paid a visit to Kadhimia, eh, Mikhaelef, and met your mother. Maybe that would account for our likeness.'

I smiled politely. 'Yes, it would, Your Excellency.' I could hardly take offence and those assembled in the room, including Akram, joined in with Saddam's hearty laughter.

Looking closely at him for the first time, I was struck by the extraordinary aura of energy that he appears to exude. When his mouth is closed he has an intense, reflective appearance, but his open, expansive smile changes his countenance completely. His dark hair is combed back and waved and sits above a brow that shows remarkably few signs of his middle years. He has a solid, dimpled chin, and if our likeness and my own modesty precludes my calling him handsome, he nevertheless presents an imposing figure.

In contrast, Udai is long and lean and owes much of his appearance to his mother's side. While his nose is sharper than his father's, he shares Saddam's deep and penetrating eyes. I took an instant dislike to him, an impression that was to be reinforced as he matured and I got to know him better. It was a feeling that became mutual.

Saddam carried on in a playful manner for another few minutes, sometimes inviting those gathered around to compare our features. It was noticeable how cautious everybody was not to imply the slightest slur on Saddam. Although he is five years my elder, whenever comparisons were made those assembled clearly stressed he was just that touch more youthful. Young Udai made several derogatory remarks that were out of place for a boy of his age, but he is an extrovert in every way that his father is not.

'I do not think he looks like you at all, Father,' he said, displaying that cynical smile I was to become so familiar with. 'His nose is too thin and his eyes are weak. I believe he has the courage of a mountain sheep.' He stood up and stepped forward, gazing down on me from his already considerable height. 'Tell me, Mikhaelef Ramadan, do you have courage? Would you be able to do what my father has done? Could you stand against the might of the most vicious enemies with nothing more than the love of your family to protect you?' It was an impossible question to answer and my heart skipped and my hands trembled as I sought a way to extricate myself from the predicament in which I had been placed. It was Saddam who came to my salvation.

'Udai, be seated and show the man some respect. He is here as our guest. You should not tease him.'

Udai sat down again, smirking arrogantly as he looked to the guards for their approval. He had thoroughly enjoyed my discomfort and Saddam had to put his hand over Udai's arm before he spoke again.

'Please excuse my son's youthful exuberance, Mikhaelef, but perhaps it is natural for a son to be proud of his father. Do not take offence.'

'No offence has been taken, Your Excellency. He is a fine boy.' I had a natural flair for diplomacy.

'Indeed. Now, let me come to the point of your being here today.' He clicked his fingers and was approached by a house-servant carrying a large box of Havana cigars. He took one and lit it, at the same time indicating to the servant to offer the splendid box to Akram and myself. We both politely declined. 'You will understand,' Saddam continued, 'that my daily routine is congested. I know the people of Iraq idolise their President, but my responsibilities are such that I do not have the time I would like to spend with my people. Maybe, Mikhaelef, this is where you can help your President. Would you do me and, of course, the great people of Iraq an enormous service and perhaps stand in for me on occasion?'

'I do not understand, Your Excellency,' I said, bemused. I really could not comprehend what he meant.

'It is very simple,' he said, with his reassuring smile. 'Sometimes I like to be seen among the ordinary people of Iraq. Although I have overcome great difficulties in climbing to the mountain top, I do not forget that I was once at the foot of the valley. I was not, as the British used to say, born with a silver spoon in my mouth.' He looked up to those gathered around us.

'My mother owned just a wooden ladle for stirring the *mathruda* that we ate with our fingers!' As Saddam laughed, so did everyone else. 'My point is that I want the people to know I do not forget them. I am one of them, but it is difficult for me now to spend time doing the things my heart tells me I should. Opportunities are rare. Perhaps you could do this for me?'

'Of course, Your Excellency,' I said with a conviction that disguised my apprehension. 'But what exactly could I do?'

'You could do so much!' he exclaimed. 'You could visit hospitals, go to the poorer quarters of Baghdad or perhaps visit the children in the schools. Nobody would know the harmless truth and it would give so much pleasure to so many people. If you can do this, Mikhaelef Ramadan, I promise you will be generously compensated.'

It was dressed up as a request, but I was not so naive as to think I had any choice but to agree.

'If you wish it, Your Excellency, I will do it.'

Saddam clapped his hands. 'I never doubted you would help. No man could be so like me on the outside and be so very different on the inside, whatever Udai says.' He gestured to one of the guards, and only seconds later a tray

of coffee was brought in. 'As a young man I was imprisoned for nearly two years when fighting for my
nation's freedom—'

'The sacrifices you made, Your Excellency,' interrupted
Akram, all his sycophantic passion coming to the fore, 'are
well known to the Iraqi people.'

Saddam seemed to notice Akram's presence for the first
time.

'And you are Akram Salem, the brother-in-law, are you
not? The person responsible for bringing this man to my
attention?'

'Indeed, Your Excellency.'

'Well, Akram, you are, of course, correct.' Saddam
stubbed out his cigar, having taken only three or four
draws from it, before he went on. 'Many sacrifices were
made in those days, one of which was being denied the
pleasure of drinking coffee in prison. We were permitted
only bitter, black *chai*. My old friend, Izzat Ibrahim, was
with me back then.'

I do not enjoy coffee at the best of times, but took the
first of the three sips regarded as a courtesy when accepting
Arab hospitality.

Saddam spoke again. 'You are a teacher of young
children, Mikhaelef?'

'Yes, Your Excellency.'

'My wife, Sajida, teaches at a primary school, although
she is now a head principal. My uncle also. It is a most
important job. Nothing is as important to a nation as the
education and welfare of its children. Don't you agree?'

'Very much so, Your Excellency.'

Saddam then turned to Akram. 'You are not from
Karbala?'

'No, Your Excellency, I am a native of Baghdad.'

Saddam nodded. 'You have both enjoyed an urban
upbringing, whereas I was raised in a place too small to be
on the map.' Before he continued, he once again called for
his cigars. This was a habit of Saddam's with which I was
to become familiar. During the course of a day he may go

through as many as a hundred Havanas, seldom smoking the same one for longer than a few minutes.

Often when speaking, Saddam seems a little inhibited or detached, but now he spoke of his youth with pride. His early days are shrouded in mystery. He claims he was born on 28th April, 1937, in a small settlement by the name of Shu'waish, near to the town of Takrit. Lying on the banks of the Dijlah river, some 150 kilometres north of Baghdad, Takrit was sacked by marauding Tartar invaders some 600 years ago and a huge monument was erected there from the skulls of the vanquished. Later, a formidable fortress was built on the site.

Saddam claims Hussein Abd al-Majid, who allegedly died just before he was born, as his father. This is, in fact, a cover for an illegitimate birth. The real identity of his father is unknown and thus Saddam is, quite literally, the bastard that he has so often been loosely called. For this reason his opponents in Iraq often refer to him simply as Saddam al-Takriti, the absence of a paternal or family name being a direct insult to his parentage.

His "widowed" mother, Subha al-Talfah married Ibrahim Hassan al-Takriti, supposedly a relative of his 'father', whom Saddam detested. He was regularly beaten and humiliated by his stepfather. As he grew older, he took great satisfaction in revealing that to the men of the local community he was known as 'Ibrahim the liar'.

Saddam's official date of birth is also fiction. Prior to 1957, there was no precise registration of birthdates in Iraq. All babies were recorded as being born in the half-year commencing 1 January or the 1 July and Saddam was actually born in the second half of 1939. Prior to his first marriage he decided to add two years to his age so that he would appear to be the same age as his wife-to-be, Sajida Khairallah. In Iraq, it is unusual to marry a woman older than oneself. By pretending that he was born in April two years earlier, Saddam was also aligning his birth in the Hijri calendar with that of the Prophet Mohammed.

He was raised in an area where the main demographic unit was something in between a town and a tribe, known as *al-ashera* – a collection of close-knit communities. Despite being a Sunni Moslem, he later claimed the Imam Ali, grandson of the Prophet Mohammed and an early leader of the Shi'a faction, as a direct ancestor, thus making him a descendant of the Mohammedan Quraishi, tribe of the Prophet Mohammed. Since there are at least ten million people in the Islamic world who claim to be *al-Ashraf* – 'the honoured ones' – descended from the Prophet, it is hardly an exclusive club.

The nearest school was some fifteen kilometres away in the town of Takrit and it was his mother's family who overcame his stepfather's desire to have him working in the fields. At the age of ten he was sent to school and thereafter received a full-time education. He became a close friend of his cousin and fellow pupil, Adnan Khairallah, and later moved to Baghdad to attend the Khark Secondary School. There he lived with Adnan's father, his uncle Khairallah al-Talfah, a staunch Arab nationalist and a man who was to have a profound influence on Saddam's political development.

When martial law was imposed in 1956 by the government of Nuri al-Said, Saddam regularly took part in the street riots in support of the Arab nationalist revival inspired by Jamal Abd al-Nasser in Egypt. He became embroiled in the issues of the day and in 1956 joined the Ba'ath Socialist Party. He was no doubt in the thick of the rioting mobs in July the following year, when King Faisal II, the constitutional monarch, was murdered and his mutilated body dragged through the streets of Baghdad to be impaled on the gates of the Ministry of Defence.

The new government was led by Abdullah Karim Qassem, whose waning popularity led to a failed assassination attempt in October, 1959, in which Saddam was said to have taken part. Although bleeding profusely, he told Akram and myself he stitched his own wound and escaped, with the blessing of Allah, aboard a willing donkey fortuitously standing close by. He did not refer to the widely broadcast rumour that he was dressed as a woman at the time.

Later he fled to al-Qahirah (Cairo) via al-Dimashq (Damascus) and there enrolled at the university to study law. Saddam returned to Iraq without completing his degree, an omission he rectified in 1979 when he awarded himself a First Class Honours degree from Baghdad University.

In February 1963, Qassem was finally removed by a Ba'ath revolution and executed, his dead body displayed on national television. Saddam played a major part in the removal of Qassem and his ministers when he led a small group, armed with machine guns, into a government cabinet meeting. As Qassem was led to his death, his ministers were conducted to the airport and deported.

Shortly afterwards, he married Adnan's sister, his cousin Sajida Khairallah al-Talfah and for several months played a part in the purges of the National Guard until the Ba'athists were themselves overthrown and he was forced into hiding.

The following September, Saddam was arrested for plotting against the country's new leader, Colonel Abdullah-Salam Arif, but later escaped. When the colonel was killed in a helicopter crash in 1966, control passed to his elder brother, Major General Abdullah-Rahman Arif, an alcoholic and a man without the necessary guile and virulence for leadership in the Middle East. The Ba'athists prepared to seize power once again. On the morning of 17 July, 1968, Saddam led a tank assault on the presidential palace and the Ba'athists took control. Ahmad Hassan al-Bakr, a distant cousin to Saddam's mother, became President and, Saddam, as Deputy Chairman of the RCC, was installed as his Vice-President.

When Saddam became President himself, he coupled his determination to govern ruthlessly with a desire to be recognised as a paternal figurehead. He frequently staged visits to the homes of ordinary Iraqis for the benefit of the

Baghdad media, thinly disguising himself as a journalist. I watched him on television on numerous occasions, asking people what they thought of their President, his identity being blatantly obvious to everyone except, it seemed, those being questioned. Of course, they would say the most complimentary things imaginable. After a few minutes of engaging in this charade, Saddam would remove his hat, turn down his collar and all would gasp in amazement. I was always greatly amused by this, but it used to drive Amna's eldest brother, Latif, to distraction.

As well as Udai, Saddam has another son, Qusai, who was thirteen in 1979, and three daughters: Raghd, then eleven, Rana, nine and Hala, four. Saddam, with his wife, Sajida, was frequently photographed in the company of his adoring children, the family unit being of enormous importance in Arab culture. It was Saddam's dearest wish that his sons would follow him into government and Udai was already being groomed for high office.

Throughout the time it had taken Saddam to relate the story of his early life, he was not once interrupted. Much of what he told us was known to all literate Iraqis, but the manner in which he spoke was a revelation to me, showing him to be a man of enormous passion and great mental strength. Those who had underestimated him had not lived to regret it. They had not lived.

On the way back into the city, I was pleased with the way the meeting had gone. I found Saddam to be far less intimidating than I had feared, yet, perversely, I would have been disappointed had I not sensed the innate menace simmering within the man. I know that the people of the West cannot comprehend Saddam's popularity among certain sections of the Iraqi population and wonder if it is not entirely staged. It frequently is, but it is important to understand the region's traumatic history and how Arabs expect strength in their leaders, not compassion. This is deep-rooted in Iraqi culture and comes from centuries of conflict in one of the most turbulent regions of the Middle East.

Since ancient times, the land we now know as Iraq has been both among and surrounded by a constant succession of warring empires. On the 'fertile crescent' between the Dijlah and Furat rivers, the great empires of Babylon and Assyria established the earliest cradles of civilisation. For two hundred years, the two dynasties clashed in fearsome wars until, at the end of the 11th century BC, the Assyrians conquered an area stretching to the Mediterranean.

To the west lies the Holy Land of the Jews, Christians and Moslems, where more than 3,000 years ago the territory of the Hebrews was divided into the two kingdoms of Israel and Judah until defeated by the Assyrians. To the north was Asia Minor, from where the Hittites came to destroy the first Babylonian dynasty at the beginning of the 16th century BC. To the east, Cyrus the Great of Persia defeated the Medians in the 6th century BC and founded an empire from the foot of the Himalayas to the Aegean Sea. To the south are the barren sands of Arabia, upon which the fractured tribal domains of the hardened Bedouin people have been for centuries, unsafe to all outsiders, and where once had been the hidden Sabaean city of Shabwa, home of the Queen of Sheba. Thus, Saddam is only the latest in an historical succession of powerful leaders who have attempted to dominate the Arab peninsula.

I tried to ignore Akram's prattling as he made up now for his reticence in Saddam's presence. For my brother-in-law, it was very much the first day of the rest of his life, and he waxed lyrically on how the fortunes of our two families would now be forever changed for the better. He saw additional significance in the fact that the Hijrah calendar was entering a new century. The sighting of al-Helal, the new moon, had ended the twelfth Islamic month of Thw al-Hijjah and brought in al-Seneh Gedidah, the new year, with the month of Muharram, in the Hijrah year of 1400. In Akram's superstitious eyes, this surely indicated a divine blessing on our families.

For myself, I looked forward to the novelty of my new

occupation. Saddam had ordered me to take long-term leave from my teaching, but I was never to go back to the classroom. With my mother, I was immediately provided with a luxury government apartment in Baghdad and made plans to bring my marriage forward so that Amna could follow me as soon as possible. After being allowed a few days to settle, I was to attend the palace daily to be schooled in the subtle techniques of presidential behaviour.

Chapter Two

1980
Safar 1400 – Safar 1401

For the first few months of the year I was coached daily in the mannerisms of Saddam Hussein at the presidential palace on Karradat Mariam. My tutor was Mohammed Qutaibi al-Jenabi, introduced to me as an aide from the presidential office. Together we watched endless video newsreels of Saddam. I would practice his handshake, his walk and the way he laughed. I watched him closely on film as he acknowledged the adulation of large crowds assembled before him. At such times, he raises his right arm from the elbow, with the palm opened towards the crowd, in a manner similar to that adopted by Adolf Hitler. Every day, I watched and practised conscientiously. When I was provided with audio tapes of Saddam being interviewed and making speeches, I did not at first suspect there was perhaps a deeper, more sinister role for me to play.

Saddam frequently came to monitor my progress in the office set aside for the purpose of my training, a place that came to be known as the 'Dark Room'. The lights were frequently turned off as I watched video tapes with Mohammed, but that had nothing to do with the name. Members of the palace staff not aware of my existence had been told the room was a photographic developing studio for sensitive government material, and they were strictly prohibited from entering.

Initially, I found it difficult to perform while Saddam was watching. I was terrified I might offend him. He was, though, more amused than anything else and gradually, with Mohammed's encouragement, I grew in confidence. I spent many a long hour working on the manner in which Saddam orders, smokes and puts out his Havana cigars, and when Mohammed thought I was ready, we introduced this into my demonstration. I was worried that this would be going too far, but Saddam was highly amused.

'You are making remarkable progress, Mikhaelef,' he told me, smiling broadly. 'Soon you will be able to fool even my mother!'

Once I was rid of my inhibitions, the general tone of these sessions was light-hearted and entertaining. Few people realise that despite his fearsome reputation, in private Saddam has a lively sense of humour. He is a compulsive practical joker and it is often impossible to know whether or not he means what he says.

One morning he came into the Dark Room to announce he had an idea.

'I want to have you smuggled over the border into Iran,' he said with credible enthusiasm. 'You will be taken to one of the larger towns or cities early in the morning, perhaps to Khorramabad or Ahvaz. There we will place you outside one of their sacred mosques and have you photographed. We will then send a copy to that Islamic madman in Tehran with our best wishes. I would pay a fortune just to see his face.'

I thought the idea was insane and was about to splutter some polite objection when Saddam burst out laughing. 'Do not worry, Mikhaelef, it is my idea of a silly joke. The thought amuses me, but it is more important we keep you under wraps and use you for the greater purpose we have already discussed.'

Mohammed also began to teach me Kurdish, a difficult language for an Arab to master. As I struggled with my lessons, I would frequently object, seeing no purpose in it. Mohammed brushed away my protests and argued that I should never reject an opportunity to learn another tongue. As a former schooltecher, part of me agreed. I did not know then that Mohammed's insistence would one day save my life.

My new position was obviously shrouded in secrecy. I had been instructed to tell my friends I had successfully applied for a position with the Ministry of Education in Baghdad. Apart from Saddam's own elite inner-circle, only Amna, Wahab, Akram and my mother were initially aware of my new occupation. I was not permitted to move around freely and had to be escorted to and from the presidential palace in a private limousine with the windows blacked out. On the few occasions I ventured outdoors, I was made to wear a heavy false beard. It transformed my appearance utterly. When outsiders were present I was not allowed to be seen in Saddam's company, and even my movements within the palace were carefully monitored.

I was dedicated to my role and keen to justify what I thought was a grossly excessive salary for the work I was doing. I spent hours of my own time impersonating Saddam, much to the amusement of my mother. Had I done such a thing a few months earlier, she would have berated me for my disrespect. Now it was my job.

It was pointed out by Mohammed, subtly at first, that although Saddam and I were very alike, we were not identical. One afternoon, shortly before I was to return home for the day, he had me standing in front of a full-length mirror alongside a life-size cut-out of Saddam, of which there was an abundant supply.

'What do you think?' Mohammed asked. 'Where are the differences between yourself and the President?'

I studied the cardboard replica carefully, but could pick

out nothing of significance. 'The President wears a much better suit than I do,' I finally offered.

'Yes, very good, Mikhaelef,' Mohammed said, shaking his head in amused frustration, 'but I was thinking more of your physical appearance.'

'The President is taller.'

'Yes, perhaps. How tall are you?'

'One metre seventy-five.'

'You are a little shorter, yes, but we can easily stack your shoes. What about your face?'

I looked closely. 'The President's nose is slightly thicker than mine.'

'Yes, it is, although I think perhaps we should phrase that a little more tactfully in his presence, don't you? What else?'

'I have pock-marks.'

'Yes, you do, and the President does not. Sit down, Mikhaelef.' I took a seat in front of the desk by a window that looked across the palace compound and onto the River Dijlah. 'I've noticed you are putting on weight.'

'Yes, thanks to my mother. Since my sister married and my father died she has only myself to concern herself with. Now that she can buy what she wants, she feeds me as if every meal may be my last.'

'I am not complaining, Mikhaelef. What is your weight?'

'About seventy kilos,' I guessed. I did not check it very often.

'You are still a few kilograms lighter than the President,' Mohammed remarked. 'Tell your mother to carry on.'

Of the changes imposed on my life in those first few months, the considerable improvement in my diet was easily the most pleasant adjustment I had been asked to make.

Mohammed sat down on the other side of the desk and picked up a file. He flicked through the pages before looking up at me. 'What do you know about cosmetic surgery?' he asked me with a smile.

'Nothing,' I replied honestly.

'You must have heard of it.'

'Yes, of course. I believe Western women are obsessed by it.'

'Indeed, but it does have another purpose. Sometimes faces can be totally reconstructed. After serious accidents, for example. But the standards are high now and more frequently people in the West are having minor adjustments made to their appearance to help them feel better about themselves.'

'Like breast implants, for instance?'

Mohammed laughed. 'Yes, like breast implants. The women of the West are a strange breed, are they not?'

'I think it is immoral,' I answered, a little pompously.

'And I do, too. But I was thinking of something a little different for you. It would require only minor surgery, but with a couple of almost insignificant adjustments to your face, you would be identical to the President. How do you feel about that?'

'I'm not sure,' I replied. The idea of undergoing plastic surgery would have seemed ludicrous to me only a few short weeks earlier. 'Do you think it is necessary?'

'Think about it. It would be no problem at all to bring in a top plastic surgeon from West Germany who could fix your nose and repair your cheeks in the blink of an eye. It would all be done under local anaesthetic. You wouldn't feel a thing.'

'Should we not ask the President what he thinks of this?' I asked.

'It was his idea,' Mohammed answered without hesitation.

It was a *fait accompli*. I could see clearly now where the conversation had been leading for the past few minutes. 'The President would like me to have plastic surgery?'

'Yes.'

'And if I refuse?'

'You know him well enough now, Mikhaelef.'

Those who did not comply with Saddam's wishes were

usually soon found to be surplus to requirements. Whilst I had not yet personally encountered the darker side of his nature, I was well aware how he was not to be deflected from having his own way. Even though I believed I was already important enough to him to be able to negotiate the point, I was not so strongly opposed to the idea of facial reconstruction to make it an issue. In all honesty, I did not see what harm it could do and, if it improved my standing with the President, so much the better.

'You can tell the President I will do it,' I said finally.

'Excellent!' Mohammed responded happily. He had obviously been uncomfortable with the subject. My resistance would have caused him problems with Saddam. The tension of the moment visibly left him. 'I will tell him straight away.'

A week later, Dr Helmut Riedle was flown in from Hanover and I was introduced to him on the morning of his arrival. He was a tall man in his late-fifties and typically German. He carried his head high and spoke in clipped, staccato phrases. As he did not speak Arabic, nor I German, we had to converse through a translator, an Iraqi doctor by the name of Ayad Jihad al-Asadi. A small but well-equipped operating theatre had been set up in the palace to reduce the number of people aware the operation was taking place. Earlier in the day I had asked Mohammed why an Iraqi surgeon was not being used.

'They do not have the courage,' he answered laughing. 'If an operation were to go wrong . . .'

'Go wrong?' I looked anxiously towards him. The thought that anything might 'go wrong' had not occurred to me.

'Please, Mikhaelef, I am talking in general terms. You have nothing to worry about here. As I was saying, if an operation were to go wrong, Iraqi surgeons are too terrified of the consequences. Even the most minor operations performed on or on behalf of the President are carried out by foreign doctors.'

'But surely this is different,' I protested. 'How can the

President be sure Riedle will keep quiet about the operation once he is back in Germany?'

'He has been paid $250,000 to do this,' Mohammed replied, 'and politely told that if details of the operation come to light in the West, he can expect a visit from the Mukhabarat.'

'It is a lot of money,' I conceded, 'but why would such a man involve himself with an arrangement like this? He cannot be poor.'

'Such men always exist,' Mohammed answered. 'Two years ago, Dr Riedle was arrested in Langenhage, a town just to the north of Hanover, and charged with indecently assaulting two nine-year-old boys. The case never came to court, but he was struck off and has not openly practised since. When the President heard about it, he thought we might have a use for him one day. As usual, the President was right.'

I would have much preferred Mohammed had kept this from me until after the operation, but I now had no choice but to put myself in the hands of this foreign child molester. Dr Ayad went through the details of the operation as Riedle made the preparations.

'The doctor needs to thicken the bridge of your nose. After he has given you a local anaesthetic, he will insert a silicone strut through a vertical incision he will make in the mid-line of your columella. This is the piece of skin . . . here . . . between your nostrils. It will take but a few minutes. Then he will remove the pock-marks on your cheeks by using a mechanical abrasive cylinder. You will probably feel some discomfort, but no pain.'

I felt no pain, it was true, but the thirty minutes that followed were decidedly unpleasant. I was mightily relieved when Riedle indicated to Ayad that he was finished. My entire face was bandaged and I was given painkillers to take when the anaesthetic wore off. I then went home and retired to my bed feeling very sorry for myself.

For the next two weeks, my mother clucked around me, praising the courage of her son who would make such sacrifices for his country. I was far more concerned with whether or not I had been permanently disfigured. I suffered constant nightmares, none of which were quite the same. I was always standing in front of a mirror when the bandages were taken off, but each time a different, hideous face was revealed. On one occasion, the face was my sister's, which says as much about what I think of her as anything could. On another occasion, there was no face at all, just an empty space.

When Dr Ayad finally removed the bandages, my fears were proven unfounded. Apart from some slight bruising, I looked very much the same as I had before. After the swelling had completely disappeared it was possible to see the subtle difference, and I was now uncannily like Saddam. We had become more alike than twins.

As soon as I returned to my normal duties, Mohammed supplied me with a case, inside which there was a quantity of splendid false beards and several pairs of dark glasses.

'You must get into the habit of disguising yourself whenever you are outdoors and not impersonating Saddam,' Mohammed instructed me firmly. 'I know you have become used to being stopped in the street, but that must cease. Try them on. The beards are from the United States. They are real hair, the best that money can buy.'

For the next hour, I entertained Mohammed with a variety of impersonations.

'When Saddam tires of me,' I joked, 'perhaps I will find employment with Fidel Castro!'

In those early months in the presidential palace, I was kept fully occupied and progressed well. It was suggested I might make my debut as 'Saddam' at a function being organised to celebrate the 12th anniversary of the Ba'ath party in July, but Mohammed demurred. He was not convinced I was ready. This postponement caused me no distress. Within the sanctuary of the presidential palace I was becoming adept at aping the President's manner and mimicking his speech, but the thought of acting the part in public still unnerved me.

As I settled in, I became more familiar with Saddam's method of government and the nature of the security departments that surround him. In 1963, the Ba'ath party's short reign had been sustained by the Republican Guard, at that time a relatively small militia group. It had been comprehensively crushed by the army and when the party returned to power in 1968, Saddam was given the task of forming a special security unit called the Jiha'z al-Khas ('Special Agency'). It operated under the codename Jiha'z al-Hanain ('Messenger to the Prophet'), and consisted of a number of dedicated party activists operating within independent 'cells', or active service units. It was correctly assumed by foreign intelligence agencies to be Saddam's instrument of abduction, torture and murder. In 1971, Saddam formed the Elaqat al-Amma ('Public Relations Office') and three years later the Da'irat al-Mukhabarat al-Amah ('General Intelligence Department'), more commonly known as the Mukhabarat. Military intelligence remained the responsibility of the Istekhabarat, established in 1958 with the collapse of the monarchy.

Once Saddam had assumed control of the RCC, he wasted no time in placing his favoured associates in positions of prominence. Having never entirely trusted the command council, he effectively created an inner-cabinet by promoting six RCC members to the post of deputy prime minister, with one, Taha Yasin Ramadan al-Jazrawi, named senior to the others. Although I found it intimidating just being in the man's presence, Taha does apparently possess some personal qualities that endear him to his colleagues. At the outset, he went to great lengths to convince Saddam he had no ambition beyond his present standing.

The other five newly appointed deputy prime ministers were Tariq Aziz, Adnan Khairallah, Sa'dun Ghaydun, Na'im Hadad and Adnan Hussein al-Hamdani. The promotion of Tariq was particularly fortuitous for my brother-in-law, Akram. He had been assigned as an aide to Tariq shortly after my own appointment, so Tariq's promotion to Deputy Prime Minister amounted to a promotion for Akram, a point not lost on Wahab. Although Akram was never a part of Saddam's inner-circle, anyone spending more than five minutes in my sister's company would have believed the President passed no laws without first consulting her husband.

Tariq's association with Saddam goes back to their early days in the Ba'ath party and he was with him when they forced the early Ba'ath leadership into exile. Al-Bakr neither liked nor trusted Tariq and in 1969 had him removed from his post as editor of the Ba'athist newspaper, *al-Thawra*. For three months Tariq returned to teaching English before Saddam brought him back as a member of his staff. In 1971, Saddam made him an auxiliary member of the RCC, Minister of Information and a full RCC member within three years. He became invaluable when articulately defending Saddam's early pogroms.

The rise of Saddam's cousin and brother-in-law, Adnan Khairallah, was an early example of Saddam's obsessive nepotism when it came to selecting his close political allies. Adnan had acquired great wealth standing alongside Saddam and had been able to indulge his compulsive passion for motor cars, having a collection in excess of two hundred vehicles and, some said, a similar number of lovers. By the time of the Ba'ath revolution, Adnan had joined the army, but had moved on to the air force and the rank of staff colonel when appointed Minister of Defence and a member of the RCC.

Colonel Sa'dun Ghaydun had been commander of the Republican Guard's armoured division under the previous administration. He had been astute enough to support the Ba'ath party when President Abdullah-Rahman Arif was overthrown. He was a founder member of the RCC and former Minister of the Interior. In 1973, he had been kidnapped and wounded during a plot to assassinate al-Bakr and had supposedly been rescued by Saddam personally. His support for Saddam had been unwavering ever since.

Na'im Hadad, as a Shi'a Moslem, was a political pawn used unashamedly by Saddam. He was installed as head of the court of inquiry set up in 1979 to try the 'plotters' in the Ba'ath party, with the sole purpose of securing the conviction and execution of the two most troublesome Shi'a members of the government: Muhi Abd al-Hussein Mashhadani, Secretary General of the RCC, and Adnan Hussein al-Hamdani, the fifth of Saddam's new deputies.

The rapid rise and fall of Adnan Hussein illustrates how even a promotion cannot guarantee security in Saddam's regime. As a senior member of the RCC, Minister for Oil and one of Saddam's closest advisors, Adnan had been in the post of Deputy Prime Minister for barely a week when he was arrested and charged with being one of the chief conspirators against Saddam.

The red-haired Izzat Ibrahim al-Duri, a former ice-block salesman and devotee of Saddam, had been Minister of the Interior when Saddam became President and was immediately promoted to Vice-Chairman of the RCC and Head of the Revolutionary Courts. He was also, in theory at least, the constitutional successor to the presidency. Saddam's choice was not difficult to understand. They had been imprisoned together in the mid-sixties and Izzat was probably the least charismatic and most lacking in personal ambition of the RCC members. Despite his elevated position, he remains largely anonymous and is seldom seen or heard of in the Iraqi media. His most recent claim to fame occurred in November, 1998 when he narrowly escaped being killed in a terrorist explosion in Karbala, an incident given wide press coverage in the West.

Having organised the RCC personnel to his liking, Saddam then sought to further dilute its power by resurrecting a law passed a decade earlier for the formation of a national assembly . The law allowed for all Iraqis over the age of eighteen to elect a parliament of 250 members. In reality, voting was restricted to those native Iraqis over twenty-five who could demonstrate before a committee their support for Ba'athist principles. In an effort to placate the Shi'a Moslem community, more than sixty members were Shi'a, including the Speaker, Na'im Hadad, but each had been carefully vetted for their support of Saddam.

With my mother, I settled into my apartment off the appropriately named Arbatahsh [14th] Ramadan Street in the prosperous al-Mansur district of Baghdad, near to where the racecourse and many of the foreign embassies are located and uncomfortably close to the headquarters of the Mukhabarat. Amna, who was vehemently opposed to almost everything Saddam represented, was distinctly unimpressed by my new employment. As an intense, intelligent woman, she had developed strong opinions under the influence of her father, Pasha, and as the Ba'ath Socialist Party was essentially neo-Fascist, it offered little to which she was not ideologically and pragmatically opposed. I did not share her passion for political intrigue in those days, but there was little else she espoused with which I could not nod in agreement.

Amid far greater pomp and ceremony than my father had been able to afford for Wahab's wedding, I married Amna in Baghdad at the end of July. Many old friends and members of the family travelled from Karbala and Kadhimia for the day. I was a little concerned that some comment might be made about my slightly amended appearance, and I could hardly sprout a 'beard' overnight, so I concocted a story about having to undergo minor facial surgery following a car accident. As it happened, my slightly altered features were disguised by the weight I had gained and nothing was said.

My mother was fond of Amna and was delighted to see her son wed at last, but she spent most of the evening crying for my father. In a country where so many couples are married by arrangement, theirs had been a true love-match and was the reason my father had never pressed me to marry against my wishes. During the celebrations, I received a personally signed message from Saddam, conveying his best wishes to Amna and myself. It was thought prudent not to share it with anyone outside my immediate family.

One entertaining side-show during the evening was the performance of Akram. Most of our friends knew he worked in the city hall in Baghdad, but few had paid much regard to his arrogant and exaggerated tales of self-praise. Now, he strutted around in the company of the newly-appointed Mayor of Baghdad, Samir Mohammed Latif Abdullah al-Mufti, as if they were lifelong friends. Saddam had tactfully moved his uncle, Khairallah, from the mayoral post to the Iraqi Drivers and Vehicle Licensing Department where he was able to cream off much of the $80 dollars paid for a driving test by each applicant. Samir replaced him as mayor and Akram had been quick to ingratiate himself with the man.

I was approached by Abdullah Yunis, an old friend who lived in the apartment block I had recently left in Karbala.

'If I did not see it with my own eyes,' he said, looking across at Akram and Samir sharing a joke together, 'I would not believe it.'

I particularly liked Abdullah and wished I could reveal to him the full details of my recent good fortune. He found humour in most things and would have enjoyed the irony of it. He had four children and I was particularly fond of the youngest, Sa'dun. He had recently turned eighteen and I had watched him grow up with nearly as much pleasure as had Abdullah himself.

'Please tell me, Miklef,' Abdullah said, being the head of the only family who referred to me in this way, 'that Akram is not responsible for finding you a job with the Ministry of Education.'

'No, Abdullah,' I answered smiling, 'he is not.'

'Good. I can, in that case, remain proud of your success.'

I had been called Miklef by members of Abdullah's family since Sa'dun, as an infant, had been unable to pronounce my name properly and "Miklef" was as close as he could get. In Abdullah's household, it stuck.

Of the Arab nations, only Egypt had previously embarked on a serious nuclear research programme, only to abandon it following the Arab-Israeli war of 1973. Three years later, Saddam picked up the gauntlet. Iraq bought a 70-megawatt test reactor from the French, at the time one of the most advanced experimental models in the world. It was delivered to the complex at Tuwaitha, fifteen kilometres south-east of Baghdad on the Dijlah, and the total cost to Iraq was $275,000,000, which included 12.3kg of Uranium 235, enriched to 93%. Known to the French as Osiraq, from Osiris the Egyptian god of life after death, Saddam renamed the reactor Tamuz, from the Islamic month of the Ba'ath revolution.

The French always insisted that the reactor would not be used in the production of nuclear weapons, but the Israelis in particular were decidedly unhappy about the entire contract. Saddam was aware that Mossad, Israel's overseas secret intelligence agency, had been instructed to closely watch for developments. Their covert presence in Baghdad far exceeded any of the world's other security agencies at that time.

In April, 1979, the French company *Constructions Navales et Industrielles de la Mediterrane* (CNIM) based at La Seyne, near Toulon, completed the work on the Tamuz reactor. However, some essential parts were sabotaged and shipment was delayed for several months. Many believed Mossad were also responsible for another strike against Iraq's nuclear ambitions in June, when Professor Yahia al-Meshad was murdered in Paris. The professor, a forty-eight-year-old nuclear scientist employed by Saddam, was one of the world's leading experts in nuclear research and his death, in the Hotel Meridien near the Arc de Triomphe, Paris, was a serious setback for Iraq.

Saddam could have done without such distractions during a period when another crisis was developing with Iran. The border between Iraq and Iran has been one of hostility and warfare since pre-Islamic times and the Shatt al-'Arab waterway, which links the Dijlah and Furat rivers of Iraq and the Nahr al-Karun (River Karun) of Iran to the Arabian (or Persian) Gulf, was a permanent focus of Persian Gulf attention. As recently as 1975, Saddam, as Vice-President, had entered into an agreement with the Shah of Iran to maintain peace at the expense of the Iraqi Kurds. Unable to put down a Kurdish revolt while the rebels were being armed from Tehran, Saddam had reluctantly agreed to surrender Iraq's claim to the eastern bank of the Shatt al-'Arab waterway in return for Iran severing its links with the Kurds.

When Khomeini seized power, he was generally opposed towards those with nationalist aspirations, and only pragmatically recognised state authority and boundaries. His dream of a glorious Islamic empire was a constant threat to Iraq and, in response, more than 100,000 Shi'a Iraqis, many of them respectable businessman, were rounded up, labelled as 'Persians' and escorted to the Iranian border for deportation. There was no appeal.

From April, thousands of Iraqi Shi'a Moslems were expelled every day. Those whose identity papers decreed them to be 'of Iranian origin' were liable for deportation, even though the classification was a relic of Ottoman bureaucracy and went back several generations.

The Islamic underground group, al-Da'wa al-Islamiyah ('the Islamic Call'), retaliated with assassination attempts on the lives of Tariq Aziz, at Baghdad's Mustansirriyah University, and, a fortnight later, Latif Nusseif al-Jasim, Minister for Culture and Information. Both men came perilously close to being murdered. Saddam made membership of al-Da'wa al-Islamiyah a crime punishable by death. Ayotollah Baqr al-Sadr, one of the leading Shi'a dissidents, and members of his family were arrested and tortured prior to their execution.

War with Iran seemed inevitable. At the end of September, Saddam ordered a pre-emptive strike. An aerial bombardment of Iranian air force bases was followed by twelve Iraqi divisions crossing the border into Iran, from Mohammarah in the south to Qasr-e-Shirin, more than

300 kilometres to the north. Iran responded with sporadic air attacks on Baghdad, al-Basrah and Kirkuk, but they were accomplished little as their ill-equipped air force rapidly ran short of vital replacement parts.

A few days into the war, two Phantom jets fired air-to-ground missiles at the Tamuz nuclear research centre. The aircraft were said to have Iranian markings, but intelligence reports strongly suggested the initiative came from the opposite direction, namely Israel.

The war soon became known as 'Saddam's Qadisiya', a reference to an historic Arab victory over the Persians in AD 635. Once the air raids ceased, black-outs were lifted and the unprecedented high standard of living enjoyed by Iraqis before the war was, for a while at least, maintained. This era of economic growth, brought about by the oil-boom of the seventies, had been accompanied by a similar expansion in the population, more than double what it was in 1960, and Saddam went to great lengths to disguise the effects of the war. Public spending rose by 40% in the first full year of the war and most of that was spent on domestic goods and foodstuffs. Casualties, however, were one consequence of the war that could not be obscured. Saddam spent enormous sums compensating the families of those men killed at the front.

The early fighting was concentrated north of Mohammarah, around the towns of Dezful, Bostan and Susangerd, where more than a quarter of Iraq's forces were deployed. In pursuit of the oil-rich province of Khuzistan, the Iraqi army crossed the Karun and claimed to have destroyed the Abadan-Tehran oil pipeline. By the end of October, Mohammarah was occupied and Abadan was under siege, but the Iranian defences stiffened. Towards the end of the year, Iraqi progress ground to a halt and the first sounds of mutinous dissent was heard among the troops. Whereas the Iranians were attracting thousands of teenage volunteers for their nation's al-Jihad (Holy War), Iraq was suffering from an increasing number of deserters and draft-dodgers.

With the front line in stalemate, Saddam offered Khomeini the first in a succession of cease-fire proposals. It was firmly rejected. The Iranians made it clear they would not negotiate with Saddam and required his removal as a prerequisite to talks.

Thus, the war continued.

Chapter Three

1981
Safar 1401 – Raby' al-Awwal 1402

My first official function in the service of Saddam came in January when I paid a visit to the hospital in tal-Mansur, close to my apartment. I had been kept under wraps for nearly a year, but I was now ready to make my public entrance. I was terrified and had convinced myself that no one would be taken in. Mohammed, though, having noticed a little idiosyncrasy of mine when I was particularly nervous, was a pillar of great support.

'If you can stop scratching your ear so much,' he joked, 'you have nothing to worry about. You have been through this a thousand times.'

'Yes,' I replied, 'but they were rehearsals. What happens if I make a mistake?'

'What mistakes can you make? Nobody suspects anything, so nobody is looking for anything. You simply have "first night" nerves, Mikhaelef. Nothing more than that.'

When we arrived at the hospital, we were met at the main entrance by the hospital's chief administrator and a number of senior doctors and surgeons. Several children in wheelchairs suffering from a variety of ailments were also in evidence. Three of the children had cancer and were in the care of Dr Sa'dun al-Thakati, a tall, pleasant-looking man in his forties. He stepped forward and introduced me to the children individually. The most striking was an eight-year-old girl named Fatima. She was quite beautiful, but obviously unwell. The doctor explained that she had leukaemia and had been in the hospital for five months. To one side, he added she had only a few weeks to live.

I crouched down to talk to her and found it difficult in such humbling circumstances to impersonate Saddam. As I held her hand, she gave me a smile that broke my heart.

'And your name is Fatima?' I asked her quietly.

'Yes, Mr President,' she replied with a cheerfulness that belied her condition.

'You have been very brave.'

'Yes, Mr President.'

'In this country brave people are rewarded, Fatima. What would you like as a reward?'

'I'd like to get better, Mr President, and I'd like my mummy to stop crying.'

A lump rose in my throat and it was all I could do to hold back the tears myself. She had asked for perhaps the two things that I, even in Saddam's name, could not give her.

Similar scenes were repeated throughout my visit. The future of many of the patients was as limited as Fatima's, but I was convinced they were all receiving the best medical treatment available. Though nobody appeared to suspect I was anyone other than Saddam, I was relieved when the ordeal was over.

In the months that followed, I toured many hospitals, schools and factories, and even appeared once on television playing Saddam's game of 'incognito'. Less foolish were the visits to the hospitalised casualties of war. In each of the city's hospitals, several wards had been set aside to look after the army's wounded and the picture was the same throughout the country. I went to the al-Husseini

General Hospital in my old home town of Karbala, which, as one of the most westerly cities of Iraq, was as far from the front as anywhere. Even there, a distressing number of men had been admitted with the most dreadful wounds. Some of them were not expected to survive, many others would be maimed for life.

As always, I was followed around the hospital by a collection of senior doctors and hospital administrators. I had little to say to them. I reserved my words for those most in need of some comfort. A number of men had lost limbs or been blinded, but the most distressing patients to see were those suffering from head or internal injuries.

One man I saw, whose left leg ended just below the knee, was sitting beside his bed, but did not look at me as I approached him.

'What is your name?' I asked him.

'Mustapha Hahmad,' he replied. I ignored the absence of any formal acknowledgement of who I was, or rather, who I was supposed to be.

'Where were you fighting?'

'Abadan,' he answered, in a detached, surly tone.

'Do you know who I am?'

He looked at my face for the first time. 'Yes.'

'Who am I?'

'You are my father.'

Two of the administrators moved forward in alarm, but I raised my arm for them to stay back.

'Do you know where you are?'

'It is a stupid question. I am here.'

When I heard one of the doctor's behind me gasp, I turned and smiled, indicating that I was not offended. In fact, I was angry, though not with the young man before me.

'Do you know why you are here?' I asked, turning back to face him.

'It is my reward. Nobody can hurt me here. I have seen too many things, but now I am in peace. You cannot hurt me here.'

'I have no wish to hurt you, Mustapha.' I could see the terror still burning in his eyes.

'Everybody wants to hurt me!' he cried, becoming suddenly quite animated. 'Especially you, Father. You lied to me. You told me I would find glory. I found many things, but not glory. We never met.'

I turned and looked at the most senior of the doctors behind me. 'What is wrong with this man?'

'He lost his foot to a landmine on the outskirts of Abadan, Your Excellency,' he replied.

'When?'

'About six weeks ago. He was admitted to a hospital in al-Basrah, but he is from Karbala and his family asked that he be transferred here. He arrived two days ago.'

'Why is he not receiving psychiatric care?'

'We have not had time to assess his condition fully, Your Excellency. He was admitted as an amputee. We had no notice of his mental status.'

I felt the anger rise inside me. 'Do you know how much medical training I have received in my life, doctor?'

'No, Your Excellency, I have no idea.'

'Absolutely none!' I roared at him. 'And yet I, who have never so much as picked up a first aid manual, can see this man is in need of psychiatric help!'

The doctor attempted to stutter a response, but I did not allow him to speak.

'I hold you personally responsible. You will move him to a private ward and have him assessed by a competent psychologist within one hour. You will treat him with all the care and compassion that he deserves and that your profession demands. You will nurse him as if he was your brother, doctor, because he *is* your brother. He is *my* brother. He is the brother of *all* Iraqis. Do you understand?'

The trembling doctor nodded frantically in silence.

'You will be contacted daily by a member of my presidential staff and I will be provided with a full, updated assessment on what improvement he has made. And I do not want to hear that he has made no improvement. Am I making myself clear, doctor?'

I had so terrified the man, he could barely speak. 'Most . . . most certainly, Your Excellency. What you instruct me to do will be done.'

'Good. I will be back in one month. There will be no repetition of this incident.'

'Indeed, Your Excellency.'

Once I was back in the car, I immediately regretted my outburst. It was more typical of Saddam than myself, but there was nothing theatrical about my behaviour. I was genuinely incensed at the way the young soldier had been ignored, yet I realised that the hospital staff were overworked and seriously underpaid. Had I given the doctor the chance, he would have explained why the man was not being properly treated. I also believed I had overstepped the mark within the 'terms' of my employment. When I turned to Mohammed to begin an apology, he was smiling broadly.

'What is so funny?' I asked him nervously.

'You were magnificent, Mikhaelef. Saddam will be delighted when I tell him.'

'You have to tell him?' I asked, fearing the repercussions.

'Of course, but you need have no cause for concern. He will be very pleased. It will make very good propaganda. The story will already be racing through the hospital that Saddam himself was furious at how a hero of the war was being maltreated. By the morning, it will be in the papers. In fact, I will make sure it is in the papers. You were outstanding, Mikhaelef!'

The following morning, Saddam burst into the Dark Room carrying copies of both *al-Thawra* and *al-Jumhuriyah*, another government-controlled newspaper. With him were Tariq Aziz and Akram.

'Mikhaelef, this is wonderful!' he enthused, shaking the papers at me. 'This is exactly what I had in mind when I first asked you to come and see me. Look at this.' He first passed me the copy of *al-Thawra*. I read the headlines across the top of the front page:

'THE COMPASSION OF A GREAT LEADER'

The story that followed gave fairly accurate, if somewhat coloured details of what had taken place the previous day. The *al-Jumhuriyah* article was written in a similar vein with a similar message in its headline:

'OUR PRESIDENT'S FURY AT THE TREATMENT OF A WAR HERO'

Saddam embraced me and then held me at arm's length. 'This is wonderful, Mikhaelef. I am very pleased with you. You reacted in just the way I would have done had I been there myself. Tell me, were you impersonating your President or where you genuinely angry?'

Despite his broad smile, I suspected there might be an underlying motive behind this apparently innocent question. I answered as tactfully as I could.

'Perhaps a little of both, Your Excellency. I was unhappy with the indifference of the hospital staff, but I am always mindful of the fact it is you I represent.'

'Excellent, excellent,' Saddam exclaimed. 'Now, in future, you will address me by name. There is no longer any need for such formalities between us. You will call me Saddam.'

I was taken aback by this great honour bestowed upon me. Although the Iraqi people usually refer to the President as 'Saddam', few are permitted to address him so informally. I looked across at Akram, who was red-faced with jealousy. Clearly, the privilege had not yet been conferred upon him.

I always believed there was a patronising element to the way Saddam treated me in those early days. It was as if he did not take me entirely seriously and, on the face of it, there was no reason why he should. At that time, I was something akin to a court jester in that I did little of true significance, but could be relied on as a source of amusement.

It would be foolish to imagine that he might ever have considered me a threat to his position, but over the months and years to come a relationship developed between Saddam and myself that I never saw duplicated with any of his other associates. He rarely confided in me with regard to affairs of state and, wisely, never asked for my political opinion. Yet he would often talk to me in an open, uncomplicated way which I felt was increasingly genuine. I wondered if, because of my looks, I was in some way playing the part of his alter-ego. When we were alone together he would often talk to me as if he was thinking aloud, as if we were both one and the same person.

Saddam was obsessed by his public image and ever conscious of the impression he gave others. The most usual topic of conversation between us was how he could improve the way he was perceived by the average Iraqi citizen, and he encouraged me to behave in a compassionate and caring manner when I was impersonating him.

The early months of the war had been effectively ignored by the United Nations. Iran had seriously antagonised the international community generally and the United States specifically when fifty-eight American hostages were taken at the US Embassy in Tehran in November 1979. Having been held for 444 days, they were finally released in February 1981. Washington had broken off diplomatic relations with Iran and imposed economic sanctions. When their cries of indignation over the Iraqi invasion were met with global apathy, it began to look as if Saddam had judged the political climate correctly.

At the start of the new year, the Iraqi army occupied at least five Iranian towns and were some thirty kilometres east of the Shatt al-'Arab waterway. Five Iraqi divisions were deployed to the northern sector of the fighting with a further seven to the south. Facing them were fifteen Iranian divisions. Iran, as had been expected, launched a counter-offensive from Khorramabad and Dezful towards Mehran in an attempt to cut off the Baghdad to al-Basrah road, north of al-Kut. The first assaults failed and although Susangerd and Ahvaz were recaptured, it was to take the Iranians a year of bitter fighting to reverse earlier Iraqi successes.

In April, the Iraqi forces were forced to abandon some important ground following the battle for Dezful, though we enjoyed some compensation with successes at Serbil and Zahab. In July, recognising that the longer the war went on, the more conditions would favour Iran, Saddam proposed another cease-fire. This was during Ramadan, a holy month of abstention in the Islamic world when it is not permitted to eat or drink between sunrise and sunset. It made no impression on Khomeini, however, who once again rejected Saddam's overtures.

The war had already lasted much longer than Saddam had foreseen, and I did not see much of him during this period. Our paths had not crossed for the best part of a month when he surprised Mohammed and myself one morning in May. He entered the Dark Room in the company of Abdullah Qader Izzadin, the new Minister of Education, with whom I had had to become familiar for the sake of appearances. Mohammed immediately switched off the tape to which we had been listening and we both stood up. Saddam waved us back into our seats.

'Please pardon the interruption, Mikhaelef, but there is a small matter I would like to bring up with you.' He went to the window and turned a little theatrically to face us. 'I am pleased with your work. You know I am a demanding man, but you have exceeded my expectations. I would not have dreamed you could be as effective as you undeniably are.'

'Thank you . . . Saddam. I do my best.'

'Well, your best is very good, but there is something else I would like you to take on.'

'If it can be done, I will do it.'

He nodded and, walking across the room, pulled up a chair and sat beside me.

'When we first spoke last year, you may recall that I told

you everything you will do here is in the service of this great country of ours.'

'I remember it clearly.'

'As you know, Mikhaelef, civilisation started here. Here was Rafidain and the site of the great empires of Babylon and Assyria. In the ancient city of Ur, the prophet Abraham was born. At Qurna was the Garden of Eden and on the slopes of Mount Ararat did the ark of Noah finally come to rest. But even great nations such as ours go through difficult times and must make great demands of its people. At such times, we have to demonstrate how proud we are of our homeland and in order to protect it, to show our enormous appreciation, we have to make sacrifices. Do you not agree, Mikhaelef?'

'I agree with every sentiment,' I replied, although the intensity of his little speech worried me. I greatly feared I was being lined up for a task that would prove beyond me.

'This is such a time for Iraq,' Saddam continued, 'and we must each of us look at ourselves and determine what we can do. The playboy American President, John Kennedy, was a man for whom I had little regard when I was younger, but I recall him saying one thing which perfectly articulates what I am thinking now: "Ask not what your country can do for you," he said, "but what you can do for your country." Fine words, Mikhaelef.'

'Indeed, Saddam, in the context in which you place them.'

He looked at me intensely.

'You, Mikhaelef, can do a great service for your country now. I want you to spend time with our brave young men who are going to war.' He got up and walked back towards the window, standing there, hands clasped behind his back, shoulders squared, as if he were inspecting a parade of troops. 'They need to see their President. They need to know he is with them.' He turned around. 'I myself am unable to undertake this duty, Mikhaelef. The war is run from here. No move is made by any senior officer without my personal approval. The responsibility is a great

46

one and I do it gladly. But it leaves me with little time for anything else. Will you help me? Will you help Iraq in this way?'

'You want me to visit the front?' I asked. My throat was dry.

'Eventually, Mikhaelef, yes, but first I want you to visit the men in their barracks as they themselves prepare to go to the front. Reassure them that I am with them. Will you do it?'

Later, I discovered this to be a typical ploy of Saddam's. Whenever he wished someone to do his bidding, he would first make the task appear to be the most difficult and dangerous imaginable. Having thus prepared his 'victim' he would make the task sound scarcely more onerous than a walk in the park. Naturally, I agreed without hesitation. In any case, I was hardly being given the opportunity to refuse.

A few days later, I travelled north to the headquarters of the 1st Army Corps at the Khaled Camp in Kirkuk. From there I was driven east towards Chamchamel where the infantry and tank brigades were billeted. Just short of Chamchamel, on the hills of Ban Maqan around the villages of Qarah Hanjeer and Qoran where the infantry battalions of the 36th Brigade, part of the 2nd Infantry Division. The commander, a staff brigadier whose name escapes me, assured me the men were well and those I met seemed eager to play their part in the 'heroic' struggle.

I was taken to see some men of the brigade's 2nd Infantry Battalion, recently returned from the fighting at Zahab. Things had gone well for them and I was there to decorate four officers and eleven men for their courage during the early stages of the battle, when success had seemed unlikely. They were each fiercely proud of their achievements, and I was humbled by their gracious attitude towards me. Mohammed, never very far away, had to constantly whisper in my ear to remind me whom I was impersonating. The real Saddam would never feel humbled.

It was expected that I would only personally address the more senior officers present, but I was keen to show Saddam to be a man of the people and also spoke to many ordinary conscripts. It was while I was speaking to a small group of conscripts that I spotted Sa'dun Abdullah, the eighteen-year-old son of my close friend and neighbour in Karbala, Abdullah Yunis. I had not seen Abdullah since my marriage and had no idea his son had been conscripted.

I had known Sa'dun all his life and I looked anxiously toward Mohammed as the young man pushed through the soldiers blocking his way, wondering if he would expose me as an impostor. Mohammed noticed my anxiety and the direction of my glances and as Sa'dun drew near he pounced on him and wrestled him to the floor. Other members of my entourage joined in. Sa'dun was hauled to his feet and searched. I wished the boy no harm, but I remained seriously worried that he would recognise me. As it turned out, my fears were baseless.

Sa'dun vehemently protested his innocence and was found to be carrying nothing more harmful than a pencil and some loose change. Mohammed relaxed but looked at me enquiringly.

'Is everything in order, Your Excellency?' he asked me, obviously puzzled by my behaviour. I nodded in reply as Sa'dun shook himself free of his captors.

'What is the matter?' Sa'dun demanded. 'I am only trying to shake the hand of my President.'

Mohammed was not used to being addressed in such a way, especially by a conscripted private in the army. He moved threatening towards Sa'dun, but I stepped forward between them, and put a restraining hand on Mohammed's shoulder. This had already gone too far.

'Please, Mohammed,' I said, 'let the man be.' I took Sa'dun by the hand. 'Please accept your President's regrets with regard to this little misunderstanding.'

Sa'dun stood transfixed as I released his hand and embraced him, kissing him on both cheeks.

'Mr President . . . Your Excellency,' he stammered. 'I am deeply honoured.'

I smiled back at him. 'How is the war treating you, young man?'

'Very well, Your Excellency, although I miss my family.' He hesitated before carrying on, but then decided to say what was on his mind. 'It is remarkable, Your Excellency, but a friend of my father looks so very like you. I had always thought he was like your twin, but I can see now that you are not identical.'

I laughed, more in relief than anything else.

'This friend of your father is a popular man, no doubt?' I asked, smiling with mock arrogance.

'Yes, indeed, Your Excellency, but we do not see him now. He has moved to Baghdad to work with the Ministry of Education.'

Once we were safely back in the car, Mohammed playfully accused me of fishing for compliments and would not accept my pleas that I was looking only to confirm that Sa'dun did not recognise me.

As the year progressed, Iraq came closer to becoming a nuclear power. Unfortunately for Saddam, the development programme received a severe setback on 7th June as a result of an aerial bombardment of the Osirak nuclear reactor complex at Tuwaitha, south-east of Baghdad. Fifteen Israeli F16s, protected by F15s, attacked in a low-level bombing raid, the first strike ever against a nuclear installation. The raid lasted little more than two minutes, but the damage was extensive. Only a quantity of fissionable material stored deep underground survived. The reactor was within three months of completion. Had the attack taken place a month or so later, considerable nuclear fall-out would have resulted, wreaking havoc on Baghdad. Major General David Iuri of the Israeli air force claimed every bomb found its target. Even in Saddam's inner circle, no one disputed this claim.

In September, the Iranians lifted the siege on Abadan, but

not before both sides sustained heavy casualties and some 1,500 Iraqi soldiers were taken prisoner. Our army was also driven back to the Karun from Dahkhavineh to Abadan and the roads from Mansuri and Ahvazto to Abadan were reopened to Iranian traffic. Saddam's offer of a cease-fire was once again rejected. By this time, the Iranian Arabistan offensive in November had recaptured Bostan and the course of the war was turning in their favour.

Casualties on both sides were high. Although the figures were never properly revealed in newspapers such as *al-Jumhuriyah*, I was aware that we were suffering fatalities in excess of 1,000 men a month. Iraq had been receiving massive financial aid from Saudi Arabia, Kuwait, Qatar and other Arab nations and was seen by Arabs generally as 'the guardian of the eastern gateway', but it was a war which most non-Arab governments hoped both sides would lose. An old Arab proverb aptly described their attitude: Let the venom of the scorpion kill the snake. Even our neighbours bearing gifts privately hoped we would be given a bloody nose.

The Americans were still reeling from the loss of a close ally in the Shah of Iran following the Shi'a revolution. Iran had played a strategic role in a ring of US 'fortresses' surrounding the Soviet Union and as an important oil producer, its stability was vital to Western economies. The US feared that a powerful Islamic Iran could close the Gulf to the West, and many qualified observers believed the US had engineered the war with Iraq. Certainly, their policy throughout the war was to support the side on the defensive, supplying Iran with Hawk missiles in the early part of the year and then refusing to forward the necessary spare parts for maintenance when the tide began to turn in their favour.

Shortly after the reverse at Bostan, I was sent to the front to boost the morale of the troops. If the soldiers believed that Saddam was prepared to put himself at risk to come and see them, they might once again believe in the war they were fighting. With Mohammed, by this time my friend as well as my constant companion, I was driven to the front, taking the al-Basrah road as far as al-Kut. There we turned east towards al-'Amarah, where we were met and taken by Land Rover to the front line, some fifty kilometres away. I was in full army uniform in the rank of Field Marshall and created something of a stir as we drove into the border town of Dasht-e-Azadegan on the Karkheh river. It was to here the army had retreated after their defeat at Bostan and even now, we passed many dead along the roadside.

At the front line itself, I struggled to maintain my composure at the sight that confronted me. The Iraqi line was a mass of earthworks and trenches torn out by bulldozers from which the infantry fired ceaselessly at the Iranian line a few hundred metres away. No-man's-land was a devastated wasteland of corpses, shell-holes and abandoned vehicles and artillery. Most of the dead were Iranians, young men wearing red bandannas who had thrown themselves fearlessly on the Iraqi guns. An invasion by a foreign army had been the national crisis Khomeini had needed to restore public order and rally patriotic fervour once support for the revolution had waned, but their losses were terrible, frequently amounting to tens of thousands in a day.

My appearance among our fighting men initially stunned them, but once word of the arrival of al-Qaed al-Muhib, 'the fearsome leader', had spread, I was greeted with great enthusiasm. The effect was precisely what Saddam had intended and the joy in the men's faces as their President walked among them was simultaneously heart-warming and, because I was there under false pretences, shaming.

On my second morning at the front, I left my tent during a lull in the firing in the company of Mohammed and a number of senior officers. Despite being some distance from the front line trenches, my left thigh suddenly felt as if a red hot brand had been applied to it. Looking down, I saw blood seeping through the green cotton of my uniform trousers. I had been shot. I fell to the ground and stayed there, too shocked to be afraid.

As I later learned, three Iranians had concealed themselves behind a small rocky rise in the ground about two hundred metres from the line. The sniper and his companions, no doubt believing they had been chosen by Allah for the task, had no other target but myself and Mohammed, who was a few paces to my rear. Seconds after the shooting, the three men momentarily disappeared, reappearing from behind a cloud of sand aboard an army jeep making directly for the Iranian line.

The glory of my would-be assassins was destined to be short-lived. They could not have covered much more than a hundred metres, when I heard first a series of explosions and then the cheering of troops as the vehicle was blown to the sky. Thanks to the accuracy of an Iraqi howitzer, the trio would not live to gloat over their success.

Once my entourage realised what had happened, I was surrounded by hysterical attendants. Mohammed, however, kept a clear head and had me carefully lifted onto the back of a troop transporter. I was losing a lot of blood and simply lay there, in a dreamlike state, as the soldiers about me shouted and screamed in confusion. Then I passed out.

When I came to, I was in a private room of the Ibn Seina Hospital, Baghdad, where I was to spend the next three weeks. Amna was with me almost constantly and I wanted for nothing. The most painful part of my recovery was having to endure the frequent visits of my gushing sister, Wahab, who would repeatedly tell me what a fine and courageous brother she had and then discuss in my presence how she and Akram might profit from my misfortune.

Saddam called in to see me one evening, accompanied by the usual team of bodyguards and sycophants. In the presence of Amna, my mother, Wahab and Akram, I was decorated with the Medal of Rafidain for my 'courage in upholding the principles of Ba'athism in the face of the enemy'. All I had done was to get myself shot; an award for carelessness might have been more appropriate. The ceremony was informal, but despite Saddam's apparent good humour I knew him well enough by now to see he had much on his mind. The war was not going well.

My mother cried and Amna, although uncomfortable in Saddam's presence, smiled politely and maybe just a little proudly. As Saddam stood up to leave, he placed a brotherly hand on my shoulder.

'We are now more alike than ever, Mikhaelef,' he said gravely.

'Because of the medal?' I asked, knowing there was no civil or military medal of significance that Saddam had not awarded himself.

'No,' he replied, pointing to my injury, 'because of the shot wound in the leg.'

According to Saddam's official biographies, in 1959, when he was just twenty-two, he had taken part in a plot to assassinate President Qassem. His role had originally been to cover the retreat of the assassination group, but when a machine-gun jammed, he became involved in the main assault and was apparently shot in the leg. I know not whether the claim is true, but we did not compare scars.

Instead, we embraced.

'We may not be blood brothers, Mikhaelef Ramadan,' he said, 'but we are surely now brothers in blood.'

Chapter Four

1982
Raby' al-Awwal 1402 – Raby' al-Awwal 1403

In January, Saddam launched a major offensive in the
central zone of the war and captured the Iranian town of
Gilan-e Gharb, forty kilometres from the border on the
Kabir Kuh mountains and 200 kilometres north-east of
Baghdad. This promising success was broadcast widely and
for a while it was hoped the Iraqi army was regaining the
initiative. Alas, the trend did not continue.

During this period of my recuperation, I was able to
spend more time with Amna and almost inevitably she
became pregnant. Following a regime of daily physio-
therapy I was close to full recovery by the start of
February, which was when Amna first openly expressed
her distaste at my being directly connected to a regime of
terror. She had always objected to the President's methods,
but by now she was distraught over the continuing arrests
and the horror stories that were seeping out from the
prisons. Her anxiety deepened when an old friend of her
family, Aswa al-Rawi, now living in al-Basrah, came to
Baghdad.

By then, I had returned to my duties at the palace and had been told by my doctor to walk at least three kilometres each day, gradually extending the distance as my leg got stronger. On this particular day, I had covered more than five kilometres and returned to my apartment to find Amna talking to a clearly distraught woman, cloaked in a traditional black abaya.

I had not met Aswa before and Amna introduced us briefly. I was wearing my false beard and dark glasses and the woman did not appear to see through this thin disguise.

'Aswa's elder sister was a close friend and neighbour of my mother's in Karbala,' Amna told me. 'I have known the family since before I can remember. She has gone through a terrible experience, Mikhaelef. You must listen to her.'

I sat down opposite the woman, as Amna related to me some of the details.

'Aswa lost her husband, Hassan Hamid al-Asadi, ten years ago, when he was killed in an accident at work. He was an engineer. She has two sons, Yasin and Ahmad. Yasin followed his father into engineering. Ahmad was a medical student.'

'Was?' I queried.

'Yes,' Amna replied, 'Ahmad is dead and Yasin may well be dead also. Ahmad was arrested by the Mukhabarat in the week following Shab-e Yalda.' This is a celebration of the winter solstice that dates back to pre-Islamic times, when families and friends sit together long into the night eating, drinking and talking.

Amna turned to Aswa. 'I know this is difficult for you, but, please, tell Mikhaelef what has happened.'

As Aswa related her story to me she never once raised her head, staring constantly at the floor.

'I was told Ahmad was being held in the Abu Ghraib prison here in Baghdad,' she began, 'but after I had spent three days applying to the governor for some information, I still did not know for certain if he really was there or not. In the end, I had no choice but to return to al-Basrah. I heard nothing.'

Amna sat down beside Aswa and put a comforting arm around her shoulder. Aswa looked up briefly at Amna and tried to raise a smile in response to her compassion, but her gaze soon returned to the floor.

'Why was he arrested?' I asked.

'I have never been told. There are some students who involve themselves with politics, but Ahmad was never one of them. He was only interested in medicine. I tried everything I could think of to find him. I applied to every government and security department I thought might have anything to do with his arrest. I went to the Mukhabarat's al-Hahkimiya prison, in the al-Karada district more times than I care to remember. It is a dreadful place. If you stand outside the Passport Office, you look across and see three floors, but there are another two floors underground. From there I used to walk each day to the Mukhabarat headquarters in al-Mansur, but was never told anything. It was not until I bumped into Amna today that I knew you lived here. I dearly wish I had known it several months ago.

'I could not believe that Ahmad was dead,' she continued, 'and I kept looking for him. Then, three weeks ago, my eldest son, Yasin, was also arrested. Again I was told nothing. With both of my sons missing, I was out of my mind.'

Relating the story was taking its toll on Aswa, but she forced herself to carry on. 'The day before yesterday, I received a visit from some piece of human excrement from the Ministry of Information. He told me I could . . . I could collect Ahmad's body from the Baghdad city mortuary.'

This was not an unfamiliar story. The difference was that it had been brought into my home, to confront me. I pitied the poor woman.

'How long had Ahmad been dead?' I asked her, as sensitively as I could.

'I cannot be sure,' Aswa replied. 'They told me nothing. I think maybe only a few hours. Maybe a day. He had been in prison for two months, but even now that he is dead, they will not tell me why they were holding him. I arrived at the mortuary at eleven in the morning and there were more than a hundred people waiting. Each had been told to collect the bodies of their dead loved ones. Nothing happened for several hours. I just waited outside the mortuary with the others and talked. Everybody told the same story. Their husbands, fathers, brothers and sons had been arrested for no good reason. We waited and waited. The stench of the dead was dreadful. People were ill with the smell.

'Eventually, my name was called and I was allowed into the mortuary and taken into a small room. The officer there ridiculed me. He said I was the mother of a coward and a traitor. He spat in my face. I was told to fill in a form and then I was left alone in the room for perhaps another hour. I was so shaken, I lost all sense of time. Finally, I was told I could collect my son's body. I was told I was not permitted to cry or hold al-Fatiha [public mourning]. I was then taken to the cell where his body was laid out.'

For a moment, I thought she would break down. Instead, she took a deep breath and, fighting back the tears, came to the most chilling part of her story.

'Inside the cell, there seemed to be bodies everywhere, but I was not prepared for what I saw. I could never have imagined such horrors with my own mind. One young man's chest had been sliced lengthways into three sections from the neck to the stomach. Another's limbs had been crudely hacked off and another's eyes were gouged out and his ears and nose sliced off. Another lay with the skin peeled off his body from his neck to his ankles and what remained of his body seeped with pus. His exposed muscles showed the bruising on his neck, arms and legs from having being tightly strapped. One had been hanged, but his stretched neck indicated death by slow strangulation rather than a broken neck. Then I saw Ahmad.'

At this point, Aswa wrung her hands together and rocked the upper half of her body back and forth. Amna stroked her hair and asked if she wanted to rest. She shook her head.

'No, I am all right. There is not much to tell now.' She closed her eyes tightly, perhaps conjuring up in her mind the image of her son as she had found him. 'His body was burnt and his face so blackened even I . . . even I, his mother, could barely recognise him. His hands were still strapped behind his back and his face . . . his face had stiffened in the expression of agony in which he had died. He was lying on his side on a metal bunk. Underneath there were the remains of a fire. They had . . . had tied him to the bed and then started a fire beneath him. They had cooked him alive.' Aswa finally succumbed to her anguish and wailed with grief, overcome by the brutality of the memory. I was only able to mutter some incoherent words of condolence before Amna waved a hand for me to be silent.

If my narrative of Aswa's recounting of her dreadful experiences gives the impression of great fluency, I must correct it. Her words throughout were halting, and punctuated by weeping and wailing, and almost an hour passed before she came to a stop, in yet another burst of tears.

'Aswa is desperate to know about Yasin,' Amna said quietly. 'He is all she has left to live for. Can you find out what has happened to him?'

'How can I do that?' I asked, my mind still filled with images of burned and mutilated bodies.

'Mikhaelef, you know people now. Ask them to find out.'

Later that night, I argued with Amna for the first time ever in our marriage. She was furious at my reluctance to ask questions about Yasin. The truth was I was too scared. Even a hint of association with anybody who had been arrested by the Mukhabarat could put me at risk. With little conviction, I suggested that Saddam and his ministers were unaware of what went on in the prisons and that it was unlikely anybody in the palace would be able to help.

'Are you brain-dead, Mikhaelef? Do you really believe that Saddam Hussein does not know exactly what goes on inside his prisons? If you do not come to power through the ballot box, you can only keep power by means of terror. It is only by the indiscriminate arrest of thousands of innocent people that Saddam can hope to identify those few in number who plot against him. You must be able to see this!'

'I cannot believe,' I replied, my head still spinning with Aswa's revelations, 'that Saddam is a party to what has happened to the son of your friend. He is ruthless, yes, but he would not authorise the murder of innocent students. What is the point? Cruel as he is, everything Saddam does has a purpose.'

'In the name of Allah! How can you be so naive? Of course, there is a purpose. Terror is the purpose. What has happened to Ahmad and hundreds of others is a message – a message to all enemies of Saddam. "If you dare to stand against me, this is what will happen to you and your family." You cannot hide from this, Mikhaelef. It will not go away because you refuse to face up to it.'

I could think of nothing to say. I was just as moved by Aswa's account as Amna, but desperately wanted to believe Saddam was not responsible.

When I returned to the palace the next day, I felt that Mohammed was the only person I could talk to about Yasin. We had been running a video tape of a recent visit of Saddam's to Karbala and it reminded me sharply of a time when my life was less affluent but infinitely less complex. When it was finished, Mohammed switched off the television set and turned to face me.

'What is the matter, Mikhaelef?'

'What do you mean?'

'I have got to know you well over the past few months and I can see when you have something on your mind that bothers you. You have hardly said a word all morning. Tell me what is wrong.'

I hesitated, but having already decided I could safely confide in Mohammed, began to tell him of Aswa's visit. He did not say a word until I had finished.

'It is a problem, Mikhaelef, but it is not the mountain you make it?'

'Well, what do I do? Go to Saddam and ask him to look into it personally?'

'Why not?'

'Are you mad? If I am lucky he will kick me from the palace and tell me never to return! And if I am not so lucky . . .'

I did not need to elaborate on my probable fate in the event that Saddam took umbrage.

Mohammed disagreed. 'Not at all. You underestimate your position and the regard and the need the President has for you. Be courteous, of course, and be sure he is in one of his better moods, but ask him.'

With that the subject was closed, and I know I would never have had the courage to ask Saddam anything about Yasin had Mohammed not taken it upon himself to do so on my behalf.

Saddam paid one of his sporadic visits to the Dark Room later that morning, in the company of his younger son, Qusai, clearly in a mood to be entertained. We exchanged small-talk for a few minutes, then Mohammed broached the subject without preamble.

'Mikhaelef has a problem, Your Excellency, a dilemma even, with which you may be able to help him. Tell the President, Mikhaelef.'

I froze with fear as Saddam looked across at me, his gaze curious yet not without compassion.

'What is it, Mikhaelef?' Saddam asked. 'What troubles you?'

'It is nothing, Your Excellency.' I began to sweat and had no idea what to say next.

'Please, Mikhaelef, do tell me.'

I swallowed hard. 'My . . . wife. . .'

'Yes?'

'My wife has a friend from Karbala . . . she lives now in al-Basrah . . .'

Both Saddam and young Qusai eyed me intently, nodding with a smile as I spluttered out my story. 'This woman's husband was killed ten years ago in an industrial accident and she has brought up her two sons alone. They were both recently arrested and the youngest was recently executed. She has no idea what has happened to her other son. My wife has asked me if perhaps I could find out where he is.'

'I see,' Saddam said, still smiling. Did I imagine it, or had the smile become fixed, a travesty? 'And why were these two men arrested, Mikhaelef?'

'I have no idea . . . Saddam, but the mother believes they were arrested by the Mukhabarat.'

'And no doubt she insists they are both entirely innocent of any wrongdoing?'

'Yes, she does.'

'What is his name? The eldest son?'

'His name is Yasin Hassan al-Asadi.'

'How old is he?'

'I'm not sure. I think perhaps about twenty-one.'

'From al-Basrah, you say?' He took a few casual paces across the room, looking thoughtfully at the floor. 'I will look into it, Mikhaelef,' he said finally. 'But I cannot guarantee anything. We do not know how serious were his crimes, but it seems to me that this friend of your wife, the mother of Yasin Hassan, perhaps deserves to be treated with some sympathy. If Yasin's crimes are not too serious, perhaps we can show a little leniency on this occasion.'

It occurred to me that Qusai's presence was no bad thing. Saddam's youngest son, sixteen by this time, was as different in personality to Udai as it was possible for two brothers to be. I did not see him very often and on the rare occasions I did, he had little to say. He seemed happy to let his father take the spotlight and did not attempt to impress or intimidate in the way Udai had, at the same age. Consequently, Saddam was always more relaxed and paternal when with Qusai and I hoped this would be reflected in his handling of my request. I was not optimistic.

'I will do what I can, Mikhaelef,' Saddam said, putting his arm around young Qusai's shoulders. 'I am a man of my word.' He looked at his son and smiled fondly. 'Now we must go, Qusai. Your mother is expecting us.'

As soon as the door closed behind Saddam and Qusai, I collapsed into a chair, drained by the ordeal I had just been through. I decided to say nothing of the conversation to Amna, as I did not want to encourage any expectations and I was, in any case, highly sceptical I had achieved anything. I was wrong. The following day, when I arrived home, Amna ran to me and threw her arms around my neck.

'Mikhaelef! Mikhaelef! What did you do? What did you do?'

'What are you talking about, Amna?' I asked, bemused. She was a rather reserved woman and such a welcome home was completely out of character.

'Yasin!' she exclaimed. 'He is free!' Delight was spread across her face.

'Free? You are sure?'

'Yes, I am sure. He came here today with Aswa.'

I was aghast. 'You have seen him?' I asked 'How is he?'

'He is not well, Mikhaelef, but he is alive and will recover.'

'How do you know I had anything to do with it?'

Amna's joy was contagious and I began to feel something of her elation.

'It could only have been you! The governor of the prison called him to his office to tell him he was free. He asked Yasin what friends he had in high places. Of course, Yasin said none. The prisoner governor shrugged and said it was most unusual. He had received an instruction directly from the presidential office ordering Yasin Hassan to be released immediately. How did you do it, Mikhaelef?'

I gave Amna a modestly edited version of my conversation with Saddam and explained why I had not mentioned it to her the previous evening. In reality, my surprise in the outcome of my appeal to Saddam was absolute. It proved that he was human, if only to a limited degree.

'I know how difficult it was to do what I asked,' Amna said, looking directly into my eyes, 'and I apologise for the things I said to you the other night.'

'It is nothing, Amna. Put it behind you.' I confess I enjoyed the adulation and felt I had recovered much of the dignity I had surrendered two days earlier.

'No, listen, Mikhaelef. You took a personal risk in bringing up such matters with Saddam and I respect you for that. Thank you.'

'Please, Amna, you embarrass me.'

'I embarrass you? This is nothing.' She smiled and put a hand gently to my face. 'Aswa has taken Yasin to the hospital. Then she is coming back here to thank you personally for saving her son. She will devour you with gratitude.'

In March, a large area west of Dezful in the south, was lost with heavy casualties on both sides. At Mohammarah, 70,000 Iranian troops gathered. We had three divisions inside the city and one on the road to the north-west along the Shatt al-'Arab waterway. The battle opened on 21 May and was lost after four days, with 30,000 Iraqis taken prisoner. *Baghdad Radio*, of course broadcast only the most heroic details, but the people of Iraq were tiring of the war. Their young men were not coming home and conscripted recruits were becoming younger. Saddam's public statement that the purpose of the war had been to inflict heavy casualties on Iran, which had been achieved, was not convincing. In addition, the Iranians were now at the border for the first time, and al-Basrah came under heavy artillery fire.

While I was working towards full fitness, Saddam re-cruited another 'double': Mahdi Mahmud al-Thakabi was from Ba'qubah, about seventy kilometres north-east of Baghdad but, despite having plastic surgery, it was quite obvious to anybody who had met Saddam that the new man was an impostor. Consequently, he was only ever used when he could be kept some distance from potential enemies. Some referred to him as 'sniper-meat.'

Mahdi was some ten years Saddam's senior and having worked in the fields for much of his life, his weathered skin bore little resemblance to that of the President. He was, however, a pleasant, humorous man, delighted to have been plucked from the obscurity and hardship of his rural life. With no sons, he had worried for years what fate awaited him in his old age. Now his worries were behind him.

I was a little curious as to why Saddam had decided to employ another double. Presumably it would mean a reduction in my workload, but since my duties were not especially demanding, there seemed little point in splitting them. It did not occur to me then that Mahdi might be an insurance policy in case I succumbed to an assassination attempt.

Mahdi was a simple man, but he could not have tried harder to please me had I been Saddam himself. He had acknowledged that my likeness to Saddam was much closer than his own and generally deferred to me as the 'senior' double. I brought this up with Mohammed when we were alone.

'He cannot tell the two of you apart,' he suggested, 'so he treats you both the same.'

An example of Mohammed's humour, not to be taken seriously.

Saddam was prone to amuse himself with his doubles and made particular use of me in this fashion. Frequently, he would fool his own ministers with his practical jokes. On one occasion, an order came through from the presidential office to report to Saddam's private study immediately. At the time, this was most unusual. In those days, I was seldom allowed anywhere near the inner-sanctum of the palace. When I arrived, Saddam was alone and clearly in a playful mood.

'Ah! Mikhaelef! Excellent. I am pleased that you could come so quickly.'

Before I had a chance to reply, he walked across to the window and pointed to the garden below. 'Go down into the garden and walk about as if you are admiring the flowers. Occasionally, look up to this window. Shortly, you will see Tariq and Taha standing here. Wave up to them and shout that you will be with them in a few moments. Make sure that you do not stray from their view for a moment. Go now and hurry. They will be here at any minute.'

I did not understand what was behind Saddam's odd request, but obediently made my way down to the gardens. Strolling between the flower beds, I felt quite self-conscious, but I had been there for just a few moments when, as Saddam had prophesied, Tariq Aziz and Taha Yasin Ramadan appeared at the window above me. I raised a hand to them.

'Tariq! Taha! Please, I will be with you in just a few minutes,' I called out. By this time I was able to impersonate Saddam's voice flawlessly.

They both waved back at me and stayed at the window talking as I carried on inspecting the flowers. Looking up again, I saw Saddam suddenly appear between his two ministers who both turned, clearly startled by the duplication. Saddam dissolved into a fit of laughter and the three heads withdrew from the window. Saddam often played childish games of this nature, but they were not without motive. I had no doubt he used such opportunities to eavesdrop on his governmental colleagues, perhaps hoping they would utter some indiscreet remark, or even that he would uncover a plot to usurp him.

There were several changes in government personnel at this time and altogether eight members of what was now a sixteen man RCC were removed. Unlike in previous reshuffles, six of the eight were neither jailed nor executed, but given generous positions elsewhere. General Sa'dun Ghaydun, however, an old friend of Saddam and the last serving member of the revolutionary administration of 1968, did not live long enough to enjoy his retirement. As a parting gift, Saddam gave him a beautiful carpet enriched with a uranium solution. The General died three months later from radiation.

In another notable exception to this phase of tolerance, another minister was removed from the RCC in July in a style more in keeping with Saddam's usual methods. I was with Mohammed in the Dark Room when we heard a single gunshot ring out from somewhere within the palace.

'Stay here, Mikhaelef,' Mohammed told me, walking towards the door, 'I will go and see what has happened.' He rushed out, but was back within minutes.

'Riyadh is dead!' he announced. 'The President has just shot him.'

It was beyond belief, but it turned out to be true. The official story later released to the Iraqi media was that Riyadh Ibrahim, Minister of Health, had been executed for the importation and distribution of unsafe and illegal medicines. It was also rumoured that Riyadh, no relation to Saddam's half-brothers, was an ambitious, headstrong man who, during cabinet meetings, persisted in proposing that Saddam should temporarily stand down as President in favour of his predecessor, Ahmad Hassan al-Bakr, so that a peace settlement could be negotiated with Iran. While Saddam was in power, the Iranians would not entertain talks. The debate continued over several weeks until finally, on this morning, an irate Saddam suggested to Riyadh that they should continue their discussion privately and they left the cabinet room together. A few moments later a gun was fired and the matter of Saddam's resignation was permanently closed.

The truth was somewhat different and far more credible. Saddam was determined to use the Ministry of Health as a means of importing chemicals in the quantities required for his illegal weapons. Riyadh, as a man of principle, refused to co-operate. Saddam saw no point in taking the man outside to shoot him. He put a bullet through his heart as he sat before him, in full view of the other RCC members.

Saddam was certainly not slow to pull the trigger when

he felt it necessary. A few weeks after the shooting of Riyadh, he was addressing the National Assembly when he suddenly drew his revolver and shot dead two men sitting in the front row. It later transpired, at least officially, that the two were associates of Riyadh and were exchanging information with a view to an assassination attempt on Saddam.

There were other similarly ruthless expulsions during this period. More than 300 senior offices of the armed forces were executed on a variety of trumped-up charges, generally attributed to poor performances in the field. But Saddam had been criticised by the military for insisting all operational planning was cleared through the presidential office and those who objected the loudest were 'coincidentally' prominent among those executed.

During the Ramadan offensive of July, the Iranians crossed the border to the north of al-Basrah and, as the year ended, they occupied territory in the Mendali and Mehran regions. Despite this success, the Iranian infantry, dependent on tank support, were unable to make progress in the al-Huweizah marshlands of southern Iraq, where the Ma'dan tribes, descendants of the ancient Babylonians, had lived for thousands of years. The Iranian Revolutionary Guard, many of whom were passionate but ill-trained teenagers, were mown down by superior Iraqi gunfire in the wetlands. Nevertheless, they did inflict an embarrassing defeat on Iraq when 4,000 of our troops fled their defensive positions around Kut and al-'Amarah in Iran. I heard that as many as 50,000 Iraqi soldiers had been killed since the outbreak of the war to some 200,000 Iranians, but with a population nearly three times smaller than the enemy, our losses in manpower were no less difficult to replace.

Iran had for some time enjoyed air and naval superiority around the Gulf, but towards the end of the year Saddam had managed to acquire five French Super Etendard aircraft with Exocet missiles. This, he hoped, might even things up. Saddam declared a military exclusion zone around the Iranian oil terminal on the Jazireh-ye Kharkh (Kharg Island) and, in a bid to 'internationalise' the war, several foreign ships were sunk.

With the loss of his nuclear potential a year earlier, Saddam developed a second-string to his war-waging capacity and a relatively inexpensive deterrent to Israel's nuclear threat. When vice-president he had been instrumental in founding Iraq's chemical weapons industry, and invested heavily in mustard gas, Tabun and Sarin. He brought more than 4,000 foreign scientists and technicians to Iraq in the mid-seventies and organised the procurement of the necessary components for chemical research and development. All this was undertaken by Iraqi agents posing as business excutives in the pesticide industry.

As the Egyptians led the field in chemical research in the Middle East, Saddam placed a $12 million contract with Egypt's main pesticide factory, and had it reactivated as a chemical weapons plant. When the Egyptian premier, President Sadat, intervened, many of the research and development scientists left and set up in Iraq. Although signatories to the extension and ratification of the Geneva Convention in 1978, which outlawed chemical weapons, the Iraqi leadership saw no moral dilemma in their use. If Israel was prepared to vapourise the enemy, Saddam was content to poison them.

Mustard gas was produced in large quantities at Falujah, eighty kilometres west of Baghdad on the Nahr al-Farut. Introduced as a military weapon by the Germans during the first world war, its manufacture is a simple process. Ethylene oxide is combined with hydrogen sulphide and then mixed with hydrolic acid. Meant to disable armies rather than kill them, mustard gas causes painful skin eruptions and inflamed lungs. The damage is often permanent and occasionally fatal, but as a weapon its effects diminish rapidly within a couple of hours.

Tabun and Sarin were nerve agents produced at Samarah. Whether inhaled or absorbed, they attack the body's nervous system and death is almost inevitable.

However, they remain effective for under an hour and in the hot climate of the Middle East, where the evaporation process is so rapid, their effective life is even shorter.

Binary chemical weapons, also manufactured at Samarah, are a combination of two often harmless chemicals, which when combined produce a deadly mixture. Sarin XV, first produced in Egypt, is a potent binary weapon, much more virulent and persistent than its predecessor. Because they are generally safe in transit and can be manufactured under the cover of pesticide industries, Iraqi chemists have experimented with more than fifty chemical combinations in order to develop efficient binary weapons.

Biological and bacteriological weapons were developed at Salman Pak, near to the nuclear reactor complex at Tuwaitha, eighteen kilometres south-east of Baghdad. Researchers here developed anthrax and botulism toxin, as well as other common viruses, such as typhoid and cholera. Unlike chemicals, biological weapons do not require heavy industrial facilities, but they are volatile in transit.

Saddam believed that the development of chemical and biological weapons was a legitimate response to the Israeli nuclear threat. They were afford- able, easily developed and psychologically menacing.

But more than anything else, they were available and they worked.

Amna was deeply distressed by the rumours, gaining currency within government circles, that the Iraqi President was prepared to unleash such chemical weapons on the people of Iran. Once again, she said, ordinary people were to be the victims when two warring dictators clash.

I did not know it then, but the seeds of our undoing had been sown.

Chapter Five

1983
Raby' al-Awwal 1403 – Raby' al-Awwal 1404

On the fifteenth day of the Islamic month of Raby' al-Awwal, in the Hijrah year of 1403, Amna presented me with a daughter, Nadia, weighing a healthy three-and-a-half kilos. She was born with a shock of black hair and the deepest blue eyes and for a while she brightened my life more than I can describe. I thought my life was complete.

I knew that Amna had dearly wanted to present me with a son and such is the nature of Iraqi culture that only the birth of a son is celebrated with great thanks to Allah. Indeed, when I told my mother later in the day that we had a daughter, she cried for an hour bemoaning our misfortune. She had waited in vain for a number of years for Wahab to produce a son, having delivered three daughters, and she was deeply disappointed at the arrival of yet another granddaughter.

'Girls! Girls!' she cried. 'Why can my children give me only girls?'

'Please, mother,' I said, more than slightly irritated, but

trying vainly to soothe her. 'It is more important that everyone is well. There is plenty of time for sons yet.'

'Plenty of time?' she barked in response. 'You tell me there is plenty of time? Wahab is forty-four and you will soon be forty-one. Wahab has finished with having children and I have to rely on you, a middle-aged man who thinks there is plenty of time!'

'Amna has only just turned thirty, mother,' I pleaded defensively.

'Yes, and she produces a girl. Maybe I should resign myself to never seeing a grandson carrying your name to the next generation.'

There was no point in talking to her when she carried on in this fashion. In any case, I knew that once the child was brought home she would fuss about her as if she were destined to be Queen of Iraq, had there been such a thing. For myself, I was content that the birth had been a straightforward one and my daughter had no defects. I could wait for a son.

While Amna was still in hospital, I received a telephone call from Mohammed, who broke the news that Mahdi, the other 'double', had been assassinated in al-'Amarah. He had been travelling through the centre of the town in a secure convoy when they were stopped by an explosion outside the town hall. The details of what followed were somewhat sketchy, but it seems a gun battle broke out during which Mahdi was shot dead. The killing had only just missed being filmed by an American television news team in the area, but rumours of Saddam's demise proved premature when he appeared on live television in Baghdad later that night. I was shaken by Mahdi's death. Only a handful of people were aware of Saddam's use of doubles, but from this time I began to hear of occasional rumours being aired that there might be more than one 'Saddam'. This, I feared, could make me as much a target as Saddam himself.

As I was far more accessible than Mahdi had ever been in his short career as a double, his death was particularly worrying. He had only ever been seen by the public from a distance, whereas I tended to mingle with crowds, shaking hands and talking to the people. Amna, too, was deeply anxious about the dangers I was facing and she urged me to talk with Saddam.

'You do not ask him for much, Mikhaelef,' she argued, as she breast-fed little Nadia in her hospital bed. 'It is not right that you should have to take such risks.'

'What is right has nothing to do with it, Amna,' I replied. 'It is my job. I cannot say to Saddam I am frightened of being killed. We are at war. There are men being killed every minute. He will see me as a miserable, selfish coward if I voice concerns about my own safety.'

'It has nothing to do with that. You have demonstrated your courage many times. But you are a father now and some consideration has to be given to Nadia's future.'

'Yes, of course, but if I were not in the service of Saddam, I might now be serving at the front as a soldier. Do you not think there are many men fighting for Iraq at this very moment who would rather be at home with their young children?'

'Of course, but this is different.'

'Why is it different, Amna? Who am I that I should be regarded any differently? How many times have you reminded me that I am just a schoolteacher from Karbala?'

Amna went quiet, finally conceding the point. I had no wish to cause her more anxiety than was necessary when she was still recovering from the birth of our child, so, to placate her, I said, 'If it makes you feel better, I will talk to Mohammed. He may be able to suggest ways of keeping my head below the parapet for a while.'

To speak to Mohammed would have been a waste of breath. The threat of assassination was a permanent feature of my job and the main reason I was paid so well. I had no intention of raising the matter with Mohammed or anyone else. I would accept whatever fate had in store for me with stoicism, I hoped, should I ever come to an untimely end in the service of Saddam.

The following day I was with Mohammed in the Dark Room. We found ourselves discussing what had happened to Mahdi. He was an ordinary man who could brighten a room with his simple, naive humour, but we would laugh with him no more. Growing depressed as we mourned our dead colleague, I eventually changed the subject by asking for Mohammed's opinion on the newly-announced promotion to Foreign Minister of Tariq, who had replaced Sa'dun Hammadi, standing down on the grounds of ill health – genuinely for once. Sa'dun had been at the foreign office for nine years, was a complete devotee of Saddam's and would continue to act for him on matters of state. He had a unique qualification for dealing with the US in that he was the only member of Saddam's inner circle to have received an education in the West, gaining a PhD at Wisconsin University for agricultural economics in 1957.

Mohammed suggested we should go over the diary of engagements for the next few days and look at how we might be able to tighten security. Before we could make a start, Saddam came into the room, escorted by Udai and his new foreign minister, Tariq.

Saddam looked troubled. Possibly he was unsettled by the assassination of Mahdi Mahmud. The bullets were, after all, meant for him.

'You are aware of what happened yesterday to Mahdi Mahmud,' he said, a statement not a question.

Mohammed and I nodded.

'It is a terrible tragedy,' Saddam continued, 'and you can be sure no stone will remain unturned in search of those responsible.'

'What will happen to his wife?' I asked and Saddam smiled warmly.

'It is typical of you, Mikhaelef, that you should ask such a question at this time. Mahdi's wife will be well compensated for the loss of her husband. He will be posthumously decorated and she will receive a generous war widows' pension. She will be able to grieve over her husband without having to worry how she will feed herself.'

I was confident that Saddam would keep his word. He was capable of enormous generosity towards those who served him loyally. Mahdi's wife would not go short.

'With the death of our friend,' Saddam continued, 'we have to be even more vigilant than we have been so far. We were fortunate that an American film crew did not shoot the whole incident. We must, however, not take such good fortune for granted. What happened is the will of Allah, but we would be foolish in the extreme if we did not take heed of the lesson he wishes to teach us.'

Although there were three other people in the room, Saddam was addressing me directly. 'It is important that the outside world does not know that I have people such as yourself standing in for me, Mikhaelef. For a while you must stay out of sight. All your engagements for the next few weeks will be cancelled or rescheduled.'

A wave of relief ran through me and I knew that Amna, too, would be delighted with Saddam's decision.

'Obviously, I have your welfare at heart,' he said, 'but it is a practical step also. I cannot afford to lose you. The loss of Mahdi is terrible, but he was not as close to me in appearance as yourself, therefore of less use to me. If the same fate were to befall you, Mikhaelef, it would be an irreplaceable loss to me.'

These were sentiments of pragmatism, not affection.

As this scene was being played out, I noticed that Udai, now nineteen and about one ninety-five in height, looked decidedly unimpressed at his father's reluctance to throw me to the wolves. I wondered when he might say his piece. We did not have to wait long.

'I think everybody is missing the point here, Father,' he said boldly, when it was clear that Saddam had finished speaking. 'Surely the object of the exercise is for the look-alike to go where it is not safe for the President to go. Our man from Karbala is the solution to a presidential dilemma. In a time of war, there are many more things that our nation's leader should do but cannot, because the risk to his life is too great. The country cannot afford such a loss, but what is the point of employing a look-alike if you protect him as you would protect yourself?'

'Your point is taken, Udai,' Saddam answered, 'and it pleases me that you can think so clearly, but you are over-simplifying the problem. If I were to send Mikhaelef out with no regard for his safety, I am endangering the presidency as well as his life.'

'I do not see why, Father.'

'Then I will explain. Let us say I do as you suggest. I send Mikhaelef to the front and with a large number of people to witness it, he is killed. It is, you will agree, difficult to be killed inconspicuously at the front. We tried using Mikhaelef once before, remember, and he was shot. We were lucky that time that our stratagem was not discovered.'

'Yes, Father,' Udai said, looking sulky and clearly still uncomprehending.

'But, to return to the point I am making. If Mikhaelef were to be killed, the people would be in deep mourning because their great and courageous leader has been killed when supporting his army in the thick of the fighting. And then I appear and declare that all is well, because I am alive. The man who was killed was only my double, standing in for me because it was too dangerous to visit our soldiers at the front. What will they think, Udai? I will tell you. They will think that perhaps I am not so courageous after all. They will think that perhaps they have a coward for a President. Once the people believe I have lost my nerve, Udai, it is all over. Our soldiers will lose their nerve too. Believe me.'

When on his metaphorical soapbox, Saddam is impressive. His passion and sincerity can be infectious. Despite my growing concern about his true nature, I would be less than honest if I did not admit I admired him intensely at such moments. For me, Saddam Hussein was the greatest contradiction of my life. The more I learnt of the dreadful atrocities he had committed and the terrible crimes perpetrated in his name, the more reason I had to despise him. Yet I desperately wanted to like and respect him. I cannot justify those feelings. I am not able to properly explain why I felt this way towards him. Even now I find myself thinking back on something or other that he said or did, to which I was a witness, and smiling to myself at how he handled it. I was as seduced by Saddam's personality as anyone and it was difficult for me to free myself of his potent spell.

Before this meeting with Saddam, and again while Udai was speaking, I had assumed it would only be a matter of time before I was sent back to boost the morale of our troops at the front. I was much relieved that this was no longer the case. I had hardly expected Saddam to reflect my anxieties, even if our reasons were different.

In the early weeks of the year, the fighting had lessened in its intensity, but when the Iranians launched their Val Fajr offensive in February towards Fakkeh in the south, the death toll was as high as it had been since the outbreak of war. Fierce fighting continued in the months that followed, but the Iranians were repeatedly repelled.

The militant elements of the Shi'a movement had seen the war as an opportunity to put pressure on the presidency and during the first half of 1983 Saddam set about putting the problem behind him. Hojjat al-Islam Mohammed Baqr al-Hakim, who was to become the head of the Supreme Council of the Islamic Revolution of Iraq (SCIRI) the following year, angered Saddam by moving from Jordan to Iran. Saddam had sixteen members of his family, still living in Iraq, tortured and executed. A message was relayed to Hojjat that the executions would carry on if he continued to agitate against the Iraqi government. When Hojjat formed SCIRI in 1984, another ten family members disappeared forever but, now resident in London, he remains active to this day.

I spent several weeks doing little more than turning up at the palace each day and chatting with Mohammed. When eventually, I began to appear again on minor public occasions, I was surrounded by much more security than in the past. Then came the surprise announcement of a wedding in the Saddam Hussein household.

At the age of just fifteen, Saddam's eldest daughter, Raghd, married Hussein Kamil Hassan al-Majid, Saddam's rising star and the son of Kamil Hassan al-Majid, Saddam's 'cousin'. In 1983,

Hussein Kamil was just a sergeant in the Iraqi air force and used as a driver by its commander. When Saddam called the men of Takrit to join the Republican Guard, Hussein Kamil transferred and became a chauffeur to Saddam's wife, Sajida. From this privileged position, he began courting Raghd and quickly rose through the ranks to captain.

For many observers, this confirmed Saddam's intentions to groom Hussein Kamil as a future successor, possibly as an interim President as Udai matured. The marriage did not therefore meet with universal approval. Saddam's three younger half-brothers saw it as a direct challenge to their place within the Iraqi hierarchy. Barzan Ibrahim and his two brothers, Watban and Sabawi, were the sons of Saddam's stepfather and largely due to the influence of their mother, Subha al-Talfah, had enjoyed enormous privileges under Saddam. Barzan had been made head of the Mukhabarat in 1979, Watban was the governor of the province of Salah al-Din, which included the town of Takrit, and Sabawi was the deputy chief of the Amn al-A'am, General Police Security in Baghdad.

The al-Majids represented a different branch of the family. While Subha was alive, some degree of control was brought to bear on the two factions, but there was little love lost between them.

In August, Subha died. The open grieving was tempered with the knowledge that the power struggle within the family would soon come to a head. Saddam had to make a choice between the two families and, not surprisingly, came down on the side of the al-Majids. It was Mohammed who broke the news to me.

'The Ibrahims are out,' he told me, as he came into the

Dark Room one morning. 'Barzan demanded to see Saddam alone to find out where he stood. Well, he knows now all right. He has been dismissed from the Mukhabarat and placed under house arrest.'

'What has happened to Watban and Sabawi?' I asked.

'Dismissed also.'

'What will happen to them?' My curiosity was only out of politeness.

'It is too early to say, but it seems some kind of arrangement has been made.'

'Do you think there might be more to this?'

'Perhaps,' Mohammed replied, his expression indicating he thought it likely. 'There are rumours that the Ibrahams have been involved in an army conspiracy against Saddam, but that is nonsense.'

'How can you be sure?'

'Because they would have been executed without a second thought. There is also no truth in the tale that Barzan has been reprimanded by Saddam for failing to uncover a plot against him. I believe Saddam has asked Barzan to step out of the limelight for a while.'

'He was given an option?' I asked sceptically.

'I am sure he was, but it may not have been a particularly attractive one. Barzan will be back, mark my words. This is Saddam's way of solving a problem that could not be overcome by conventional means. It also possible Barzan has not been dismissed. It might well be a clever ploy. Perhaps by appearing to push him out into the cold, Saddam is hoping he will be approached by those who conspire against him, believing he will resent Saddam and be sympathetic to their cause. Whatever the case, Saddam will stand by his "blue-eyed" son-in-law for now, but Barzan is not gone for good. He will have his day yet.'

'You do not like Hussein Kamil?' I asked in surprise.

Mohammed shook his head. 'I do not trust him. Barzan may have a dark side to his nature, but he plays with the one deck of cards. I do not believe Hussein Kamil is interested in anything but his own advancement.'

I did not know Hussein Kamil well and had only been in his company perhaps three or four times. Yet I always found him intelligent and articulate and not at all disagreeable. Despite his modest physical stature, some ten to fifteen centimetres shorter than his younger brother, Saddam Kamil, he was imbued with tremendous presence and was extremely popular with the officers and men under his command. I was intrigued as to why Mohammed had such a low opinion of him.

'What you say mystifies me, Mohammed. I have never before heard anyone say a word against him.'

'It is instinct, Mikhaelef. I cannot really rationalise it. I know he is married to the President's daughter, but that is just an arrangement to secure his future. He represents trouble and I believe the President will regret the trust he has placed in him.' Mohammed then looked up at me as if realising he had been somewhat indiscreet in his criticism. 'These thoughts of mine,' he added cautiously, 'are for your ears only, Mikhaelef.'

'Do not concern yourself, my friend,' I replied. 'Nothing you say to me will ever be heard by others.'

Personally, I thought Saddam had made the correct choice between the two. I would have followed Hussein Kamil wherever he led me, but I had no regard for Barzan who, in my opinion, was nothing more than a psychopathic thug. There was, though, another possible element to Saddam's decision to favour Hussein Kamil over Barzan. For the best part of a decade, the Ibrahims had amassed enormous wealth and influence, and Saddam was ever alert to the dangers from within. Perhaps Saddam feared Barzan as a potential usurper and could not 'retire' one brother without removing all three.

It would have also been typical of Saddam to pretend that Barzan and his brothers were out of favour for the reasons Mohammed had suggested. Despite my closeness to Saddam, his family and his ministers, only one person ever saw the full picture at any given moment – and that person was Saddam Hussein.

There had been whispers, mostly in the north and mostly unfounded, that Saddam was losing his grip on his cabinet ministers. In truth, he was as strong as ever, a fact confirmed by the dismissal of the Ibrahim brothers and the murder of Riyadh. In the September, though, Saddam had arranged a show of strength with a public speech to a rally of supporters in Arbil, an old Kurdish town situated some 300 kilometres to the north of Baghdad. Dominated by an ancient fortress, Arbil was deep in the heart of Kurdish country.

On the morning of the rally, Saddam fell ill. For some years, he had suffered from severe bouts of migraine for which the only remedy was to spend several days in a darkened room. He frequently had premonitions of an impending attack and at such times would spend a few hours rescheduling his appointments. Such a prescience occurred shortly before he was due to leave for Arbil and I was quickly summoned to replace him. Under normal circumstances, it would have mattered little to cancel the event, it happened frequently, but his non-appearance at this critical moment would have led to credence being given to the rumours. Saddam insisted I replace him.

Generally, when I stood in for Saddam, it was easier and more practical for me to travel by road, but given that Saddam's private jet was standing by, I was taken instead to the Muthand presidential airfield close to Zowrah Park. From there I was flown directly to al-Mawsil. Mohammed, as always, was by my side, as were a number of Republican Guards. Two of them, Jassim Abdullahlah and Taqi Ghadanfar, were to escort me everywhere, shoulder to shoulder, until I was returned safely to Baghdad. For both men, it was a great honour. Although they did not know it, they were chosen for the task because they were the most recent additions to the presidential guard and the least likely to notice any subtle differences in my mannerisms. Of those aboard the aircraft, only Mohammed was aware I was not the genuine article.

At al-Mawsil we were met by Hassan Muwafeq, a local

Ba'ath party member, who drove us the remaining eighty kilometres to Arbil. The speech had been meticulously prepared. Even so, as I stood before several hundred members of the Ba'ath Socialist Party my knees trembled. It took me some fifteen minutes to deliver the speech and it was followed by a twenty-five minute ovation. When it was over, I was left mentally and physically shattered. Jassim and Taqi were at my side during the entire proceedings and afterwards I was met by Mohammed and Hassan. Our party immediately set off for al-Mawsil for the flight home.

We covered some thirty kilometres without incident. Ahead were the lights of what appeared to be a small town. I was about to ask Mohammed its name, when Hassan gave an exclamation of annoyance.

'There is a road block up ahead.'

Road blocks peppered the approach roads to major towns and cities in Iraq, so none of us were alarmed.

'Where are we?' I asked Mohammed as I peered into the darkness.

'We are coming to the bridge crossing the az-Zab al-Kabir river,' he replied, wiping the condensation from the window. 'It separates the provinces of Arbil and Ninawa. It is the usual practice to be stopped here.'

During the daytime, the residential insignia on any vehicle carrying the President was easily visible and the barrier would have been raised before we reached it. But on unlit country roads at night our limousine was indistinguishable from any other large car. The barrier remained down and we were waved to a halt.

Jassim was seated in the front passenger seat and started to climb out of the car, shouting obscenities at the patrol. He was immediately shot through the forehead. He slumped to the ground without so much as a cry of pain. A second later, automatic gunfire opened up on the car. Hassan was hit several times in the face and chest and Taqi, seated to my left, was shot through the chin and neck. I was convinced I was next and tried to throw myself to the floor. As I did, I felt Mohammed throw himself over me.

The firing stopped as quickly as it had started and within a few seconds both rear doors were opened. Taqi was dragged from the car and Mohammed was lifted from me. Looking up, I saw one bullet had passed through his cheek below his right eye and blown away the back of his head. He had also been shot several times in the chest. He was unquestionably dead. I was now the only survivor.

It was my guess that we had been ambushed by the peshmerga, Kurdsish revolutionaries, and knew that the instant they saw my face properly, they would take great delight in killing me. I prayed to Allah they would not wish to enjoy some sport with me first. Instead, I was spoken to by the man obviously in charge of the events taking place.

'Your Excellency,' he said, with a sweeping mock-bow. 'Do please join us. We have been waiting for you, though we expected you to be in the company of a somewhat more formidable escort.'

'That was the idea,' I replied, with as much bravado as I could muster.

My hands and feet were bound and I was put into the boot of another car. Although I could see nothing, as we moved off I sensed we were headed directly for al-Mawsil. Less than an hour later, we crossed the Dijlah and I could hear the sounds of the city until all was quiet again and I assumed we were heading for the town of Tall 'Afar, fifty kilometres west of al-Mawsil. Within half-an-hour we passed through the town and shortly afterwards took a left turn and headed south. Unless I had totally lost my sense of direction, I reckoned we were now on the eastern edge of the al-Jazirah desert, travelling towards al-Hadr.

My mind drifted back to Mohammed and, although I tried to suppress the feeling, I was deeply upset by his death. We had grown close over the previous few years and I had thought of him as my friend as much as my mentor. Until that day, I had never seen a murdered body and the image of Mohammed's bloodied face will live with me forever. I knew I would miss him. If I lived long enough, that is.

We pulled off the road and drove for an hour or so over sand. Finally the car stopped and, amid a great deal of commotion, the boot was opened and I was hauled out onto my feet. We were in a desert camp and from having travelled south for less than an hour, I thought we were probably still about thirty kilometres north of al-Hadr and some twenty kilometres west of Qayyarah and the Dijlah. I was taken to a large tent to one side of the camp and held under armed guard. Although I was given some rice and water, I was not reassured by this gesture and expected every moment to be my last. I was wrong. After being allowed to relieve myself over a hole in the sand, within a circle of five sniggering guards, I was left alone and eventually fell asleep. Nobody disturbed me until after sunrise the following morning.

When I was finally interrogated, I was told that my kidnappers were now aware the real Saddam was in Baghdad. They had informed the government that my escort had been wiped out, but that I was still alive. If they wanted me back, it would cost them $1 million. Otherwise, I would be tortured and shot.

It was a king's ransom, and I was no king. The government declined to pay.

Chapter Six

1984
Raby' al-Awwal 1404 – Raby' al-Thaany 1405

Negotiations between the Kurds and the Government were drawn out for more than five months, during which time I lost the ten kilograms in weight I had gained over the previous four years plus a few of my original kilos. I was not starved by my captors, eating much the same as they did themselves, but my diet was restricted to little more than bread, rice and tea. I was neither abused nor beaten and found my captors to be reasonable men, dedicated to the cause of liberating their people from the Ba'ath oppression that had undoubtedly blighted their lives for three decades.

The man I spoke to immediately after the murders of Mohammed and the other men of my escort was Mullah al-Barzinji, leader of this desperate group of rebels. I saw more of Mullah than anybody else in the camp and over a period of time we spoke about many things. He was an articulate, intelligent man and although I vehemently disputed his attempts to justify Mohammed's murder, I was forced to concede the validity of his grievances.

The Kurds are also Moslems, but they are non-Arabs, racially and culturally distinct from other Iraqi Moslems. For generations, they have been the political pawns of the Middle East and they will know no peace until the most reasonable of their claims have been satisfied. There are more than three million Kurds in Iraq, and a further twenty-million are spread across Iran, Syria, Turkey and the Republic of Azerbaijan, at that time part of the Soviet Union. No single race of people who are yet to win the right to self-determination is greater in number.

In 1918 they were promised an 'absolute unmolested opportunity for autonomous development' by President Woodrow Wilson and in the 1920 Treaty of Sevres, the powers of the League of Nations agreed that the Turkish Kurds should be permitted to form a nation-state. It never happened.

Instead, the British ignored the protestations of both the Turks and Kurds and annexed the region to the new state of Iraq. The Kurds, under the leadership of the self-declared king of Kurdistan, Sheikh Mahmud, rose up in rebellion, but their villages were destroyed by the Royal Air Force. Among the British weapons used to defeat them were bombs with delayed fuses, set to detonate when the fleeing Kurdish families had returned to their homes.

Mullah accepted that the nation-state of Kurdistan was an impossible dream. It would contain too many of the rich oil resources of Iraq, Syria and Turkey and would never be permitted, least of all by the US. In 1977, the Iraqi Kurds had been granted a limited degree of local autonomy and the Kurdish language was officially recognised by the al-Bakr administration, but Mullah insisted that his people had to be properly represented at government level both at home and abroad.

'We should be an integral part of any conference regarding the affairs of the Middle East,' he argued, 'and be granted observer status at the United Nations. Palestinians have been granted this and are far fewer in number.'

During such conversations, Mullah would become quite

animated and passionately defended his people's right to exist in freedom.

'We are treated as outcasts in our own homeland and thrown into prison for demanding what is rightfully ours. Do you know what goes on in the prisons, Mikhaelef?' he asked.

I nodded. 'I have a good idea. I once spoke to a friend of my wife. Her two sons were arrested by the Mukhabarat. One was killed in prison, but the other was released.'

'That is most unusual,' Mullah said, with raised eyebrows. 'When one brother is murdered, the other is usually killed also. They are rarely so careless as to release a man onto the streets with vengeance in his heart.'

'I think I may have had something to do with it,' I said. I related to him the story of Ahmad and Yasin al-Asadi.

'Had you told me this tale when we first met, I would not have believed you. It surprises me that Saddam Hussein possesses even a morsel of compassion. Do you regret becoming involved with him?'

'Yes, but I had little choice in the matter. Saddam asked me to join him and I agreed, but I do not think refusal was an option. It would take a stronger man than I to refuse a request from the President.'

'I am sure you are right,' he said unsmilingly.

He went on to tell me of his own experience at the hands of Saddam's security forces, having spent six months in prison in al-Mawsil in 1981 before he was able to escape.

My expression revealed my own scepticism. 'Not many have escaped, Mullah.' In fact I knew of none.

'It happened while I was being transported to the Qasr al-Nihayah prison in Baghdad. You know it?'

'Of course,' I replied. Everybody knew the "Palace of the End." It had once belonged to the Iraqi royal family. When Iraq became a republic, it was converted into a brutal detention centre, so feared an establishment that few Iraqis dared even speak of it.

'In al-Mawsil,' Mullah continued, 'I was treated badly, but I knew I would not last long in the Qasr.'

'What happened?' I asked.

'I was being transferred with two other Kurds from the town of Ash-Sharqat. We had been on the road for an hour and were near Qayarah. A taxi travelling north had a blow-out and swerved across our path. It forced our vehicle off the road and we flipped over and rolled into a sand dune. If I am honest, I was terrified of the fate awaiting me in the Qasr, and in those few short seconds I was half hoping I would be killed. When we came to a stop, one of the guards was dead and lay sprawled across me. My fellow-prisoners were dead also, as was the driver, who had gone through the windscreen. The other two guards were at least unconscious, but I did not wait around to see if they were alive. I was able to take keys belonging to the dead guard and removed my shackles. My right arm was broken and I was bleeding badly from my forehead.' He pointed to a curved mark just above the eyebrow. 'As you can see, I still have the scar. The taxi that had caused the accident was still there and I made the driver take me to al-Mawsil on three tyres.'

'You were tortured in prison?' I asked, overawed to be in the presence of a man who had been subjected personally to the terrors I had heard so much about.

Mullah laughed. 'Perhaps one day you will introduce me to someone who has been imprisoned by the Mukhabarat for six months and not been tortured. Of course I was.'

'What did they do to you?'

'The Mukhabarat do not lack imagination when it comes to means of extracting the information they require,' Mullah said bleakly. 'You know of al-Falaka?'

'I have heard of it,' I replied, my stomach turning. This widespread form of torture consists of tying the victim's feet together and beating his soles with a club until they bleed.

'It is one of their friendlier methods of persuasion. On one occasion, I was confined in a metal drum, little more than a metre and a half in height and maybe fifty centimetres wide. It was not high enough for me to stand upright and not wide enough for me to sit down.'

'How long were you in there?'

'For three days, with nothing but my own urine and excrement for company: I wondered at the time why they fed me so heartily. Still, I should not complain. I was one of the fortunate ones. I have lost many good friends who were tortured in the most dreadful ways you can imagine. Burning is a speciality. They might fasten your hand to an electric ring and turn it on or they might strap you to an oil heater. One favoured method is to tie you to a metal bedstead and then light a fire beneath it.'

I nodded in acknowledgement as my mind drifted back to Aswa's son, Ahmad.

'They hang people from the ceiling by their hair, feet or worst of all, by the wrists after they have tied your hands behind your back. They amputate hands, feet and whole limbs. They push needles under your fingernails. They pin you to a wall by driving nails through your ears. They drill holes in your head, hands and feet. They put your head in a vice until your skull cracks.'

Mullah paused to light a cigarette. As he resumed his frightful account of the Mukhabarat's atrocities, his voice changed, becoming gruff, and his eyes glistened with tears. 'Two years ago they killed my younger brother, Hamid. He was arrested by the Mukhabarat in Rawandiz, where he was working for an uncle. Hamid had done nothing, never raised a finger against the state, but he was my brother. They dragged him from my uncle's house and tied an arm and a leg to the bumper of one car and the other arm and leg to the bumper of another. In front of my mother's family, the vehicles were then driven slowly in opposite directions and ripped him apart. He was fifteen-years-old.'

Nothing I could say seemed appropriate and I remained silent, the image of his brother's final agony all too vivid in my mind. After a short silence, Mullah spoke again.

'Do you know what they do to our women?'

I confessed that I did not.

'Then someone else will have to tell you, my friend, because I cannot.'

My captors frequently talked loosely in my presence, unaware that I could by this time understand Kurdish quite well, thanks to the programme initiated by Mohammed Qutaibi. All of my conversations with Mullah had been in Arabic and I did not reveal to him my ability to speak his language.

Although I never felt threatened during the time I was held, I was under no illusions. While I was alive, the Kurds had a commodity that might be of use to them, but once it was clear Saddam would not play their games, I knew I would be eliminated. After five months of on-off negotiations, my time was running out.

I had no doubt in my own mind that Saddam would not pay for my release. He had often categorically stated in my presence he would never give in to the ransom demands of terrorists. Yet clearly some form of bargaining was taking place. Perhaps Saddam was temporising while the Republican Guard scoured the country looking for me. They had effective methods of extracting information.

During my months as a hostage of the Kurds I never once attempted to escape and after a while was given some degree of liberty within the perimeters of the camp. Most afternoons, once I was fed and watered, I took to walking around the tents for exercise in the company of an armed guard who would amble along a few metres behind me. One afternoon in March, the Kurds were having trouble starting the one vehicle they possessed, and the guard accompanying me was called over to lend a hand. Alone for a few moments, my attention was drawn to an argument taking place within the largest of the tents and I slowly made my way towards it, doing my best not to appear that I had an objective in mind.

The conversation I overheard was a realisation of all I had feared since my capture. As I came within earshot, I recognised Mullah's voice.

'I tell you Saddam is playing games with us,' he was saying, almost shouting. He spoke rapidly, but I was well able to pick up what he was saying. I praised Allah for Mohammed Qutaibi's determination to teach me Kurdish so long ago and ignore my objections. 'He has no intention of meeting our demands,' Mullah continued. 'But that is no reason to kill Mikhaelef Ramadan. We should not take out our frustrations on a man because he looks like Saddam.'

'Why not?' another voice answered. 'He is one of them.'

'He breaks bread with Saddam,' said another. 'Why should we lose sleep over him?'

These were strong arguments for killing me, but Mullah was fighting my corner. 'If we kill him, then we are no better than Saddam!'

An older voice interrupted. 'You are a decent man, Mullah, and your humanity is admirable. But there is no dilemma here, moral or otherwise. We have no choice but to kill the prisoner. If we do not, then Saddam will laugh at our weakness. We have found out one thing during our negotiations. He may not be prepared to submit to our ransom demand, but Saddam wants this man back. He would have broken off contact with us a long time ago if that was not the case. If we kill him, we hurt Saddam. It is not much, but we cannot walk away from this without our pride intact. I am sorry, Mullah. You have befriended this man, but that was a mistake. We have no choice.'

His sentiments were met with a chorus of approval.

'What shall we do with the body?' a voice asked.

The proposal that my dead body should be photographed and the pictures released to the international media met with general approval. Then the world would know that Saddam uses doubles. They were, though, more creative when it came to disposing of my body and my skin went cold as they clinically discussed it. Finally though, they decided I would be returned to Baghdad and dumped near to the main gates of the Karradat Mariam.

At that moment, the car's stubborn engine burst into life behind me, and the guard, noticing my absence, came hurrying across and ushered me away from the big tent. It did fleetingly cross my mind to attack him and try to escape, but my nerve let me down. Instead, I allowed myself to be meekly led back to my tent to ponder my fate. I was terrified by the thought that I would be shot within minutes and nearly passed out when it occurred to me the Kurds might instead decide to cut my throat. But more than an hour passed and nobody came.

Lost in self-pity, I sat curled up, whimpering quietly to myself. I had been in this position for perhaps an hour when a noise that sounded at first like a roll of thunder in the distance shook me out of my self-pity. As the noise grew louder, I realised I was listening to the sound of approaching jet aircraft. I rushed outside. First one and then another roared immediately over the camp. The Kurds ran around in panic and confusion, shouting, some firing into the air in a hopeless attempt to bring the aircraft down. The jets circled round and flew back over the camp, strafing the tents with gunfire. I dived back inside my tent, though it afforded little protection. As I measured my length with a force that squeezed the air from my lungs, a series of explosions made the ground shudder beneath me. Now screams mingled with the shouts.

I was beginning to think the Iraqi air force might deny the Kurds the opportunity of killing me when an explosion just a few feet away brought the roof of the tent down onto my head. I grappled with the canvas and crawling out from under it, came across the guard who had been standing outside. His face was covered in a hundred tiny shrapnel wounds and he was quite dead.

He was not the only one by far. I was surrounded by a scene of carnage and utter confusion. There were bodies scattered everywhere and those not dead or injured were scampering about the camp looking for cover where none existed. Nobody paid me any attention, so turning onto my stomach, I began to crawl away. Scrambling into a small dip in the ground just outside the perimeter of the camp, I stopped and looked behind me. I had not been seen.

As the aircraft came swooping in for a second strike, I rose up and, turning my back on the camp, ran for my life. For what seemed like an enormous distance, but was probably no more than 500 metres, I ran. My lungs burned, but still I ran, instinctively ducking my head with every explosion to the rear. I had not run so far without respite since I was a boy and only fear and adrenaline kept me going. After covering perhaps two kilometres, I collapsed in a panting heap, gasping for wind. It was only then I noticed the planes had departed; all that remained of them was two dwindling specks in the clear blue sky.

Many parts of the camp were in flames and from my slightly elevated position I could see the Kurds – those that were still on their feet – rushing hither and thither. There were no signs that I had yet been missed.

I began walking, as quickly as my exhausted legs could carry me, away from the afternoon sun. By moving east, I was keeping away from al-Hadr and heading towards the al-Mawsil – Baghdad road. If I could find no assistance there, I would make for the nearby town of Qayyarah.

Inevitably, the Kurds came in pursuit, and on one occasion passed within fifty metres of where I was hiding. Lying flat behind the crest of a sand dune, I pressed my head onto the sand and listened as their car roared past. Having access to a vehicle enabled them to catch up with me quickly, but it also gave me fair warning when they were close. Whenever I heard the screaming engine, I took to a ditch or darted behind a rocky outcrop. Luckily, there was no shortage of places of concealment.

As the afternoon wore on, of greater concern to me was the need to get to the town before nightfall. My clothing was unsuited to the freezing desert nights and unless I could find assistance quickly, I might be in no condition to move at sunrise. I could see Qayyarah on the horizon, but estimated it to be still some fifteen kilometres away. I had to use what few hours of daylight were left to find adequate shelter.

After more than two hours of slow progress, I came

across a tributary to the Wadi ath-Tharthar and saw in the distance a southbound train on its way to Baghdad. I knew the line was close to the road, though it would still take me the best part of three hours to get there. By then it would be nightfall. I was desperately tired and found progress difficult, but I had no choice but to push on.

Crossing the wadi, I stooped to drink and bathe my neck and face in the little water it carried at that time of the year. Where possible, I walked on rock to avoid leaving tracks and made use of any shelter I could find to rest up and look over the landscape behind me.

There had been no sign of the Kurds for a couple of hours. Convinced I had shaken them off, I casually moved around a rocky outcrop and stumbled straight into the company of five armed men standing beside their parked car, Mullah among them. To run would have been pointless even if I were still physically capable of such exertion.

I dropped to the ground in anguish and disbelief. After all my efforts to evade capture, I had strolled into their midst. Utterly despondent, I wondered only whether they would shoot me dead where I lay, or take me back to the camp for a ritual execution. My question was answered when Mullah walked across and stood over me, a gun in his hand.

'I am sorry, Mikhaelef,' he said, his tone sympathetic. 'If there was another way, I would take it.'

He raised the gun and I wondered if I should beg him to spare me. I did not. Nor did I think of anything profound or courageous to say. Instead I thought of Amna and Nadia. It seems ridiculous now, but in the few seconds of life that I believed remained to me, I imagined Amna talking to Nadia some time in the future, telling her about the father she never knew. What would she tell her? How would Amna remember me?

I do not know how long it was I sat there, my head lowered. Seconds become distorted when they are all that is left and thoughts of my wife and daughter did not distract me from the dreadful reality that confronted me. I was absolutely terrified. I prayed Mullah would at least allow me death both quick and painless.

'I cannot do it,' Mullah said at last.

I looked up. He had lowered the gun and was shaking his head, as if he could not believe his weakness.

Then a shot did come. But not from Mullah, or even his colleagues, one of whom fell to the ground, clutching his side.

'Take cover!' Mullah shouted, but even as the warning left his lips a rattle of machine-gun fire sent another Kurd spinning. Yet another was pinned to the side of the car as the impact of the bullets held him upright for several seconds before he too slumped to the ground. The last of the band threw himself over the car to seek shelter behind it, but never made it. The machine gun stitched a line of red dots down his back and he slithered down the bonnet and onto the sand.

Only Mullah remained uninjured. He had dived to his right to seek the protection of the rocks and when an army Land Rover, crammed with soldiers, emerged from a gully, he loosed off a few despairing shots before standing, arms held high. The Land Rover skidded to a stop and four soldiers tumbled out. Mullah was punched to the ground and about to be shot by one of them when the officer-in-charge, who had remained with the vehicle, rapped out an order.

'Wait! I want a prisoner!' He stepped down and walked across to the four Kurds lying by the car, kicking each in turn. Two showed signs of life. He shot them both in the head without ceremony. He then walked across to where Mullah was being restrained. 'This one,' he said, smiling sardonically, 'we will keep.'

He then turned his attention to me as I staggered to my feet and I wondered what he would make of seeing his President in the middle of nowhere in such desperate straits.

'I am relieved to see you are safe and well, Mikhaelef

Ramadan,' he said instead, his smile now completely sincere. 'I will be handsomely rewarded for finding you.'

Slightly bemused, I asked if his dramatic and timely appearance was simply good fortune and was told he had earlier received a radio message giving details of the aerial attack on the camp. He had been instructed to search the surrounding area and look out for a relative of the President. They had spotted the Kurd's vehicle approaching and had set up an ambush in the gully. By chance, I arrived on the scene as they were about to spring the ambush.

'Your name was given to me, as was the fact that you bore a remarkable resemblance to you cousin, Saddam. When I saw your face through my field-glasses, I knew you had to be a relative of al-Qaed al-Muhib.'

His men seemed a little bewildered by my appearance, but when one of them asked if I was Saddam himself, the officer slapped him across the face. No more questions were asked.

I was immediately taken back to Baghdad and was met first by Dr Ayad Jihad, one of Saddam's personal physicians whom I had known since having plastic surgery four years earlier. Apart from my being undernourished and somewhat dehydrated, my physical condition was not bad.

'Nothing wrong with you that your mother's cooking will not remedy,' Ayad quipped.

On my return to the capital, I had telephoned Amna, and when I was finally restored to her, she greeted me in a flood of emotional tears. My mother, too, was overjoyed to see me alive. Nadia was asleep and as I looked down her I was astounded by how much she had grown in just five months. I had almost grown resigned to never seeing her again, and I was overcome by the sight of her beautiful little face. I broke down and wept.

In my absence, radical steps had been taken to restructure the security systems surrounding Saddam. His new son-in-law, Hussein Kamil, had been given the task and his measures covered three basic areas: the Baghdad Emergency Forces, responsible for civil order, were reinforced; the Republican Guard was increased; and the Special Republican Guard (SRG) was formed.

For the SRG, Hussein Kamil recruited almost exclusively from fourteen and fifteen-year-old Takritis, many of whom were illiterate. They were sent to military college in Baghdad and indoctrinated in the principles of 'Saddamism'. Hussein believed, correctly, that within five years these young men would form an impenetrable barrier around the President.

Their responsibities are now threefold: approximately 3,000 guards cover any movements of Saddam and his family; another 3,000 monitor the area around Saddam's palaces and private residences; and 5,000 more patrol Baghdad and a ten kilometre ring around the city. There are fourteen SRG battalions, numbered one to fifteen; Saddam is too superstitious to have a "13th Battalion".

Other changes in 1984 included the introduction of a new branch of the Istekhabarat called the Amn al-Askari (Military Intelligence Agency') and the formation of the Amn al-Khas ('Special Security Agency'). The Amn al-Askari were responsible for military intelligence within the Iraqi army. The Amn al-Khas were charged with guarding Saddam and his family inside the palaces. They also accompanied ministers abroad, acting as agents for the regime. Saddam rightly mistrusts his ministers when they are out of sight, and the Amn al-Khas watch their behaviour closely and report back to the presidential palace.

In a bid to bolster the army's depleted numbers, Saddam introduced the novel measure of conscripting students who failed their final examinations. Many young men, with no real hope of graduating, had taken to further education in a bid to avoid military service. Saddam also felt that these young academics, many of whom had criticised the campaign against Iran, should be given a patriotic task to concentrate their minds on.

Iran had retaken the uninhabited but strongly defended

al-Fao peninsula, a fifty kilometre stretch of land that forms Iraq's only physical contact with the Gulf, but the war swung back in Iraq's favour during 1984. In February, the aerial conflict intensified into what became known as the "First War of the Cities" when missile attacks were launched on the Iranian towns of Dezful, Shushtah, Andimeshk, Ahvaz, Kermanshab, Ilam and Abadan. Iran retaliated by shelling al-Basrah, Khanaqin and Mandali. The high civilian casualties were reported around the world and, following UN intervention, both sides agreed to stop the shelling. At least for the time being. In more than one instance during the war, Saddam confounded many observers with his reluctance to press home his advantages. My own thinking at this stage was that he did not want to escalate the scale of the conflict until he was assured of winning it.

The Iranians then took some 100 square kilometres of Iraqi territory in the al-Huweizah marshes around Majnun, an area of vital importance to Iraq with its fifty unworked oil wells. Saddam decided it was time to deploy chemical weapons.

Such weapons were banned under the Geneva Protocol of 1925, but this did not deter Saddam from having mustard gas dropped over large area around Majnun. General Maher Abdullah al-Rashid had no misgivings in carrying out the order.

'Give me a pesticide to destroy a swarm of insects,' he declared, 'and I will use it.'

He was not deterred by the prescence of many Iraqi soldiers and civilians in the target zone. Not surprisingly, an international outcry resulted, but Saddam was quick to accuse the nations of the West of double standards. The ingredients required for mustard gas had been obtained from Britain and the claim by the manufacturer that they had been sold for agricultural pesticides was barely credible. Another British company had sold 10,000 protective kits and breathing equipment to Iraqi specifications with the full knowledge of the UK Ministry of Defence.

After a week's rest, I was collected by car and driven to Samarah, eighty kilometres to the north of Takrit. No reason was stated. As well as being an area of ancient Mesopotamian civilisation and an important archaeological site, Samarah is also the centre of Iraq's chemical industry, both legitimate and covert. As we approached the town, we passed endless kilometres of excavations on both sides of the road.

We drove through the gates of an industrial chemical production plant and parked outside a heavily guarded annexe away from the main factory. Once inside, I was taken along a corridor and into a dark room in which there were already several men present. I recognised Saddam's eldest son, Udai, now twenty and in charge of the proceedings, and to his right, Fadel Barak Hussein, Barzan's replacement as the head of the Mukhabarat. Looking to my left, I was startled to see Mullah al-Barzinji hanging from the ceiling by his wrists, his body suspended two metres above a large, stainless steel tank. The tank was about two metres deep and filled to within a half-metre of the rim with what Udai took great delight in informing me was sulphuric acid.

Mullah had been badly beaten, but he was conscious and watched me enter the room with dull eyes. Udai approached me.

'He looks a little different now, does he not, Mikhaelef?' he spouted, his arrogant smile firmly in place. 'I thought that as this man caused you so much personal discomfort and murdered your good friend, Mohammed Qutaibi, you might enjoy a little sport.' He turned to his accomplice. 'Please, Fadel, let us not delay any longer.'

Fadel approached Mullah and struck him hard across the thigh with a steel baton.

'What is the name of your immediate superior in your pitiful organisation?' he demanded.

Mullah spat out his answer. 'Death to your children!'

Fadel hit him again, this time much harder, and Mullah screamed out in agony. 'I will ask you again. I want names.'

'I will give you names!' Mullah screamed. 'Your father is an illegitimate thief and beggar and your mother a Baghdad whore!'

Fadel responded by administering a beating of such ferocity that I wondered if there was more than a grain of truth in Mullah's insults. Finally, Udai intervened.

'Enough, Fadel! We don't want him to pass out before the main event begins.' Udai had to raise his voice to be heard above Mullah's moans. He nodded to the guard holding the rope on which Mullah was hanging. 'Lower him a little.'

As he neared the acid bath, Mullah raised his feet in a frantic struggle to stay clear. With amazing physical dexterity, he managed to raise his feet and lock them behind his outstretched arms. His lower back was now presented to the acid.

Udai approached Mullah. 'I will not lie to you,' he said dispassionately. 'Your life is over. You may, however, decide how much agony you will endure. If you co-operate, you will be dropped into the acid. If you do not, you will be lowered inch by inch. It is up to you.'

Mullah glared at Udai with hatred in his eyes. 'I will tell you nothing but that you are a sorry piece of shit, Udai Saddam! Do what you will, but after me there will be many more. I curse you and your family. One day your evil will come back on you a thousandfold!'

Udai said nothing and backed away. He signalled for the rope to be lowered. 'Take him all the way, but do so slowly. Very slowly.'

As Mullah touch the still surface, setting up ripples, the acid bit into the skin of his back, corroding the muscles around his spine. His screech of agony made the hairs of my neck rise and I shook violently, and turned away. Although Mullah continued to spew out his virulent expletives, the lowering process continued and he was soon completely incoherent. Udai and Fadel smiled as the process continued and Mullah's buttocks, spine, and intenal organs were progressively dissolved by the acid. He was screaming continuously now and he continued to scream until, quite suddenly, he appeared to lose consciousness, or more likely, he died as vital organs simply ceased to exist. As silence fell the guard speeded up the lowering process, and Mullah's chest, head and finally his limbs disappeared from sight.

Udai grinned broadly at the completion of the entertainment, but without waiting for more of his sneering remarks, I walked quickly from the room. The first door I came to was a toilet. I crashed the door open and was violently sick into the pan.

I hoped and prayed Saddam was ignorant of this gruesome episode and that he would never countenance such a barbaric practice. I was soon given the opportunity to find out. Two days later, I was with the President for the first time since my escape and he praised me for my courage in breaking free from the Kurds. I would, he told me, be decorated. I thought that if courage be defined by running as fast as my legs would carry me in the opposite direction to danger, then I was a brave man indeed.

After I had witnessed Mullah's gruesome execution, something inside me died. Perhaps my captivity and the death of Mohammed had also affected me, but I felt I no longer cared what fate befell me. Fear is generated by an instinctive human desire to survive, and survival no longer seemed to matter very much. Probably I was in the throes of depression and what might nowadays be termed Post Traumatic Stress Disorder, but the effect on me was profound. I was not flattered by Saddam's compliments and as I no longer feared the consequences of my actions, I was more able to speak my mind.

'I was at a chemical plant in Samarah on Tuesday,' I said, having never before changed the subject in a conversation with him. 'I was with Udai and Fadel Barak .'

'Yes,' Saddam replied, a little uneasily I thought, 'Udai told me.'

'Mullah al-Barzinji was executed in my presence.'

'I am aware of that.'

I hesitated before I continued, not because I feared his reaction, but because I wanted to phrase my words in a way that would elicit a response free of any ambiguity.

'He was lowered into a bath of sulphuric acid,' I said.

'Yes,' Saddam, eyeing me carefully, no doubt wondering where this was leading.

'The orders were yours?' I asked, displaying more impertinence than I had ever before seen anyone show Saddam. He did not answer. I nodded in resignation. 'I would be grateful, Saddam,' I went on, 'if I could be excused such demonstrations in the future. I do not have the stomach for it.'

Saddam immediately stood up and approached me. 'My dear friend, of course. You have been through too much these past few months. I am so pleased to have you back that I have perhaps been a little selfish. You will take a vacation with your wife and daughter at my expense. I have a pleasant house and a boat near Shithathah on the Bahr al-Milh. You know it, perhaps?'

'Yes,' I said, without enthusiasm. 'The lake is quite close to my home town. My father used to take me there when I was a child.'

'That is settled then. It is yours for as long as you wish to stay there.'

I muttered some small words of gratitude and the arrangements were made. The 'pleasant house' to which Saddam referred was in fact a small palace and the boat a private yacht with facilities a world beyond anything I had encountered when visiting the lake with my father.

We stayed by the Bahr al-Milh for nearly a month and were treated by the permanent staff members at the house as if we were part of the President's family. It was a difficult period for me, however. My wife had been voicing serious doubts about the President for many years. Now I, too, was unnerved to be rubbing shoulders on a daily basis with such sadistic, ruthless men. I did not speak of it, and she did not raise the subject of Saddam and my allegiance to him. When the time came to return to Baghdad, I did so with great foreboding. The break had reminded me that I did indeed have something that made my life worth living. Amna and Nadia were precious to me and I would have to find a way to continue with my role, if only for their sakes.

As a direct consequence of the vacation, Amna once again became pregnant, but even that brought little joy to my life. In the aftermath of his tacit admission that he sanction such extreme cruelty as that to which Mullah had been subjected, I became increasingly more sceptical of everything Saddam said, and I detested Udai with passion. Although I kept my thoughts to myself, it was a burden I found more and more intolerable.

In my enforced absence, Saddam had recruited another lookalike, Nadar Rafi al-Ajili, a relative of one of the senior officers of the Amn al-Khas. The man's sudden elevation in status went to his head and he was stupid enough to make an incautious, though harmless remark in front of Saddam. He was brutally flogged on the spot by two of Saddam's guards.

Iraqi attacks on international shipping in the Arabian Gulf had continued over the past two years. In consequence, Iran threatened to close the Strait of Hormuz, an act that would have had the most devastating effect on the Western economies. The US, France and Britain sent their respective navies into the area, but the Iranian threat never materialised. Saddam had always believe the threat to be pure bluff on Khomeini's part, as the Iranians later conceded. Closing the strait would have damaged the Iranian economy beyond repair. Iraq was by this time in receipt of substantial economic aid from its Arab neighbours, as they all recognised the threat an Islamic revolution posed to the Arab world. Kuwait, in particular, put considerable funds at Saddam's disposal and in doing so, paradoxically sparked a chain of events that would lead ultimately to the Gulf War, six years later.

Chapter Seven

1985
Raby' al-Thaany 1405 – Raby' al-Thaany 1406

The attacks on Kharg Island in the Gulf continued. At the end of March the Iranians opened another terminal beyond the range of Iraqi bombers on the island of Sirri further south. In the same month, during the 'Second War of the Cities', a small Iranian force crossed the Dijlah and successfully cut off the Baghdad – al-Basrah highway. This caused near panic in the Iraqi government and a counter-attack was immediately mounted. The invading force was quickly pushed back, but the psychological damage had been done and for the rest of the war, the citizens of Baghdad were destined to live in fear of their city coming under siege.

The anxieties that now seeped into all areas of my life had affected Amna, too, and in the later stages of her pregnancy her blood pressure was abnormally high. Tests revealed protein in her urine and she was diagnosed as having pre-eclamptic toxaemia and admitted to the Ibn Seina Hospital in the Karada district of Baghdad. The blood supply to the unborn infant was severely restricted and there were fears that it would not have the strength to withstand the contractions of the uterus during labour. In the end, no chances were taken, and the baby was born at the beginning of April by caesarean section under epidural anaesthetic. It was a boy and we called him Salih.

Upon my return home shortly after the birth, my mother seemed determined to avoid me. She had convinced herself that the new baby would be another granddaughter and she was reluctant to hear the news. When I finally tracked her down in the garden, she ignored me as I came to stand beside her.

'Amna and the baby are fine, Mother,' I whispered in her ear.

'Good,' she said. 'What have you decided to call her?'

'We are calling him Salih Mikhaelef.' I answered, smiling broadly.

My mother turned her head sharply towards me, not sure if she had heard me correctly. 'It is a boy?' she asked, barely able to contain the joy she was so obviously feeling.

'Yes, mother, you have a grandson.'

She immediately threw her arms around my neck and began to wail onto my shoulder.

'Oh, Mikhaelef, I don't believe it! A boy, a boy!'

I held her closely and felt as if a great burden had been lifted from me; I had produced a grandson for my mother. 'Perhaps you will be content now?'

'Oh, Mikhaelef, do not berate me for being a foolish old woman,' she chattered. 'I am so happy. I have waited so long. I just wish your father was here today. He would have been so proud, especially as you have named the baby after his father?'

'How could I call him anything else?'

'Salih Mikhaelef al-Kadhimi,' she sighed. 'It is a beautiful name.'

My mother spent the next few days on a cloud, but Amna was still weak and had to stay in hospital a while longer to recover her strength. For myself, I was obviously proud and delighted to have a son. I may believe the significance attached to producing boys is excessive in our culture, but I could not deny the instinctive satisfaction I felt as the father of a son. I was going through a difficult period in my life, but little Salih was a true ray of sunshine through the darkening clouds over my country.

When I returned to normal duties at the palace, I was reminded, poignantly, of Mohammed's death. I spent many hours in the Dark Room thinking back over the conversations we had had, and I saw his face and heard his voice in my mind every day. Occasionally, when someone came into the room, I turned expectantly, hoping to see him. Of course, I never did. He was dead and from death there is no coming back.

His place was taken by a younger man from the presidential office, Hashim Mushir. He was pleasant enough, and did not take offence when, out of habit, I occasionally called him Mohammed.

Whether it was the years catching up with me or the trauma of my recent experiences I do not know, but Hashim pointed out to me one morning that my hair was turning grey at the temples. In some illogical way, I hoped this might mean I would be released from my obligations, but the matter was easily resolved. Udai was presented with the task of importing high quality hair dyes in a range of brown-black shades. The box that they were delivered in was so big it required two men to lift it. Saddam himself helped me select the right tint.

I tried to visit Amna every day, but it was not a straightforward procedure. If Saddam was making a public appearance or if his whereabouts were generally known, then I was compelled to stay out of sight. At such times, I had to arrive at the hospital quietly by a side entrance, wearing my false beard and dark glasses, and have my route to her private ward cleared of any casual observers. At other times, I was able to visit as Saddam himself, but in order not to arouse too much curiosity as to why the President should be such a regular visitor, a story was concocted up regarding Amna's identity. As far as the hospital staff were concerned, she was the husband of a government official who had saved Saddam's life in the fifties. It served a purpose, but was not universally accepted, as Hashim informed me one evening.

'I was in the toilet when two doctors came in,' he told me, wearing the broadest of smiles. 'As I was in one of the cubicles, they were unaware of my presence. One asked the other if he believed this story about the woman Saddam visits so frequently. "Why?" said the other. "Well," said the first, "I have seen the baby. And I tell you he is the image of the President!"'

While Amna was still in hospital, I stood-in for Saddam at a meeting of Baghdad dignitaries, which included the city's mayor and 'friend' of Akram, Samir Mohammed. I was by now quite relaxed in such situations and everything was going well as I sat at the top of the table, enjoying course after course of beautifully prepared food.

Quite suddenly, my vision blurred and I felt my throat swelling. As I tried to get to my feet, my chair fell behind me with a crash. I stumbled forward across the table. I was bent double with abdominal cramps and two of Saddam's guards rushed forward to help me from the room. Taken to an ante room, I was violently sick and continued to vomit repeatedly for an hour, bringing up blood as well as undigested food.

In hospital, I was injected with an antiemetic to control the retching and was then sedated while my stomach was pumped. I was treated with an anti-diarrhoeal mixture and an electrolyte solution to control and replace my body fluids. It turned out that I was infected with a form of botulism that would have killed me within hours had I not received such prompt treatment.

Afterwards, an intensive inquiry took place and I was told that Saddam had flown into a rage at the thought of his enemies having access to his kitchen. Saddam's head chef, Hannah Jejjo, was a trusted man who had been preparing the President's meals for years. Cleverly, Saddam employed Hannah's son, Kamil Hannah, as his official foodtaster, in the tradition of the grand viziers of ancient Baghdad. Hannah had prepared the meal that evening and Kamil had tasted it, but Saddam refused to believe that either or both of them had conspired to poison him.

Apart from the element of trust, Kamil was a close confidante of Saddam's and the man largely responsible for organising his illicit affairs. He enjoyed a position of privilege beyond his social standing, and Saddam's demise could only be to his detriment. Udai, very much his mother's son, despised Kamil for the role he played and I would have feared for Kamil's safety without Saddam's protection. For this reason alone, it was inconceivable that he would plot against the President.

Finally, and still more conclusive, Kamil and his son were, of necessity, aware of my existence and knew when I was sitting in for Saddam, so why poison my food? It seemed fantastic they would take such a risk just to kill a mere double.

As only my meal had been poisoned, the most likely perpetrator was one or more of those members of the staff who had access to my meal between the kitchen and the dining table. There were three such house-servants. They were arrested, imprisoned and no doubt tortured, but I do not know what ultimately became of them.

As a consequence of this attempt on Saddam's life, Kamil was instructed to taste food from the President's plate, rather than from the cooking pans in the kitchen, a task that induced considerable nervousness on his part for a while.

Once I was fully recovered, I was summoned to a personal audience with Saddam and awarded Iraq's highest civilian medal of honour, 'The Star of Saddam'. In the course of six years presidential service, I had been shot, kidnapped and poisoned, but at least I was putting together an impressive collection of medals. I was also given a substantial pay rise and instructed to move into an larger house, in the middle-class residential district of Amiriya, ten kilometres west of the Karradat Mariam.

The relocation may in part have been a security measure, as I had been living in al-Mansur for a number of years and it was inevitable that I would be seen occasionally by my neighbours. They no doubt also believed that Amna was the President's lover, so kept their observations very much to themselves, but now with two young children, it was felt I needed more privacy. The new house had two large walled gardens and meant that I could play with Nadia and Salih outdoors without fear of being seen.

Naturally, my mother moved with us. If I had attempted to find her alternative accommodation, it would have killed her. She was devoted to Nadia, and even more so to little Salih, who was never given a moment's peace. She tended to his every need and was there by his side as soon as he awoke. Half-hearted attempts on my part to restrict her pampering were brushed aside. As for Amna, she accepted her mother-in-law's interference with good grace, and in truth she was glad to have her around. She had been slow to recover from the birth and was suffering from mild depression. I kept a husbandly eye on her and was satisfied she would be all right in due course, but having my mother on hand to share the load was a bonus.

Udai had been playing a more prominent role in affairs of government, but in the early summer he brought on a small crisis for Saddam. For several weeks he had been pursuing the twenty-one-year-old daughter of an army colonel. She had resisted all his attempts at seduction, but one evening he became so frustrated he tried to rape her. Her father, understandably beside himself with rage, confronted Udai. According to one of Udai's servants who witnessed the event, the President's son listened to the man's ranting for perhaps a full minute before pulling a gun from under his jacket. Without hesitation, he shot the colonel dead.

Surprisingly, it was Saddam rather than Udai's mother, Sajida, who was the more disturbed by the killing. Udai had committed a crime no worse than the many committed by his father before and since he came to power, and Sajida was quick to point this out. If the man was stupid enough to show disrespect to the eldest son of the President, she argued, he should expect to receive nothing less than a bullet for his trouble. In the end, Saddam let the matter rest, but he prohibited Udai from carrying a gun for several months and saw to it that the murdered officer's family were generously 'compensated'.

During the summer, Barzan Ibrahim resurfaced and it saddened me that Mohammed Qutaibi was not present to say, 'I told you so!' Owing to his public condemnation by Saddam a couple of years earlier, Barzan did not emerge in Baghdad. Saddam had sent him to Geneva just a few months after his fall from grace for the purpose of procuring arms and chemicals, and recruiting foreign scientists. Such a position allowed him to continue with his illicit money-making schemes almost entirely without restraint. He was also believed to be responsible for planning Mukhabarat assassinations of exiled Iraqi dissidents.

Distracted by the war with Iran, Saddam had been unable to attend to the problem of the Kurds, who continued to cause trouble for his regime. As a provisional measure, he had entered into an agreement with the Turkish government to allow them access across the border in pursuit of the PKK, the Turkish equivalent of the Iraqi *peshmerga*. Saddam was given a similar facility in Turkey. Much publicity was then given to an amnesty offered by Saddam, but the Kurds' response had at best been lukewarm. The 8,000 Kurds arrested three years earlier had never been seen again and were reported to have been massacred. For most of them, the report proved ultimately to be well-founded.

All opposition elements of the state were given the opportunity to accede to Saddam's authority. In return, all pending charges against imprisoned Kurdish dissidents would be dropped and a process of releasing political prisoners would commence. In reality, the amnesty added up to a complete surrender of all the Kurds' future aspirations and there was not the remotest possibility of their accepting the proffered 'olive branch'. Saddam knew this well enough, and many saw the gesture as the opening move of a campaign of hostility against opposition elements.

Leaders of the Kurdish political organisations, excluding the peshmerga, were invited to put forward their proposals for a settlement. This invitation was not greeted with much enthusiasm, so Saddam proposed a meeting with one of the more vociferous leaders within the Patriotic Union of Kurdistan, Mohammed Mahmoud al-Khoshnawi. As a gesture of goodwill, Saddam suggested the meeting should take place on Kurdish home ground, and an informal gathering was duly arranged in Arbil.

This decision was vehemently opposed by Saddam's ministers, who argued that to attend such a meeting, where the principal Kurdish organisations had their headquarters, would be a foolhardy enterprise, even by the standards of their courageous President. Of course, Saddam was not so stupid and having heard about the meeting, I feared the worse when he called on me in the Dark Room.

He was in of his more expansive moods and I had come to realise that when Saddam is at his most flattering, he is likely to want me to play a particularly hazardous role. Such was the case.

'Without your aid and support I do not believe I would have seen this day, Mikhaelef Ramadan,' he gushed, 'I value your loyalty and admire your bravery. You have the heart of a lion.'

'You flatter me, Saddam,' I replied, contriving a humble look.

'No, you are wrong. I know of few men who could have done as you have done.' He paused theatrically, and then looked at me directly in the eye. 'I have a new task for you which I fear may be too much to ask.'

I was wide awake to the realities of my position and had a good idea what was coming.

'You are aware of my peace initiative with the Kurdish people,' he said. 'During such troubled times it is of paramount importance that Iraqis learn to live with each other. We have to recognise that we are one people.'

'Of course, Saddam.'

'It is for that reason I have arranged this meeting with Mohammed Mahmoud. It is, however, impossible for me to attend personally. The war with those Persian devils is at a critical juncture and I have to be available at all times to make vital executive decisions of strategy. You understand this?'

'Yes, Saddam, I understand. You would like me to go in your place.' It was not a prospect that appealed to me, to parade openly through the streets of Arbil in the guise of Saddam. But if that was to be my lot, such was the will of Allah. I did not fear for myself. Those days were behind me. But I had no wish for my two children to grow up fatherless.

'You are as astute as always,' Saddam remarked. 'Will you go?'

'As ever, if my President wishes me to go, then I will go. But I am not comfortable about going to Arbil, Saddam. I have distressing memories of the place.'

'Yes, of course, I am forgetting. Your friend, Mohammed Qutaibi, was murdered near Arbil. Very well. The venue will be changed. There is no reason why the meeting cannot take place in al-Mawsil. In that way, you will be closer to the airport and can avoid taking the road where Mohammed was killed.'

It was unusually charitable of Saddam to make concessions to accommodate my sensibilities. Aside from this, his decision to send me north in his place flew in the face of his fine words to Udai little more than a year earlier. He was, it seemed, now prepared to have me run greater risks than he was prepared to run himself. His decision to avoid the Kurds may well have been, as he put it, in the best interests of the nation, but I was left with the distinct impression that I was less indispensable than formerly. Perhaps it was a case of familiarity breeding contempt.

Accompanying me on the flight to al-Mawsil were Hashim, Tariq Aziz and Mustapha Hassan, an officer of the Amn al-Khas. This proved to be the only occasion I ever travelled with the Tariq and I found him a calming influence. He seemed genuinely understanding when my arrival at the airport invoked memories of my last hours with Mohammed.

'I did not know him well,' Tariq said, 'but I heard he was a good man. You spent a lot of time with him?'

'I was with him nearly every day for three years,' I answered. 'I miss his friendship.'

'Yes, he is missed also by his fellow officers in the Mukhabarat. He—'

'What is that?' I interrupted, momentarily forgetting my place. 'Mohammed was with the Mukhabarat?'

'You did not know?' Tariq overlooked my impertinence. 'Well, if I have been indiscreet, it hardly matters now.' Before he continued, Tariq glanced nervously over his shoulder to check that Mustapha was not eavesdropping. 'Yes, Mohammed was with the Fourteenth Directorate of the Mukhabarat.'

'The Fourteenth? Special Operations?'

'Yes, of course. Do you not think you are regarded as a special operation?'

'Yes, but I had no idea that Mohammed—'

'Where did you think he came from?' Tariq cut in, appearing amused by my apparent innocence.

'The presidential staff.'

'Come now, Mikhaelef, do you really believe an important specialist position such as monitoring the President's double would be left to a clerk from the presidential staff?'

'I suppose not, but . . .'

'Well, I'm sorry to be the one to disillusion you, but do not think badly of Mohammed for this. If he did not tell you, I am sure he had your best interests at heart.'

Reflecting later, I should not have been surprised. The

Mukhabarat was divided into many different directorates, but the Fourteenth was one of the largest and most important. From their offices in Salman Pak, eighteen kilometres south-east of the capital, they are responsible for the most sensitive, covert operations at home and abroad. It was entirely logical that the job of monitoring the President's doubles should be assigned to them. Nevertheless, I could not help but feel deflated to learn that a man I considered to have become a close friend and confidant, actually worked for the equivalent of the German Gestapo.

Having left me with my thoughts for a minute or two, Tariq offered me some consolation.

'Not all officers of the Mukhabarat fit the public's perception, Mikhaelef. Mohammed was a good friend to you and somebody upon whom you could depend. Such trust is a rare thing, especially in Iraq.' His sentiments reminded me of his own long-standing relationship with the President.

'Saddam trusts you, Tariq.'

'I like to think so. I have certainly never given him cause to distrust me.'

'And yet you are not a Moslem.'

'No, I am a Christian,' Tariq answered casually, 'but that is irrelevant to Saddam.'

'It is a pity,' I added, 'that not all Iraqis believe religion is irrelevant to trust and friendship.'

'Yes, indeed. Saddam has done much to lessen the tensions between the different sectarian factions, but no one man can undo what has evolved over centuries. Fortunately, Christians in Iraq are few in number and there is no element Saddam need feel threatened by.'

Tariq was an easy man to talk to and if he was the butt of occasional jokes because of his idolatrous fawning towards Saddam, he was no less a good companion on that account.

As it happened, the risk to my life on the trip to al-Mawsil was minimal. With Tariq, I was driven directly from the airport to the hall where the meeting was to take place and walked the twenty metres distance from the car to the entrance surrounded by six of the tallest officers of the SRG. As part of the security arrangements, it had been arranged that Mohammed Mahmoud would be in the hall before I arrived and leave after me. In this way, should the Kurds harbour thoughts of bombing the building, they would have to sacrifice their revered leader into the bargain.

The building was unknown to me and not identified by a sign at the entrance or in the reception area. It resembled an old government administration block. It had an abandoned air, though it was possible it had simply been cleared for the duration of the meeting, for security purposes. Perhaps even at Saddam's insistence.

I had been instructed by Saddam not to reject any proposals put forward by Mohammed. In general, I was to say his terms were acceptable and that his more extreme demands, such as complete autonomy for Iraqi Kurds, were negotiable. I was to encourage Mohammed to believe that something could be gained by prolonging the dialogue between the two sides.

Mohammed was a stern-looking man in his early sixties, and his face bore all the marks of a warrior: it was weather-beaten and scarred, with eyes like those of a hawk, forever darting, forever watchful. He was reputed to have an intelligent, active brain, and was not to be underestimated. We sat opposite each other, at a table made from imported oak in a large hall with the windows set high on panelled walls. Mohammed was flanked on either side by aides. I had Hashim to my left and Tariq to my right. At the far end of the table sat Mustapha.

Despite his unwavering subordination to Saddam's authority, Tariq was not without strength of character. As we seated ourselves, he leaned across and whispered in my ear.

'They will try to bully us, but take no notice. They have to be hostile in each other's presence. If they ask something to which you cannot give an answer, simply hesitate and invite me to respond. Saddam does this frequently. If they become threatening, appear indifferent.'

Tariq's words did much to reassure me. Although I was well practised in my impersonation of Saddam, I had never accompanied him in this type of situation and obviously there was little video record of such meetings for me to study. Tariq's advice was welcome. He is not always taken seriously by the more ambitious of Saddam's ministers, but he is an intelligent man and a survivor. The latter attribute is an essential ingredient for a minister in the government of Saddam Hussein! I nodded to Tariq, to indicate my understanding and he gave me a paternal smile in return.

The talks went on for more than an hour and nothing untoward occurred. I was able to deal with most of the issues raised by Mohammed and to generally placate him. When Tariq had to intervene, he did so with his usual tact and diplomacy. When we were done, though, Mohammed made a suggestion that caught me off guard and I hesitated dangerously in my response.

'We have seldom seen eye to eye with each other, Saddam Hussein,' he said with a thin smile, 'but I feel today we may have made some progress.'

'I would like to think so,' I replied, non-committal.

'Then perhaps you would humour an old Kurdish rebel for a while longer? I have arranged for a room to be set aside so that we may be able to share a drink together. In the name of friendship, shall we say? There are one or two things I would like to discuss with you in private.'

I felt the colour drain from my face and at the very moment I needed Tariq's guidance, he could not give it without arousing Mahud's suspicions. I had to respond.

'Very well, Mohammed Mahmoud, but I cannot give you long.'

Tariq shrugged helplessly. It was evident that he was distinctly uneasy at this sudden and unexpected development. Mustapha, too, was far from happy. Still, I had no alternative but to go through with it and hope it was as harmless as Mohammed had made it sound. He and I stood up and together we left the room. Leading me a short distance down a corridor, he opened a door, beyond which was a large square office, with modern but rather shabby furnishings.

The fact that Mohammed seemed familiar with his surroundings led me to suppose that this was his own office. If we were in offices belonging to the PUK , then no wonder the venue for the meeting had been kept from me. I began to wonder if I was being lured into a trap, but as I looked nervously about the room, Mohammed casually invited me to take a seat among four low armchairs that were arranged around a coffee table. He offered me a drink, but although I am not a devout Moslem, I have never been fond of alcohol. As a student in Karbala I had once over-indulged, as a result of which I was sick and hungover for two days, and had vowed never to tempt the wrath of Allah again. I tried to decline politely.

'Come now, Saddam. You cannot tell me you do not occasionally partake, when you must have the finest collection of wines and spirits in all of Iraq. Humour a foolish old man and share a drink with me.'

'You are many things, Mohammed Mahmoud,' I said dryly, 'but only a fool would think you foolish.'

He opened a cabinet and extracted from it a bottle of whisky and two glasses. I did not protest when he filled both.

'Perhaps I should ask you how you came across this,' I said, picking up the glass.

'It is no mystery,' he said casually. 'It comes through Turkey. It is the finest ten-year old Scotch whisky I have yet tasted. If you would like to take a case back with you, I can arrange it.'

'Another time,' I said, knowing Saddam would not approve of my becoming too familiar with this man in his name. 'What is it you want to discuss with me?'

We began talking and drinking and soon I was feeling

the familiar effects of the alcohol. I had to concentrate all the harder so as not to forget who I was, but I found myself fascinated by the depth of Mohammed's intellect. It was beyond anything I had previously encountered. We talked together for more than two hours, discoursing on topics of which my knowledge was scant. We were interrupted by occasional visits from Hashim, who reminded me of 'pressing matters' awaiting my attention in Baghdad. As, under the influence of alcohol, I became more relaxed, I was able to dismiss him with growing confidence.

It was just after yet another call from Hashim that Mohammed began to talk in earnest.

'It may surprise you to hear it, Saddam, but I feel I know you very well. If much of the window dressing is removed, you would find that we are very much alike.'

'I think not, Mohammed,' I countered. 'It is my belief we should all regard ourselves as Iraqis. But you and me? We have little in common.'

'I do not mean in any obvious way. But as leaders we have to demonstrate our strength. My own people throw their arms in the air at some of the things you have done. They call you the most terrible names.'

'I have no doubt of it,' I murmured, amused by his candour.

'But me?' he added. 'I say nothing. I know why you do what you do. I, too, have killed men. Sometimes I have had to kill my own men, but only when necessary. Only for good reason.'

'Of course. Nothing is done without a purpose.'

'Exactly. But many people, especially abroad, think you are a lunatic, a psychopath. They think you kill and torture for pleasure.'

'You have a bold tongue, Mohammed.' Even under alcohol's balmy influence, I recognised the dangers of allowing him to speak as he pleased, without rebuttal. I was, after all, supposed to be Saddam, one of the most evil dictators on earth.

'But you know it is true,' he insisted. 'And yet I see the purpose in all you do. If I wore your shoes, I would do the same!'

Mohammed continued in this vein for some time before his tone hardened.

'So we respect each other, but reluctantly. One day one of us will perhaps die by the other's hand. Only one thing will stop me killing you, Saddam, and that is if you kill me first. I predict this.'

'Is there a better time than now?' I said, my bravado derived from ten-year-old Scotch.

'It cannot be now,' he replied emphatically. 'We both need each other at this time. I owe it to my people to travel this conciliatory road you have built, if only to prove to the moderates that you build it on quicksand. You also need me for the moment. If I were to be killed, the Kurdish people would rise against you. It would be a fruitless rebellion, yes, but it is a matter you would rather not have to deal with while a more powerful enemy knocks so loudly at your eastern gate.'

I found it difficult to maintain the pretence in the company of this man. I had a role to play, which for the sake of my family I had to maintain, but I was seriously tempted to confide in him. The weakness soon passed. Shortly afterwards, Hashim called again, this time with Tariq and Mustapha by his side, and between them they insisted, as far as protocol allowed, that we must leave immediately.

Unsteadily, I got to my feet and after shaking Mohammed's hand, stumbled towards the door. I collected my wits enough to promise that proposals would be drawn up for him to consider and that hopefully we could meet again in the weeks that followed, when a formal agreement could be thrashed out between us.

'Remember, Saddam,' he called after me, 'judge me as you would judge yourself.'

I signalled assent as I left the room, under Tariq's and Mohammed's exchange of puzzled glances.

I was half carried back to the car and settled untidily into the back seat. I dozed during the drive to the airport and remember nothing at all of the flight back to Baghdad. It was not until the following morning, suffering with a hangover, that I realised Mohammed had asked me nothing of importance. From what I could recall, there seemed to have been no purpose in the private meeting, unless it was to issue the warning about killing each other. Ten years would pass before I learned the real purpose.

Chapter Eight

1986
Raby' al-Thaany 1406 – Raby' al-Thaany 1407

When the Kurds came to Baghdad in January, no news of which had been broadcast on *Radio Baghdad* or published in *al-Jurmuriyah*, Mohammed was absent. It transpired he suspected something was not right at our meeting and instructed the delegation to find out exactly what was on offer from Saddam. His suspicions were well founded.

The delegates were picked up from their hotel as planned and were expecting to be taken to the Karradat Mariam. They never arrived. The Kurdish leadership were convinced that the entire party had been kidnapped by the Mukhabarat or some other government-sponsored agency. Saddam was just as adamant he knew nothing about it and accused the Shi'a underground movement, al-Da'wa, of being responsible. While accusation was met by counter-accusation, nothing was heard of the missing delegates' whereabouts.

In all, there were eleven Kurds in the party, some of whom were senior officials. For nearly a week, they simply disappeared off the face of the earth. When such people disappear, rumours as to their fate usually abound, but I never heard so much as a whisper regarding the where-abouts of the Kurdish delegation. I tried to bring the subject up with Hashim, but he was not prepared to discuss such matters in the open way that Mohammed Qutaibi used to. It did, however, give me the opportunity to initiate some meaningful dialogue with him.

He shrugged when I asked what he thought might have happened. 'Does it matter?' he said. 'The President says it was the thugs from al-Da'wa. Isn't that enough?'

'Yes, but you know Saddam has reasons for saying such things. You must have heard something to the contrary.'

'Why? What would I hear that you do not?'

'You are an officer of the Mukhabarat. You must hear things.'

This was the first occasion I had seen Hashim shaken from his habitual indifferent manner. He looked at me intensely.

'Who told you such a thing?'

'Does it matter?'

'Of course it matters!'

'Why should I tell you? You will not share with me what you know.'

'I am not permitted to talk to you in this way.'

'Nobody is listening, Hashim. I know that you are with the Mukhabarat, so what is the problem? I also know that you are with the Fourteenth Directorate and before you returned to Baghdad to replace Mohammed Qutaibi you were based in the D14 headquarters in Salman Pak. Tell me if it is not true.'

Hashim said heavily, 'I have underestimated you, Mikhaelef Ramadan.' He got to his feet and walked to the door, opening it quietly and looking in both directions down the corridor before closing it again. 'What you say is true, but the person responsible for passing on such in-formation to you is in serious breech of security. I cannot let it pass. If you will not provide me with the name of your informant, you will leave me with no choice but to pass on your reticence to my immediate senior officer.'

I was not so easily intimidated these days. All the same, I had not desire to make an enemy of my new watchdog.

'If it is so important to you, I will tell you. It was Mohammed Qutaibi.'

'Mohammed was dead before we ever met.'

'Yes, of course, but when he was alive, he told me he was working for the Mukhabarat. I just assumed you were, too.'

Hashim nodded. 'It surprises me Mohammed would be so indiscreet, but I supposed you were together a long time and went through many things together.'

When I looked at him a little quizzically, he smiled. 'There is a fat file on you in Salman Pak. I have read it.'

'Mohammed compiled this file?'

'Of course.'

'And what did he have to say about me?'

Hashim laughed. 'Do not worry. Mohammed was very loyal to you.'

I thought that perhaps my relationship with Hashim had advanced a little. If I am honest, I had resented his presence from the day of his arrival, as I would probably have resented any replacement for Mohammed. I decided I would make an effort to cultivate his friendship from now on. For an officer of the Mukhabarat, Hashim was reasonably human.

'So – what about the Kurds?' I asked Hashim again. 'What do you know?'

He looked at me and tutted in acknowledgement of my making mischief. 'Believe me, Mikhaelef,' he replied, 'there really are some things you are better off not knowing.'

It was an answer from which I could infer whatever I wished.

The disappearance of the delegation had struck fear into the hearts of the Kurds at large and made them understandably sceptical about the sincerity of Saddam's peace initiative. I had earlier hoped, despite the enormous obstacles to be overcome, that we were entering a period when the disparate elements of Iraqi society might begin to get along. I was, predictably, deluding myself.

After a week, news filtered through from Arbil regarding the Kurdish delegation. Hashim gave me the details.

'Apparantly, the driver who collected them from their hotel was an officer of the Amn al-Khas. He took them to a house in al-Maarifa.' Maarifa is a residential district in the south of the city, across the Dijla from Baghdad University. Hashim continued. 'They were told that before they could be taken to the palace, they would have to be properly searched. Once they were at the house, they were beaten and locked up.'

A great feeling of guilt engulfed me. Perhaps because I had spoken to Mohammed Mahmoud and personally suggested the meeting, I felt as if I was somehow responsible for the fate of the Kurds visiting Baghdad in his place.

'They are dead?' I asked him, fearing the answer.

'No,' he answered, 'they are very much alive, if a little chastened by the experience. They were held for a few days and then escorted from Baghdad. They are now back in Arbil.'

'What was the point of that?' I asked him. 'They come to Baghdad at Saddam's request and are beaten and returned to Arbil without seeing him. What has been achieved?'

'Maybe Saddam wished to familiarise them with his negotiating techniques,' Hashim suggested dryly.

The early months of the year had seen the emergence of what was loosely termed the 'rebel coalition'. More than twenty armed political parties in opposition to Saddam existed in Iraq. They had never been able to agree on very much and the joke was that every time a meeting was held, one party walked in and five walked out. In the previous few months though, they had managed to reach agreement on a common aim: the removal of Saddam. Consequently, a loose arrangement had been hammered out whereby they would work together to this end.

Saddam, apparently, became aware of this almost as it

happened, and it was my belief that his initiative and the subsequent abductions of the delegates were little more than an attempt to undermine the alliance. He was clearly not remotely interested in offering the Kurds anything like independence while they sat astride some of the world's richest oilfields. He was similarly not about to become involved in any power sharing with the Shi'a while he was at war with Khomeini, the greatest and most powerful of the Shi'a leaders. He had to throw the greatest weight behind the war effort and yet simultaneously maintain peace at home. Duplicity and oppression were the tactics he chose.

Several attempts were made on the life of Saddam in this period, but fortunately for myself I was never in the vicinity of any of them. Some were more imaginative than others, though none succeeded. On three occasions he came close to being shot and the belief among some Iraqis that Saddam was protected by a Satanic entity grew in substance. Certainly, he enjoys the most incredible good fortune. The closest call was the ambush of the presidential convoy by a small group of militant Kurds, near the entrance to the presidential Palace. The entire assassination party was killed, but not before they had blown up the car they thought contained the President. Inside the car was, in fact, Nadar Rafi al-Ajili, the double recruited by Saddam less than two years earlier. Fortunately for myself, I was now being used for occasions of greater importance and, despite my earlier fears, was almost as well protected, and therefore as difficult to murder, as Saddam himself. Having lost two lookalikes, Saddam's response was to recruit more. I personally knew of four, but it was rumoured that there were others scattered about the country. They were not doubles in the true sense, generally only having a vague physical resemblance that would pass at a distance. To the best of my knowledge, none of them came as close to Saddam's image as myself. My status as 'first double' was not usurped.

During the year, there were three marriages in the

Saddam household. Qusai married Lamia Maher al-Rashid, daughter of Maher Abdullah al-Rashid, one of the army's war heroes. Saddam's daughter, Rana, just sixteen, married her sister Raghd's brother-in-law, Saddam Kamil al-Majid. The youngest daughter, Hala, aged only fourteen, married another of the al-Majid brothers, Hakim. On each occasion I stood in for Saddam throughout the day. The ceremonies were widely publicised and seen as events at which Saddam's enemies might strike. More and more, whenever a public appearance was required, I took the President's place, with Saddam attending only the private ceremonies and receptions.

As the war dragged on, without any apparent hope of bring brought to a victorious conclusion, one or two members of the government sought to place themselves in an advantageous position should Saddam fall. They were nameless faces, but were largely responsible for the coalition talks taking place between the Kurds, Shi'a and other groups opposed to the government. Assassination was seen as the only realistic means of being rid of Saddam, and Baghdad was becoming a viper's nest of conspiracy and betrayal.

Rather than assassination, though, it was nearly the events of the war that finished Saddam. In February, at a cost of some 10,000 Iraqi lives, the Iranians once again seized the al-Fao peninsula. To compensate for this disaster, a distraction was arranged by taking the Iranian town of Mehran in the central sector of the war zone. Six weeks later, the Iranians wrested it back. Iran was now seriously on the offensive and for many it seemed the war had turned irreversibly in Khomeini's favour. There was an air of desperate tension on the streets of Baghdad and this period most certainly represented Saddam's greatest crisis since coming to power.

It coincided with, and probably inspired, the first moves against the Kurdish people on a mass scale by Saddam. In November, more than 600 villages in the province of Salaimaniya had their electricity supplies cut off and their livestock confiscated. A total ban on all commercial transactions within and between the villages was imposed. The purpose was to force the people into the more manage-able large towns and cities, but they refused to move. Although life was incredibly hard, trading between villages continued because of the Kurds superior knowledge of the local terrain. Saddam was advised by his officials in the province that more serious measures would have to be taken.

One morning, Hashim was called away from the Dark Room on 'urgent business'. He returned an hour later.

'I am sorry I was away so long, Mikhaelef,' he said, 'but we have had something of a minor crisis concerning you.'

'What has happened?' I asked, trying to look non-chalant.

'A man contacted the Ministry of Education asking for you by your own name. He was, apparently, beside himself with grief and would not be put off when told by a member of the staff there that he had never heard of you. Eventually, the minister himself, Abdullah Qader, became involved. He, of course, knew exactly who the man was referring to and told him you had been transferred.'

'Who was it?'

'I am coming to that. The man said it was important he spoke to you and understandably the minister was con-cerned there had been a security breech and referred the matter to the presidential staff. They called me, and that is where I have been for the past hour. I contacted the man on a telephone number he had left and it turns out there is no problem, but I am afraid I have some bad news for you, Mikhaelef.'

'Who was it?' I repeated anxiously. 'What has hap-pened?'

'It was an old friend of yours from Karbala. His name is Abdullah. He says you once lived in the same apartment block.'

'Yes, yes,' I said, nodding. 'I have known Abdullah for many years. What has happened to him?'

'To Abdullah, nothing . . . it is his son, Sa'dun.'

There was no need for Hashim to explain further.

'Sa'dun is dead?' I asked, anticipating his answer.

'Yes. I am very sorry to be the person to break the news to you, but he was killed in action yesterday at Mehran.'

My mind immediately threw up an image of young Sa'dun as a sprightly three-year old. When he saw me returning from school, he would run down the path that led to our apartment block and throw himself into my arms shouting, 'Miklef! Miklef!' I then recalled the last time I had seen him, when I feared he had recognised me at the army barracks near Kirkuk. He was a fine young man and I was desperately saddened by his death. I had been through many things in the previous years, but for the first time since my father died, I felt the tears well up in my eyes. Perhaps the strain of what I had been going through finally came to the surface, but within a moment I was sobbing my heart out.

Hashim seemed embarrassed by my grief, as if it were an alien emotion to him.

'I am sorry, Mikhaelef. If I had known you were so close to this man, I would have informed you more tactfully.'

I could not answer him, but was able to indicate with my hand that I wished to be left alone. Hashim left the room and there I stayed until I brought my emotions under control. I took a sheet of paper from my desk and set out to write a letter of condolence to his family. It was not an easy letter to write and I was on my third attempt when the door opened. Assuming it to be Hashim, I did not look up.

'I have just been informed that the son of your close friend has been killed.'

The voice was that of Saddam. I raised my head and nodded without speaking.

'Then you must leave for Karbala straight away to be with his father,' he said. 'If he goes to so much trouble to contact you, then you should be with him. I will arrange it for you. You will be in Karbala within two hours.'

This was another example of the schizophrenic nature of

the man. To those he knew and was well-disposed towards (and I flatter myself that this included me), his magnanimity was boundless. At such moments it was almost possible to forgive him his crimes against his people.

I spent the next three days with Abdullah. I found it particularly distressing to be in the same room as his wife, Amina, who took the death of her youngest son very badly. She wailed persistently and the only temporary relief came on the occasions she fell exhausted into a fitful sleep.

My heart went out to them both. They were simple people who asked little from others but friendship. I did what I could to distract Abdullah from his grief, but the task was beyond me and our conversations always centred on Sa'dun and the little incidents of his childhood and youth that I had thought long forgotten. On the evening before I was travelling back to Baghdad, we sat alone together in his apartment and finally talked of other things.

'I have missed you, Miklef, since you have been away. You know I am pleased you have prospered, but selfishly I wish you were still just across the landing.'

'You do not know how often I have wished that myself, Abdullah.'

'Why?' he asked curiously. 'Are you not happy?'

I did not know what to say. How could I explain my unhappiness without telling him the complete truth?

'No,' I said at length. 'I am not happy.'

'Why not? Is it Amna?'

'No, no, everything is fine with Amna.'

'Then it is the job?'

I paused before answering with a sigh, 'Yes, it is the job.'

'Then no job is worth it, Miklef,' he said, quite adamantly. 'Come home. Leave the damned job.'

'I cannot leave the job. It is not that simple.'

'Why not? What job is it that you cannot leave? What is the good of the money you earn and the house you live in if they do not make you happy? Come home, Miklef.'

I hesitated, wanting to explain at least part of my

dilemma, yet reluctant to involve him. Although I had not seen him since the day I was married, I trusted Abdullah more than any other person outside my immediate relatives. We had been close friends and I frequently scolded myself for not keeping in touch. In the end, I came to a decision.

'I have seen Sa'dun since he was conscripted,' I stated.

'He was not conscripted, he volunteered,' Abdullah said, with a little frown. 'But when did you see him? He never mentioned it.'

'It was more than five years ago. He was at the barracks in a place called Chamchamel, near Kirkuk.'

'Yes, that is right,' he acknowledged. 'I used to write to him there. What were you doing in such a place?'

'I was on an official visit.'

'With the Ministry of Education?' Abdullah asked, bemused.

I looked long and hard at Abdullah before I continued, but I had needed to confide in someone for some time, perhaps since Mohammed Qutaibi had died. 'I have never worked for the Ministry of Education. That was a cover story.'

Abdullah's furrowed brows underlined his puzzlement.

'Before I say anything more,' I went on, 'you must promise me, as my dearest friend, that you will never repeat what I am about to tell you. For your own safety as well as mine. This is in absolute confidence.'

Abdullah looked offended. 'Of course, Miklef, you know you can trust me. But what is it?'

'Just before I left for Baghdad, you may recall that one morning I was picked up here by officers of the Republican Guard.'

'Yes, I was worried sick. I thought you had been arrested and I remember you being strangely evasive afterwards.'

'The truth is I was taken to see Saddam Hussein.'

'What?' Abdullah gave an involuntary chuckle. 'You have met Saddam Hussein?'

'It is a strange story. My brother-in-law, Akram, whom

you know, mentioned to his superior that I looked like Saddam. I was summoned to meet him and . . . I have been in his service ever since.'

Abdullah, though still smiling, was wide-eyed with astonishment. 'This is incredible. I can hardly believe it. What is it you do for Saddam?'

Again I hesitated. 'I impersonate him,' I replied eventually.

'You impersonate him?' He shook his head in disbelief. 'I have heard stories that Saddam uses doubles, but I thought it was just government propaganda. Do you appear as him in public?'

'Yes. When Sa'dun was at Chamchamel, did he tell you that he met Saddam?'

'Yes, he did. In fact, he told me he spoke with him. That was you?'

I smiled sheepishly. 'That was me.'

I went on to tell Abdullah much of what had happened since 1979. He fired questions back at me, the most disturbing of which concerned Amna and her brothers.

'What does Amna think about this? As I remember she despised Saddam.'

'She does not like him or his family, but she tolerates my situation.'

'The money will not interest her, of course,' he said, 'but does she not find the hypocrisy difficult to live with?'

'What hypocrisy?'

'You know her father was a Communist, so are all his children, including Amna.'

I waved my hand dismissively. 'Yes, perhaps, up to a point. But she is not an activist. '

'Are you sure?'

'Do you think I do not know what my wife does with her time?' I asked, somewhat resentful of his inferences.

In truth, I was not as convinced about Amna's passivism as I sounded. Admittedly, since Salih's birth, much of her hostility towards the regime had subsided. At first I put this down to Post Natal Depression, but even after she recovered and appeared to be returning to her normal self, she no longer mentioned Saddam. I had hoped that motherhood had diluted her political passion, but of late I had begun to harbour vague suspicions that her reticence on the subject of Saddam was calculated, rather than a reflection of indifference towards him. Abdullah, however, did not press the point.

'What of her brothers?' he enquired.

'I do not see them often, but I am sure they are not involved in anything.'

Abdullah shrugged. 'If you are sure, then it is not for me to interfere.'

The implications of Amna or her brothers being involved with the ICP were too awful to imagine and again I cast the thought to the back of my mind.

Before I left Abdullah, he assured me my secrets were safe with him and entreated me to keep in touch in the future. He had his own load to bear and I felt a twinge of guilt about having unloaded my burden on him.

'Look after yourself, Abdullah. If you need me you know where to contact me directly. Please do so whenever you wish.'

'I will. But you must be careful too. You swim in shark-infested waters.'

'I will be careful,' I promised, but my words sounded hollow to my ears.

As I was driven back to Baghdad, I was surprised by the heavy traffic moving in the opposite direction. A considerable exodus to the west towards Jordan was in progress, and indeed, with the Iranian army now advanced as far as Mehran, rumours of the city being about to fall abounded. Stories of plots and coups escalated, and if the price of peace was Saddam's head, an increasing number of prominent Iraqis were reputed to be prepared to pay it.

Military reversals nearly put to a stop the ascendancy of the al-Rashids before it gathered any momentum. General Maher Abdullah, the father-in-law of Saddam's younger son, Qusai, was called to the presidential palace to account for his failure to remove the Iranians from the al-Fao peninsula after prolonged and bitter fighting throughout the year. Maher and his officers feared the worst and let it be known that they would not prosecute the war if Maher was harmed. This unprecedented 'rebellion' put Saddam on the defensive and Maher arrived in Baghdad to a warm welcome and a medal of honour. The army was given more freedom to decide tactics in the field and the situation improved almost immediately. Saddam, though, would not forget this stand against his authority.

Towards the end of the year, Akram's good friend, Samir Mohammed, became involved in a much-publicised case of corruption and caused Akrim several weeks of high anxiety.

He came to see me one evening, for once not in the company of Wahab, shortly after a story had broken connecting Samir with an English businessman, Ian Richter. When Amna offered him tea, he declined and said he wished to talk to me alone. Once Amna had left us, he did not delay in coming to the point. He was unusually nervous.

'Have you been questioned about me?' he asked, in a quavering voice.

'By whom?' I answered, knowing quite well what he meant.

'Please, Mikhaelef, do not play games with me. Has anybody approached you?'

'No, they have not,' I said firmly. 'But if you are involved in anything with Samir, you should tell me. You are married to my sister.'

'I have done nothing wrong!' he declared with, I had to concede, some conviction. 'But I am . . . was a friend of Samir's and many of the those who know him are being questioned by the Mukhabarat.'

'If you have done nothing wrong,' I said, 'you have nothing to fear.'

'Ha!' he snorted. 'You of all people should know that is

nonsense. The fact that I was his friend may be enough to condemn me.'

'Perhaps, but you will have to cross that bridge should you come to it and obviously I will do what I can to help. But is there anything with which they can incriminate you?'

Akram gave a sigh of resignation. 'Yes.'

'What is it?'

Beads of sweat appeared on his brow.

'You must swear you will tell nobody.'

'In the name of Allah!' I snapped back, losing patience with him. 'I am your wife's brother. You are the father of my three nieces. Of course I will not tell anybody. What is it?'

'A typewriter,' he offered meekly.

'What?' I said, nonplussed.

'I have a typewriter.'

'Yes?' I prompted, encouraging him to amplify.

'That is it. I own a typewriter that is not registered.'

It was all I could do not to laugh out loud. Saddam had recently decreed it to be illegal for Iraqis to own typewriters, printers and photo-copiers not registered with the authorities. Foreigners, including journalists, were not allowed to possess them at all. His anxiety was also heightened to some degree by the recent formal implementation of the death penalty for anyone found guilty of publicly insulting the President, the RCC, the Ba'ath party or the National Assembly. Under Iraq's idiosyncratic laws, illegal possession of a typewriter could have been construed as an intention to do just that.

I laid a reassuring hand on his shoulder.

'Akram, I too have a typewriter. And I have to confess that it has slipped my mind also to have it registered. I thank you for reminding me. Tomorrow I will put this matter right and I suggest you do the same.'

I found it difficult to take Akram seriously at the best of times, but he had at least convinced me he was not involved in any of Samir's schemes; he clearly did not have the brains or the courage for it. As it happened, his expectations that he might be arrested did not materialise.

Samir was not charged with any impropriety and was, in fact, promoted to the position of Minister for Higher Education. I was aware he had accepted huge bribes from Richter in return for lucrative contracts. No one doubted he was guilty, but, as one of Saddam's favoured cronies, it was decided to move him upstairs. It would be another three years before Saddam tired of Samir and placed him under house arrest at his home on 52nd Street in the district of Karada, where he is still held today.

Richter was not so fortunate. He was charged with making illegal payments to an 'Iraqi government officer' and sentenced to twenty years hard labour.

Chapter Nine

1987
Raby' al-Thaany 1407 – Jumaada al-Awwal 1408

The course of the war was changing rapidly. In January, the Iranians attacked the area surrounding al-Basrah and were only stopped when within rifle range of the city. Many Iraqis wondered for how much longer the Iranians could be held at bay, and whether or not Saddam could survive any more military reverses. My own feelings about Saddam's prospects were decidedly mixed. In my heart I wanted him to fall, but I was wide awake to the personal dangers that would follow his demise. News of his arrest or assassination would lead to riots in the streets and Baghdad would be a dangerous place for a Saddam looka-like. The reality of the crisis made me think long and hard about my next move.

Ordinary Iraqis, however, were unaware of events taking place behind the scenes. The last thing the US wanted was for Islamic Fundamentalists to sweep through the Middle East and take control of the world's oil resources. They campaigned heavily within diplomatic circles to put a stop to the supply of arms to Iran.

Contemporaneously, and for the same reason, Saddam's arsenal was steadily growing and there were positive indications that Iran's momentum was slowing.

The crisis on the eastern border took precedence over all other issues and the abduction of the Kurdish delegation in Baghdad the previous year was only one indication of how Saddam believed the Kurds were weakening his position. If the Iranians decided to launch a major offensive through the north-eastern border, Saddam could not count on the support of the local Kurdish population. This danger was to some degree diluted by the number of Kurds on the Iranian side of the border, equally opposed to the regime of Khomeini, but it was an Achilles' heel that Saddam could not afford to overlook.

His 'cousin', Ali Hassan al-Majid, was a well-known hard-liner within the family network. His reputation had been established when ruthlessly crushing the opposition factions that were constantly emerging in the towns and cities. Saddam now saw fit to utilise his talents further. He installed him as head of the Ba'ath party's Northern Command with specific orders to Arabise the north and pre-empt any possibility of a Kurdish revolt.

For the solution, Ali looked to chemical and biological weapons, the most secret element of Saddam's armoury. My knowledge on the subject remained scant until a chance meeting with an Lebanese biologist, who did much to further my education. This occurred at a function held at the palace, to give thanks for the contributions made by foreign scientists to the cause of Arab nationalism, a slogan that was wheeled out by the Government whenever it suited their purpose. Saddam avoided such evenings whenever it was possible and as there was only to be a short speech followed by a few token handshakes, I was ordered to replace him.

In all, there were more than five hundred men and maybe twenty women present in the palace's main conference hall. They represented an elite collection of chemists, physicists, engineers, medical doctors and other worthy individuals. The evening was uneventful and I decided I had had my fill of the fawning servility that met me at every turn. With Hashim and three SRG officers for company, I slowly but diplomatically worked my way through the mass of academics towards the exit. I was speaking with a pair of Turkish engineers who had waylaid me only a metre or two from the exit, when we were interrupted by a female voice.

'Excuse me, Your Excellency. May I speak to you.'

I turned and was confronted by an attractive woman in her thirties. Consistent with Saddam's behaviour in such circumstances, I treated her to my trademark huge grin.

'Of course, my dear,' I said, moving closer. 'What is it?'

'With respect, Your Excellency, not here. Can we go somewhere?'

Hashim gave me an anxious glance and the three engineers smirked knowingly. It was not unusual for the President to be offered sexual favours, sometimes in the hope of extracting a pardon for an arrested relative.

'I am very busy,' I said casually, indicating the number of people about us. 'Perhaps you can make an appointment to see me through my office. I am always happy to meet those worthy individuals who dedicate their lives to our cause.'

'This cannot wait, Your Excellency,' she said anxiously.

My enquiring glance towards Hashim earned a shrug, which I interpreted as a go-ahead. Leaving the hall, the woman, Hashim, and I crossed the corridor to a small room, in which there was a low table and several chairs. My SRG guards followed us and took up position outside the door.

Once the woman was seated, she glanced nervously at Hashim just inside the closed door.

'I really do need to speak with you alone, Your Excellency,' she said earnestly.

'You need not fear. Anything you have to say to me, I will discuss with my aide here as a matter of course, so you may speak quite freely.'

Reluctantly, she began to voice her concerns. 'My name is Inahri Ahmad al-Bahzaz. I am a biologist from Qurnat as-Sawda in Lubnam (Lebanon). I have been in Iraq for eighteen months, working in a research laboratory on the Salmon Pak complex. My task has been to assist in the development of a variety of strains of the West Nile virus.' She hesitated and again flashed an uncertain glance at Hashim.

'As you know, Your Excellency,' she said hesitantly, 'the experiments have been successful and preparations are in hand for several deadly strains of the virus to go into full production. We now know its effects on the human body in a variety of circumstances and different environments. Since I graduated in Tarabal (Tripoli), I have experimented on the effects of foreign matter on respiratory systems and bodily functions. Always I have used animals: rats, pigs, cattle. Now I am being asked to experiment on people.'

'What kind of experiments, Inahri?' I asked, at which Hashim, already uncomfortable with the direction the conversation was taking, coughed politely.

'Your Excellency,' he said. 'We have to return to the palace shortly. I respectfully suggest that this discussion be deferred to another time—'

'What I have to say,' Inahri cut in, 'will take but a few moments. Please, bear with me, Your Excellency.'

Ignoring Hashim's warning grimace, I nodded for her to continue.

'Last year, after the army's victory in Mehran, twenty captured Iranian women were brought to Salman Pak. They were exposed to the virus, either for observation purposes or to test the effectiveness of vaccines or protective equipment. Twelve of them are now dead. Of the others, all are sick in varying degrees. I doubt any will survive. I have to live with my conscience over that, but it is not why I am here.'

I suppressed my natural squeamishness to enquire, 'How was it done?'

She looked puzzled. 'Do you not know, Your Excellency?'

I covered up my *faux pas*, with a hasty, 'Not in detail. The methods are a matter for my scientists. I am only interested in results.'

'If you will forgive my temerity, Your Excellency, you would be advised to make enquiries. The subjects are strapped down in an air-tight chamber and the virus released. If the subject dies, an autopsy is carried out. This is done from outside the chamber by means of sleeves inserted into the chamber wall. Once the examination is complete the chamber is frozen and the contents stored. The chamber is then prepared for the next test.'

Only to the inner circle of government, on whose periphery I hovered, and the higher command of the army, was it known that Saddam had first used chemical weapons on Iranian targets in 1982, albeit on a minor scale.

Inahri went on, 'Such experiments have been an integral part of the development of chemical and biological weapons since their inception into the Iraqi armoury in the seventies. Kurdish and Shi'a prisoners provide chemists and biologists with an abundant supply of 'volunteers'. Captives from the war with Iran have only boosted the numbers. We know as much about the way the human body reacts to the various strains of the West Nile virus as we ever will until they are used on a large number of people at once. That is why I am here, Your Excellency.

'I have received instructions to prepare the virus for mass production. The plan is for it to be used in enormous quantities on the Kurds in northern Iraq. It must not be allowed to happen. It is madness. We are totally unable to predict how the virus will spread. We cannot determine how it will behave once it is cast to the elements. If the virus is released in sufficient quantity it may be difficult, if not impossible, to control.'

'Surely there are vaccines?' I said vaguely, out of my depth.

'Yes, of course, very effective ones. But once the virus is

released there is a very real possibility it will mutate further into strains against which our vaccines are useless. Please, Your Excellency, I implore you with the utmost respect. If Ali Hassan is not stopped, he may cause the most dreadful disaster yet seen by mankind. The 'Final Solution' he intends could be final for the whole of Iraq, perhaps the whole of the Middle East.'

'We will investigate your concerns without delay,' Hashim said abruptly, even as I opened my mouth to speak. 'Now – please – you must leave.'

Inahri was ushered, unprotesting, from the room.

'What do we do?' I asked Hashim , once we were alone.

'You do exactly nothing, Mikhaelef,' he snapped. 'I will see Saddam tomorrow. Do not repeat one word of what you have heard here. Not even to me. Never raise the subject again. I pray to Allah that Saddam will stop this. What that woman has told us makes the entire war with Iran look like a street fight.'

Despite his cosmetic overtures towards the Kurds, I had long suspected that Saddam was bent on solving the Kurdish 'problem' by genocide. Hashim never disclosed to me what was said between him and Saddam, but I can confirm that biological weapons were not deployed against the Kurds. Instead, Hassan used chemicals. He was instructed to destroy the economic basis of their society, raze the physical infrastructure of their rural communities and eliminate all potential sources of support for the peshmerga rebels.

The first chemical bombing of a Kurdish village occurred as early as April, when Shaikh Wisan in the Balisan Valley was attacked. Within a few months, 8,000 men and boys of the Kurdish al-Barzani tribe were murdered. Huge areas in the north-eastern provinces were cleared and restricted zones set up. Anybody caught within the zones was shot on sight. Those who surrendered were shot later. Tens of thousands of Kurdish men women and children were imprisoned, deported, or relocated from border villages to the nearest towns and cities. Over the course of 1987,

 The Real Saddam

The Fake Saddam ▶

▲ August 1990: The Author with English boy Stuart Lockwood in a still from a propaganda TV broadcast, designed to reassure the outside world that foreigners would not be used by Iraq as hostages.

▲ December 1983: the Author on a morale-boosting tour of front-line communities during the war with Iran

▲ October 1988: the Author at a press conference with Hosni Moubarak and Yasser Arafat

▲ May 1989: the Author's second and last meeting with Yasser Arafat

▲ Summer 1982: with Saddam's daughter, Hala.
(Saddam himself was also in the original picture, to Hala's left,
but at his instructions was trimmed from the negative.)

hundreds of villages were blown up and bulldozed. Where Ali met resistance he did not hesitate to use gas and poison: in May, the Kurds of more than twenty villages were eradicated by mustard gas, nerve gas and cyanide; in June, similar attacks took place on the Iranian part of Kurdistan. Settlements around the Kurdish villages of Shaikh Wisan, Kela Shin, Birkin, Shahidah and Raniyah practically disappeared as Ali began sweeping a ten to twenty-five kilometre corridor along the Iranian border, from Turkey in the north towards the city of Salaimaniya, a hundred kilometres east of Kirkuk.

For ever after, Ali Hassan al-Majid was referred to as 'Chemical Ali' – but he was only warming up.

In November, at a small settlement near Ranyah, on the Zahb-e Kuchek mountain close to the Iranian border, Ali's troops revived an atrocity first carried out in Dakan in August 1969. When the villagers were rounded up, the commanding officer, Muwafeq Jihad, noted a disproportionately high ratio of men to women and children, and correctly assumed that some of the latter were hiding.

He dispatched a platoon of men to scour the surrounding area. It was not long before they came across fifteen woman and nearly as many children holed up in a small cave less than a kilometre from the village. He ordered his men to seal off the grotto with bush and timber and, after dousing the wood with petrol, set fire to it. Those who tried to escape the choking smoke were shot. As the fire intensified, those not fortunate enough to be overcome by the smoke, were burnt alive. None survived.

Ali was also instructed to experiment with a biological car bomb, which would have been a lethal weapon had it worked efficiently. The technology of such a weapon was beyond me, but the basic principle was simple enough. A phial containing a small quantity of a deadly virus, which was later popularly dubbed the 'Satan Virus,' was strategically located in a car, which was then driven into the target area and abandoned. Some time later, a small explosion would shatter the phial, releasing the virus.

Although several variations on this theme were attempted, success was limited. On one occasion near Koi Sanjaq, northern Iraq, the car containing the explosive was stolen by young hoodlums. Hashim was in tears of laughter as he related to me how the three Mukhabarat officers responsible for it were happily driving towards the safety of Arbil when the offending car raced past them. They gave chase and succeeded in pulling the lethal cargo over just outside the town. The bomb was then made safe and the joyriders were given prison sentences of a severity that must have surprised them.

Another revolutionary element returning to prominence was the ICP. As Amna's father, Pasha, had been only too willing to explain, they believed only the paradigm of neo-Marxism came close to explaining the massive contradictions that were an integral part of Iraq's existence. Without Marxism, it would be impossible to unite Arab and Kurdish Sunnis and the Arab Shi'a, all ethnically, culturally or religiously incompatible. Marxism, however, identified all as victims of class conflict exploited by capital interests.

The ICP was as independent of the Soviet Union as any international Communist party was at this time. Although the relationship between Moscow and Baghdad had cooled with the purges of 1979, Cold War realities had brought them together again by 1984 and the ICP did not enjoy the same level of funding from 'Moscow Gold' as was afforded their political counterparts around the world. The broad aim of the Iraqi Communists was to dispossess those who controlled the country's multi-billion dollar oil industry and (purportedly) expropriate it for the benefit of the people. In order to do so, they would have to assassinate not only the President but his family of ministers also.

The re-emergence of the Communists as an opposition force to be reckoned with nagged at me constantly because of Amna's family connections. My conversation with Abdullah had awakened in me a fear I had long ago suppressed. I was increasingly concerned that Amna had in some way become actively involved with the ICP.

She had also become uncharacteristically short-tempered. One evening, when I was telling her that Saddam's youngest daughter, Hala, was divorcing her husband, Hakim Kalim al-Majid, after being married for less than a year, she suddenly raged at Nadia for spilling a drink. I decided to confront her.

'What is the matter, Amna?' I asked, deliberately pitching my voice low in the hope that she would calm down.

'What are you talking about?' she snapped back.

'You know what I am talking about. For the past few weeks you have been impossible to live with. You scream at the children for the least thing. You have also been a little distant with me. What is it?'

'It is nothing. A product of your imagination.'

'Then why are you behaving this way?' I demanded. 'It is not in your nature.'

'I . . . don't know.' She glanced across at me nervously, as if realising I was not going to be easily deflected. 'It is Saddam,' she said then, after a moment's hesitation.

'Saddam?' I said.

'It is no secret what I think about Saddam Hussein. I hate him.'

I shrugged at this. 'So what is different now? You have always felt that way.'

'Yes, but I cannot take much more of what he is doing and what is done in his name. Do you remember the air disaster in America last year?'

'Yes, I think so,' I replied curiously. 'Remind me.'

'A 747 jumbo jet bound for Paris exploded shortly after leaving New York in July last year. 230 people were killed.'

'Yes, I remember reading about it,' I said. 'What has that to do with Saddam?'

'He authorised it,' Amna said, and with such conviction that I almost believed her.

'Do not be ridiculous!' I retorted. 'You forget I have access to American newspapers. If there was the remotest possibility that Saddam had anything to do with that terrible disaster, the media of the West would have been all over the story. There has been nothing.'

Amna persisted. 'American air-crash investigators have no idea what caused the explosion. They have found no evidence consistent with a bomb.'

'Exactly,' I said with emphasis. 'So what substance is there to your conspiracy theory?'

'There was a bomb, but it was very small. It was assembled on board by four foreign agents of Saddam's when the plane was travelling from Frankfurt on its way to America. They travelled as two married couples, with false passports.'

My scepticism was in no way diminished. 'So four agents in the employ of Saddam walk on board a US-bound jumbo jet carrying bomb-making equipment, quietly put a bomb together and leave it behind when they get off the plane in New York. The plane then takes off for Paris and is blown out of the sky by a bomb so small the world's best air-crash investigators cannot find any trace of it. Please, Amna, you will have to do better than that.'

She was in no way agitated by sarcasm. 'The bomb was carried on board in separate parts that consisted only of a small battery, a digital watch, an electric switch and a minute quantity of liquid explosive. They do not have the necessary equipment in Frankfurt to detect such items. The bomb was assembled in a toilet and discreetly secured beneath one of the terrorist's seats, situated immediately above the main fuel tank. There was sufficient fuel for the journey to Europe in the auxiliary tanks, so the main tank was virtually empty. Instead, it contained a potentially lethal quantity of fuel vapour. The terrorists knew this.'

Such detail had aroused my curiosity. 'Go on,' I said.

'The job of the bomb was not to blow up the plane. Between the roof of the fuel tank and the main floor of the aircraft is a space of less than half-a-metre, through which runs the electrical wiring to the main fuel tank. The initial explosion was a small one, audible only to a handful of people in the immediate vicinity, but it was sufficient to puncture the floor and cause a small fire beneath the main deck.'

'Surely such damage would have been picked up by the flight crew or, at least, by the black box recorder?' I asked, looking to pick holes in the story.

'Not at all,' Amna responded. 'The main tank was empty, so the electrics leading to it were switched off. The captain and his crew would have been completely unaware of the problem. It is likely that one or two of the passengers reported the small bang, but enquiries were probably still being made by stewards, when the plane blew up.'

'How?'

'The fire generated heat against the wall of the main tank. Fuel vapours require a temperature of approximately forty degrees Celsius to ignite. Within minutes, the temperature of the tank wall would have been greatly in excess of this. The vapours exploded, the tank blew up and the plane fell out of the sky. On the way down, the auxiliary tanks exploded, consistent with eye witness reports and the findings of crash investigators.'

My technical knowledge being all but non-existent, I was not qualified to pick holes in the detail Amna had given me. 'How do you know this?' I asked finally.

'Latif has many contacts. Most of them work against Saddam, but some will work for anybody if the price is right.'

'What movement did the terrorists represent?'

'None. This was a blind, in case they were caught. They were supposed to be affiliated to some terrorist organisation based in the Philippines.'

'But why was it done?' I said, still reluctant to believe it. 'I cannot see the point. What would motivate Saddam to authorise such an atrocity? Especially as he never claimed responsibility.'

'It was an experiment. Nobody could be sure it would work. Now that it has, Saddam has a weapon that will strike fear into the hearts of all Westerners should he ever have the need to use it. He has to be stopped.'

'Yes,' I agreed fervently. 'But who can stop him?'

'There are people,' she answered evasively.

'What people?' I asked. 'Whoever stands in his way, he removes them. What can anybody do? What can you do?'

'I can do something!' she almost yelled at me.

'You are talking nonsense!' I snapped back. 'You can do nothing.'

'Oh, yes, I can – and I have.' She did not look at me.

'What do you mean?' I demanded.

'I mean nothing.'

'What do you mean?' I insisted. 'What have you done?'

Amna finally looked into my eyes. 'Something I should have done a long time ago.'

I understood her immediately. I snorted.

'You have joined the Communist Party.'

Amna did not reply. Her silence was confirmation enough.

I rose to my feet and walked across to where she sat and held her tightly about the arms. 'Are you mad, woman? Do you want us all to be killed? You have signed the death warrants of us all! What are you thinking of? What about Nadia and Salih? Even if our marriage is of no consequence to you, you are their mother, and your first duty is to them.'

'I am doing it for them. For their future.'

'You are crazy! They have no future if you do this.'

Amna did not respond immediately. She stared hard at the floor and I could see tears welling up in her eyes. An intelligent woman, she was under no illusions as to the magnitude of the step she had taken.

'You are a good man, Mikhael' she said finally. 'You don't deserve this. I am sorry I have had to tell you in this way,'

I stepped away from her. 'And in what way would you

have liked to tell me, Amna? As we sat down to dinner? After we had made love? Would you have ever told me?'

'I have been meaning to tell you,' she said sullenly.

'Oh, of course you have. Do you take me for a fool?'

'I am serious. I have been asked to speak to you.'

I frowned. 'You have been asked? What are you saying?'

'An attempt will shortly be made on Saddam's life . . .'

'I do not believe I am hearing this.' I returned to my seat and put my hands to my head.

'I have been instructed to ask you, if it is successful, will you stand in for Saddam? Will you take the part of Saddam until a coup has succeeded and his supporters have been overcome?'

My mind was in a whirl. This was worse than I ever feared it could be. 'I am in the company of a madwoman,' I said, unable to credit that my wife was in league with a resistance movement, bent on overthrowing the President.

'This is deadly serious, Mikhaelef.'

'You are not mistaken!' I snapped back.

'Once Saddam is dead,' she went on, 'there will be chaos. It is essential that other members of his family, especially that bastard Udai Saddam and his brother, do not seize control. You can cause a great deal of confusion in those vital few hours after Saddam has been killed and help us consolidate our hold on the country.'

It made sense. Yet its chances of success were no greater than all the other failed coups that had gone before it. It was not a gamble I was prepared to participate in.

'How deeply are you involved with this?' My anger was dissipating, to be replaced by anxiety.

'As deep as it is possible to be, my husband.'

I shook my head helplessly. This was no time to quarrel. It was clear that no entreaties of mine would deflect her from her chosen course. 'Are you to be a member of this assassination party?'

'No,' she answered. I was thankful for that small mercy, at any rate.

'Do you intend to use my position to help anybody gain access to Saddam?'

'No. You must be somewhere else entirely when the plan is implemented.'

'You know this is a crazy thing to do,' I said quietly, without the slightest hope that, crazy thing or not, she would reconsider her involvement.

'It has to be done,' she responded resolutely. 'If the people of Iraq are to have any kind of future, then we must eliminate Saddam Hussein.'

I felt deflated and defeated. 'Your courage astounds me, Amna, but I can take no part in this.'

'You will not help?'

'I cannot help, but because you are my wife and for the sake of our children, I will do one thing. I will never breathe one word of this conversation to anyone. What has been said tonight will never be repeated. But I beg you, Amna, distance yourself from these people.'

'It is too late for that.'

I stayed up for many hours after Amna had gone to bed. I was terrified by what she had told me. I was also caught on the horns of a terrible dilemma. Her cause was just: something had to be done about Saddam. But not by Amna. Nor by me. The lives of my two young children were precious beyond words and I would do nothing to endanger them. Yet once Amna's part in this plot was uncovered, as it surely would be, I would be deemed guilty by association, as if I were an integral part of the conspiracy. But short of betraying her, I could do nothing to prevent it going ahead.

Over the next few days I barely spoke to Amna. In the aftermath of our last conversation, all else seemed irrelevant. I passed most of my leisure hours either in the garden or in my study, pummelling my brain over the different options open to me without ever coming close to a solution. I soon developed acute paranoia, imagining I was being followed or watched wherever I went. Much as I tried to convince myself I was being ridiculous, I had no peace from a constant, terrifying sense of foreboding.

A few days later, I was discussing the war with Hashim in the Dark Room when Saddam came in with Udai. I immediately became aware of a subtle but definable difference in the way Saddam spoke to me, and within a few sentences the worst of my fears were realised.

'I would not normally involve myself in such matters,' he said, regarding me, with no trace of his usual benevolence, 'but such is the delicate nature of what I wish to discuss, I did not feel able to delegate the task.'

Hashim immediately stood up. 'Perhaps this is a good time, Your Excellency, for me to attend to some paperwork.'

Saddam nodded. 'Thank you, Hashim.'

Once Hashim had left the room, I noticed Udai was contemplating me in a way that made me feel distinctly uncomfortable, like a cat eyeing up a mouse. Saddam moved behind me, a practice of which he was particularly fond in such situations. He placed a hand on my shoulder and came straight to the point.

'I have received some information which disturbs me, Mikhaelef. I am going to ask you some questions and you must answer them with complete honesty.'

'Of course, Saddam.' I felt my stomach turn and wished myself far away.

'Do you know that your brother-in-law, Latif Pasha, is a member of the Communist Party?'

As he asked the question, he came to stand before me, I supposed to observe my reaction. In fact, I felt some momentary relief that I was being asked about Latif and not Amna. It was to be short-lived.

'To the best of my knowledge,' I answered with as much composure as I could muster, 'he is not a member of any political organisation.'

'You know,' Saddam said, 'that your father-in-law was a Communist?'

'Yes, I do,' I replied, my confidence growing. 'But he has been dead for eight years.'

'And what about Amna?' Saddam asked. 'Was she not close to her father?'

The sudden mention of my wife's name gave me a start and I had no doubt Saddam noticed it.

'Yes, indeed, but she has never suggested or implied she shares her father's political opinions.' I hoped Saddam could detect neither the lie nor the apprehension in my voice.

'I have a problem.' Saddam walked away from me to gaze out of the window, with its panorama across the Dijlah. 'The name of Latif Pasha has been coming to the attention of our security services for some time, but that is not of enormous concern to me right now. You will not be surprised to learn that I have agents infiltrating every organisation that exists in Iraq. This morning I was given a list of names of people who attended a covert meeting of revolutionary Communists whose intention it is to cause madness and mayhem in our country at a time of great crisis. Most of the names on the list I have seen before, but there was one that I have not. That name was Amna al-Rabaka.'

I froze. I felt my heart had stopped beating. My tongue seemed to swell in my mouth. 'It is a common name,' I suggested tamely.

'Perhaps,' Saddam answered. 'But it is a most extraordinary coincidence that this particular Amna al-Rabaka should be seated at this meeting next to Latif Pasha.'

My tongue seemed to be stuck to the roof of my mouth. I was sweating and trembling, and began to shake my head in denial. 'This . . . this cannot be true,' I managed to stammer, although I knew, of course, that it most certainly was.

'I do not enjoy telling you this, Mikhaelef, but you must understand the dilemma I am faced with. What do you think I should do?'

'I do not know what to say,' I answered. That, at least, was the truth.

'Then I will tell what we have to do,' Saddam said, seeming to brighten for the first time. 'Your reaction to this news has convinced me you know nothing of your wife's activities. That was important to me. You will now go home and say nothing to your wife about this conversation. You understand?'

I nodded my assent.

'You will tell your wife that a message was left for you here telling you the Mukhabarat know of her involvement with the Communists. You can say she was observed attending a meeting at an apartment on the Hilla Road in the al-Amiriya district, not very far from where you live. That should convince her the source is a reliable one. If she asks, you will tell her the note was not signed. You must then insist she immediately breaks all her connections with these people. I can give her only the one chance, Mikhaelef. You must ensure she listens and obeys.'

I was astounded by Saddam's proposal. It was beyond my comprehension that he should show such tolerance and I would have suspected his sincerity were it not for Udai's vehement objections.

'Father, this is madness! The woman is plotting with her brother to remove you. You must have her arrested immediately.'

Saddam turned viciously on Udai, the first time he had done so in my presence. 'Do not tell me what I should do! You will be well advised to hold your tongue.'

Udai, characteristically, persisted. 'She is a Communist! Every member of her family is a Communist.'

Saddam crossed the room and confronted Udai, looking him straight in the eye. His words, although barely audible, were spoken with menace. 'If you continue to interfere, I will have you removed from the palace. Now – be silent!'

Udai simmered but refrained from responding in kind. Saddam turned his attention back to me.

'You will do as I ask, Mikhaelef?'

I nodded readily in agreement. It would be no hardship, because he and I were at one in the matter of Amna's collusion with the Communists.

That night, I ranted at her for over an hour. Long before

I finished, she had completely broken down and was weeping uncontrollably. Once she was aware Saddam had been monitoring her movements, her disbelief was quickly replaced by terror. If she wanted to live she would have no choice but to terminate her association with the ICP. To defy Saddam was tantamount to suicide. Understandably, she wanted to warn Latif, and I did not try hard to dissuade her. As she was being watched, she would have to resort to a secret means of communication they had agreed upon, in case of need.

'Latif telephones me each day at eleven o'clock in the morning,' she explained between sniffles. 'We do not speak. After ten seconds he replaces the handset. That means everything is all right. If either of us hangs up before that time, it is a signal that we have to meet in an hour at a predetermined place. If it is not safe to meet, and clearly it is not, I wait a few seconds and say it is a bad line, would the caller please try again. Latif will then know that something serious has happened and will go into hiding.'

'Isn't that a little transparent?' I suggested. 'If the line is bugged, it is fairly obvious you are passing coded messages.'

'Perhaps. But they will not know who is calling or what the message is. As for myself, they already know what I have been doing, so I will be no worse off.'

This was flawed reasoning, but it would have to do. The following day, Latif called and Amna duly passed her message.

A week went by. Latif had gone into hiding, although we had no idea where. He rang each morning at precisely eleven o'clock, but I had ordered Amna not to answer the telephone under any circumstances. If she continued to pass coded messages, Saddam would assume she was still working for the ICP and therefore was still involved in the conspiracy. Arrest would be a foregone conclusion.

I tried to continue with my life as normally as possible, but my mind was in a turmoil. Hashim made no comment on my behaviour, so perhaps I was a better actor than I thought. Looking back now, I know that I should have taken Amna and the children and fled. Not doing so is the greatest regret of my life. Abdullah would have helped me. I could have gone first to Karbala and been in Jordan in a day. There was time enough to plan it all. Yet I did nothing. Madam Inertia had me in her paralysing embrace and would not let go.

Instead, I did nothing but worry and wait. I was not totally convinced by Saddam's assurances, but as the days passed and nothing happened, I became gradually more optimistic that the danger had passed.

Then, as my heart ceased to flutter at every ring of the telephone, every knock on the door, my world fell apart.

I came home the following al-Arbe'aa (Wednesday) and Amna, my mother and the children were missing. It was obvious from the state of the house that a great struggle had taken place. I went straight to the telephone and called the presidential palace to report their disappearance. After being placed on hold for several minutes, Saddam himself came onto the line to talk, although I had not asked to speak to him. He promised he would personally instigate and oversee a search of 'urgent priority'. As soon as I hung up, I heard what I thought was a groaning sound at the back of the house.

I rushed out and found my mother. She was bleeding heavily from a gash above her ear and although not entirely coherent, she was able to tell me that four men had broken into the house and taken Amna, Nadia and Salih. Amna had tried to resist and my mother had been pistol whipped as she tried to cling to Salih. She had only regained consciousness as I spoke to Saddam.

For four days I was beset by fear and anxiety. Rumours abounded: Amna and the children had been kidnapped first by the al-Dawa and then the peshmerga, the Mossad and the CIA. Hashim, to his credit, did everything that I was unable to do. He toured the prisons, made phone calls to prominent officers of the Mukhabarat. He called in favours and threatened acquaintances in order to extract the information that might lead me to the discovery of my family. Nobody admitted to knowing anything, even by hearsay.

On the following Sunday (al-Ahad) evening, when I was at home with my mother, Udai arrived at my door. I feared the worst the moment I saw him. I could only think of one reason why Saddam's elder son would deign to visit me.

'Your wife and children have been found.'

There was not a trace of emotion or compassion in his face. On the contrary, I would swear there was a hint of a smile. 'Their bodies have been taken to the city mortuary and it is necessary for you to come now and identify . . .'

As Udai's words seemed to echo around the hallway, my mind closed down. I was later told that a tip-off had directed police to a small plot of land just outside Kadhimia, the birthplace of my parents. Amna, Nadia and Salih Mikhaelef had been found in a shallow grave. According to the official report, Amna had been raped and tortured and my children mutilated.

I remember nothing of the hours that followed. My grief consumed me and total darkness descended on my personal world.

The following morning, just before the funeral, my mother came to me as I lay fully dressed in my room. Udai's visit had left her in a seriously traumatised state, so much so that Hashim, who had rushed across the city as soon as he heard the news, called the doctor to her. She had idolised the two children, especially Salih, and had been as close to them as their mother.

Now she stayed with me as I prepared to leave for the funeral. Combing my hair in the mirror, I envisioned again the face of Udai as he broke the news to me. A slow burning anger began to rise from the well of my very being. If I should live for one day or ten thousand, I vowed I would avenge the deaths of my wife and children.

My deep suspicion of Udai's complicity was compounded by his general behaviour. Of late, he had begun to spiral out of control. Having already murdered a man in cold blood a couple of years earlier, he was at it again in a dance club in Baghdad only a week following the murder of Amna and the children. He had been openly flirting with the wife of a lieutenant-colonel, and as Udai's temper was well known, the officer tried to make a joke of it. One of Udai's guards saw it was going too far and suggested they should move on. Udai reacted furiously and squeezed the woman's breasts as if to prove he could have his way with any woman he desired. Her husband stepped forward, only for Udai to kick him in the testicles. As the man dropped to the floor, howling in agony, Udai pulled out his gun and shot him through the top of the head. He died instantly. Once again, the family of the victim were paid off and the matter was never brought before any court.

I attended the funeral of Amna, Nadia and little Salih. Arab culture allows for emotional displays of grief on such occasions, and along with other members of my family I wept openly and without restraint. Westerners, I know, think such behaviour lacks dignity, but we do not understand the European way either. To us, their stiff, motionless demeanour at funerals gives an impression of indifference.

When it was over, I drank heavily in the company of Wahab and Akram. I rashly discussed my suspicions about the identity of the person responsible for the murders with them, but so hostile was their reaction, I resolved never to raise the subject with them again. My long held misgivings regarding where Akram's loyalty lay were confirmed the following morning when instead of being driven to the palace, I was taken to the al-Hahkimiya prison of the Mukhabarat on 52nd Street in the Karada district of Baghdad and placed in a cell.

I was held for just two days and to my surprise and relief I was not badly treated. Nobody except the warder, who had the task of delivering my meals, came to see me, and even he was not permitted to speak. Whatever curiosity was aroused in him by my facial appearance had to remain unsatisfied. I tried to engage him in conversation whenever he entered my cell, but he dared not even look at me. He left the meagre fare of each meal on a stool beside the cell door and scuttled off.

My waking hours were entirely taken up by images of Amna, Nadia and Salih. I found it hard to accept that I would never see them again. The physical pain of their loss was almost beyond my endurance. I imagined the torture that Amna at least had endured, and could only hope that the children had been killed swiftly and cleanly, and the disfigurement had taken place subsequent to their deaths. I had not been requested to identify the bodies; perhaps they were not recognisable.

On the evening of the second day of my imprisonment I was transported from the prison by car, with an escort of four guards, to the palace. I was still dressed in the clothes I had been wearing at the time of my arrest; I had not been provided with soap or water and was grubby and unshaven.

Within fifteen minutes of arriving at the palace, I was seated before Saddam in his private study. With the exception of two guards standing inside the door, we were alone.

'You have been foolish, Mikhaelef,' he said sternly.

I cared little for him and his words. I was grateful I had not been tortured, but there was no harm he could inflict on me that was worse than that I had already suffered. All that mattered to me in life had been stolen from me. Without Amna and the children, I saw no point in my existence.

'The loss of a man's wife and children,' Saddam went on, after a moment's pause, 'in such a barbaric way, is bound to have a profound affect on his state of mind.'

But now I saw through the practised sympathetic expression and the fine sentiments he could conjure up with such facility. 'I also understand that you would not be human if you did not look into the eyes of every man and see their killer.'

He stood and drew close to me, crouching so that our faces were level. 'Look into my eyes, Mikhaelef, and tell me if you see the killer of your loved ones. Is this the man who took your children away and murdered them?'

I looked directly into his eyes and felt no fear. But still I lied.

'No,' I said dully.

'Then let me help you to find the murderer. Everything I have is at your disposal and we will leave no stone unturned, no questions unanswered until we have found this animal.'

I was no longer deceived by his posturing and felt no emotion whatsoever. I would find out for myself if Saddam or any member of this evil al-Takriti family were responsible for the murders of my wife, my daughter and my son. Then I would kill them.

Chapter Ten

1988

Jumaada al-Awwal 1408 – Jumaada al-Awwal 1409

Udai clearly bore me much ill-will. He suspected I was potentially dangerous to the regime, and it was common knowledge that he wanted me dead. When, some weeks after the murder of Amna and the children, he sent a message to say that a man had been arrested for the abduction and murder of my family, I was not impressed. The man confessed, of course, but was able to offer neither motive nor meaning for the foul deed. His name was Ala'a Wahib, a petty-thief and occasional black-marketeer from Shu'la, a working-class, predominantly Shi'a district on the north-west perimeter of Baghdad. Confession or not, I was sure he had had no hand in the crime.

I made a request to interrogate him myself and was personally authorised to do so by Saddam. I was in the Dark Room and preparing to leave for the prison in al-Karada when the telephone on my desk rang. My caller turned out to be the prison governor.

'I am pleased I have caught you before you left,' he said pleasantly. 'I can save you a wasted journey.'

'What do you mean?' I asked, suspicious that obstacles were already being placed before me.

'The man you wish to talk to, Ala'a Wahib?'

'Yes.'

'I am afraid he is dead.'

It took me several seconds to absorb this news.

'How is he dead?' I asked when I had regrouped my wits.

'He killed himself. His warder checked on him an hour ago and found him lying in a pool of blood. He slashed his wrists.'

I possessed more than the single brain cell required to understand that Ala'a had not committed suicide.

'How was he able to slash his wrists?' I asked, making no effort to keep the cynicism from my voice.

'He used a small piece of glass. We do know how it could have happened, but a full inquiry will take place. Somebody will be punished.'

'Yes, I am sure they will,' I sneered.

'Would you like to see the body?' the governor asked, seemingly impervious to my irony.

'No,' I answered, 'but thank you for calling.'

I hung up and slammed my fist onto the desk with frustration. It was quite obvious what was happening. The unfortunate Ala'a had been plucked from the streets and would now be posthumously convicted of the murder of Amna and the children. The matter would be closed. I sat alone, pondering my next course of action, and decided there was only one thing to do: I would make contact with Latif.

Early in 1988, I was aghast to hear that Barzan Ibrahim was being primed to become Iraqi's Permanent Representative to the UN Commission on Human Rights in Geneva. I could not begin to imagine what those fine people would make of him. During his time in Switzerland, he is believed to have been used by Saddam for a number of illicit purposes, not least of which was the removal of exiled dissidents. He has been directly linked with planning the assassination of Ayatollah Mehdi al-Hakim, brother of Hojjat Mohammed al-Hakim, founder of the Supreme Council of the Islamic Revolution in Iraq(SCIRI). Mehdi was shot dead with three bullets to the head in the Sudan at the beginning of the year.

The hypocrisy of his representing Iraq at any formal commission on human rights was laughable, but it would appeal to Saddam's perverse sense of humour. He frequently sent Tariq Aziz, a Christian, to represent him at international Islamic summit conferences.

The time was also ripe for Barzan's brothers to come in from the cold. Sabawi was given Barzan's old position as head of the Mukhabarat, replacing Barzan's successor and Mullah al-Barzinji's tormentor, Fadel Barak. Sabawi was instructed to go about his duties with the same uninhibited zeal his brother had shown a few years earlier. Watban, the youngest of the three brothers, was given a similar mandate as the newly appointed head of the Amn al-Khas, responsible for the personal security of Saddam and his family. Thus, two hard-liners from within the al-Takriti family were in position to underpin whatever draconian measures Saddam introduced. The brothers were also given a demonstration of their return to favour when Udai married Barzan's daughter, Saja. The poor girl was never happy with the arrangement from the start, and within three months was to flee to her father's home in Geneva.

Between April and August the war continued to move in Iraq's favour, due in no small part to the diplomatic initiative of the Americans, but also as a direct conse-quence of Saddam's more widespread use of chemical weapons. Another Iranian attack on al-Basrah had been comfortably thwarted in January and it proved to be Khomeini's last effective roll of the dice. Saddam unleashed a two month missile campaign on Tehran of such ferocity that many Iranians fled the city. A large number of the deadly projectiles were purposely detonated over the city to demonstrate Iraq's capacity and willingness to use chemical weapons on the Iranian capital. Khomeini came under increasing pressure from his ministers to sue for peace and avoid a national catastrophe.

From February, Saddam formally decided to elevate the destruction of the Kurdish people to unprecedented levels. The campaign was officially called *al-Anfal* (literally, 'the executions') and the people of Iraq became familiar with Saddam's attempts 'to eliminate all subversive elements in our glorious north'. The 'heroic campaign' was widely publicised in the Iraqi media.

In March, the Iranians occupied the area around the Iraqi Kurdistan town of Halabja and Saddam saw an opportunity to kill two birds with the one stone. At the same time as his air force attacked the Iranians on the ground, they dropped bombs of cyanide, mustard gas and nerve gas on Halabja. When the Iranians entered the town, they were confronted by scenes of devastation: 5,000 people in the area had been wiped out with gas. Villagers lay dead in the street, stiffened in the positions of agony in which they had died. Women were sprawled on their doorsteps clutching their babies. Groups of small children were found still clinging to each other. Surrounding the town, more bodies were found. In an hysterical dash for safety, thousands of people had tried to evade the spreading poison, some getting further than others. For those in the vicinity of the explosions, the result was the same – an agonising death.

The Iranians called in the international media and pictures of unbelievable horror were flashed around the world, though no photograph could do justice to the reality. Hundreds of thousands of Iraqis had died since the beginning of Saddam's presidency, but never before had the utter ruthlessness of Saddam been so accurately reflected. Halabja provided an open window to the evil and brutality of the al-Takriti regime.

Saddam blamed the Iranians, but few believed him. What Saddam did not say was that Iraq had recently succeeded in stabilising and adapting for delivery by missile the deadly binary nerve gas VX. He now had the ability to take chemical warfare great distances beyond the Iraqi borders. While the West heaped opprobrium on Iraq's president, manufacturers were not shy in coming forward to peddle their deadly wares. I was told that the provenance of most of the equipment for the development of chemical weapons was West Germany and that many tons of chemicals were being imported from India. China, too, was rumoured to be negotiating with Saddam over the feasibility of nuclear weapons. The multinational origins of those visiting the palace and government ministries testified to this.

Less than three weeks after the attack on Halabja, Iraqi forces under the direction of Ali Hassan bombed the villages of Guptapa and Askar. The nature of the raids was nearly always the same. First, a surveillance plane flew over the target area and released flares to confirm the wind direction. Within minutes, about six bombers arrived and dropped their deadly cargo. Throughout the whole year, a murderous campaign was waged on the Kurdish rural communities of the north.

Again using chemicals, the Iraqi army retook the al-Fao peninsula in just two days during mid-April, and the territory around al-Basrah was recovered in the course of which more than 70,000 casualties were inflicted on the Iranians. Shalamcheh, or what remained of it, on the border near al-Basrah, was retaken and the undeveloped oilfields to the west of the Shatt al-Arab waterway were once again in Iraqi hands. Baghdad, which had for the latter part of the war lived in fear of being besieged by the Iranians, was now secure following two decisive battles that had permitted the Iraqi army to advance a hundred kilometres into enemy territory.

The Iranians were in retreat over most areas of the front, terrified that Saddam's air force would drop chemicals on them wherever they were. To add to Khomeini's woes, the Iranian exiles guerrilla group, Mujaheddin-e-Khalq, were making substantial progress in the territory around Kermanshah, supported by Saddam. Saddam realised his hand was as strong as it was ever going to be. Shrewdly, he proposed peace talks, forestalling an American reaction to the dramatic change in the course of the war. In July, Khomeini conceded that he had to drink from 'the poison cup' of defeat. A cease-fire was called and the war was officially over on 20 August.

Having survived the worst crisis of his presidency and still at the top of the tree, Saddam was in high spirits. During the protracted peace negotiations he frequently instructed me to take his place at the conference table. He even suggested on one occasion I should sign the peace settlement, on the grounds that he need not be bound by a treaty to which had not personally put his name. He was finally persuaded he could only deny ever having signed the treaty by admitting my existence and attended the final session himself.

A total of 420,000 lives had been lost during the course of the eight-year war. A further 210,000 prisoners had been taken and the cost to both sides was conservatively estimated to be in excess of $600 billion. The massive oil terminals at al-Basrah and Abadan had been destroyed and oil production of both countries had at times fallen to less than 15% of their pre-war levels. Despite this, the self-esteem of the Iraqi nation had never been greater. In the eyes of the world's Arab population, Saddam was a hero. If international opinion regarded the outcome only as an honourable draw, in Iraq it was celebrated as a total victory. Saddam had a 'Victory Arch' erected at the south end of Zowrah Park by the city's Qadisiyah motorway. Two towering crossed swords were held by huge, bronze hands modelled on the President's own. The metal used came from the captured spoils of war and thousands of bullet-riddled Iranian helmets decorated the base. Beneath the road, more helmets had been buried to allow Saddam and the people of Iraq to symbolically pass over the heads of the vanquished.

Maher Abd al-Rashid, Qusai's father-in-law, had been largely responsible for the retaking of the al-Fao peninsula. He returned to Baghdad, elevated to almost as great a hero as Saddam, and was at once sent north to join 'Chemical Ali' in the eradication of the Kurdish 'problem'.

In the wake of the war, Saddam directed his ferocity at the Kurds without restraint. Ali Hassan, having already decimated so much of the Kurdish population, set about finishing the job. Hundreds of villages were attacked with the 'winds of death'. In a six month period, as many as 200,000 Kurds perished. In specially constructed villages and concentration camps, built a year earlier in the al-Jazirah desert, more than 250,000 Kurds were interned. During the course of al-Anfal, more than 75% of the 5,000 rural Kurdish villages of Iraq were destroyed.

Outrage was international. The US called for sanctions and the European Community threatened a complete ban on the sale of all weapons to Iraq. Saddam tried to present the massacre as the 'legitimate relocation' of a population ravaged by its close proximity to a war zone. His exculpatory protests were rejected outright. In the end, what remained of the northern Iraqi Kurds were saved by trade inducements: Britain promised to double its export credits to Iraq if the killing ceased. Others fell into line and the wholesale slaughter came to an end. For a while.

My efforts to contact Latif had not borne fruit. To the best of my knowledge, he did not know his sister and her children had been murdered, but a few days after her disappearance, the telephone calls had stopped. I could not be seen to be actively looking for him and my discreet enquiries in his neighbourhood through a third party brought no results. It was not until one Friday (Jumhah) in mid-September that he finally telephoned again. It was precisely eleven o'clock, the hour he had always to call Amna. I did not know if my telephone was tapped, but I had to assume so. I said nothing. The other end of the line was also silent.

After ten seconds, the caller hung up and I felt certain it must be Latif. What I could not be sure about was whether or not he would follow the old procedure and keep the rendezvous, which, according to Amna, was under the clock tower at the Central Railway Station on Qahira Street, near Dimeshq (Damascus) Square.

Within five minutes I was on my way into the city centre. To begin with I walked; after about half a kilometre I caught a bus. As Friday was a holy day there were fewer people on the streets than would normally be the case. A little before midday I arrived at the clock tower. I waited for more than twenty minutes and was beginning to think Latif would not show when I saw him approaching. As I moved to greet him, he surprised me by walking straight past, without so much as a glance in my direction. I interpreted this as meaning I should follow him and did so. He walked at an even pace towards the square and crossed the Arbatahsh Tamuz Street (14 July Street). He then walked along Dimeshq Street, towards the Art School, and turned left into Zowrah Park. Once inside the park, he made for a small wall near the lake, where he sat down. I sat beside him.

'I am glad to see you again, Latif,' I said, and indeed it gave me much pleasure to be in the company of Amna's brother; momentarily, it brought her closer to me. Latif merely nodded, and taking his cue, I sat there in silence, content to let him take the initiative from here. A few moments later another man, in a shabby grey suit, passed and nodded discreetly at Latif.

'I apologise for ignoring you, Mikhaelef,' Latif said, as the man headed away across the square. 'But as you followed me, so that man was following you. I had to be sure you were alone.'

'I am pleased you have taken such precautions. They would not have occurred to me.'

Latif's face was much thinner than when I saw him last, and there were lines and creases that were new. It occurred to me I probably looked much the same to him.

'How have you been?' he asked.

What I had to tell him had weighed heavily on my mind, but it was not possible to talk of anything else until he knew about Amna and the children. 'I am well, but I have some bad news.'

Latif raised his hand. 'I know Amna and the little ones are dead. That is why I called you.'

'How do you know?' I asked, intrigued.

'Although I have been in hiding, I have never left Baghdad. Such things do not stay unknown for long.'

'How did you know you could trust me?' I said. 'I might have become loyal to Saddam.'

'You knew the code, which Amna must have entrusted to you. In any case, I thought it unlikely you would be sympathetic towards Saddam considering what has happened.'

'You think Saddam was responsible?' I asked, a little surprised at his casual assumption.

'Please, Mikhaelef, do not pretend to be stupid.'

'It may have been Udai,' I countered, 'acting on his own initiative. It would not be the first time he has taken it upon himself to murder someone without his father's authority.'

'Well, yes, as it happens, you are partially right. Udai was involved.'

I wondered how he could be so sure. 'How do you know this?'

'Saddam is not the only one with reliable intelligence sources in Iraq. I wanted to see you because you should know what happened to your wife and children. I also want to put a proposition to you.'

I had feared as much and yet, perversely, I welcomed it too.

'I am listening.'

Latif stared at me and I could see my own pain reflected in his eyes.

'One of the men who kidnapped Amna and the children is a former lieutenant-colonel who is now a member of

Udai's personal security guard. His name is Kalid Fakher al-Takriti. He is a distant cousin of the President.'

'Yes, I know him. He is a brute of a man. But how do you know where his orders came from?'

'It is unlikely he would wipe his backside without clearing it with Udai first,' Latif said, with a straight face.

'I agree. What about Saddam. How do you know Udai was not acting independently?'

'Saddam himself ordered that Amna should be murdered.'

'How do you know that?' I persisted.

'It is better that you do not know everything, Mikhaelef. What you do not know you cannot tell others if you are ever arrested and tortured. Trust me in this. To prove it to you, I also know that Saddam instructed you to tell Amna to disassociate herself from us. Did you do so?'

'Yes.' I thought about the implications. 'If this did not come to you from Amna, you must have intelligence sources inside the palace.'

'Does that surprise you?'

It did, a little. Latif was to some degree confirming what I had often privately speculated: Saddam had enemies, both inside and outside the palace.

'What is the proposal you wish to put to me?' I asked, in some trepidation.

'I want you to join us.'

'Join you?' I said, half amused, half terrified. 'How can I join you? You are a secret organisation. I am the duplicate of the President. I would stand out like a torch in the desert night.'

'There are things you can do, but I can only tell you more if you are with us.'

I swallowed hard. 'Then I am with you.' I reminded myself, as I sat there inwardly quaking, that I had wanted to contact Latif because he would be able to help me exact my revenge. Here was the opportunity.

'The first thing you can do is meet me tonight. Now that Amna has gone, there are only three other members you need concern yourself with. Two of them you already know.'

'Rafik and Abdullah?'

'Yes, my brothers. The other is a friend. His name is Salem Mohammed. You will meet him tonight. Our movement obviously operates in great secrecy. Apart from our more prominent political officials, each of us only knows the names of the members he works with directly. In this way, we can identify only a handful of co-conspirators if we are ever caught and interrogated. You will also be required to go through a small ceremony. You will have to draw blood from your hand and smear it across the red flag of the party.'

'I am not a Communist.' It was a token protest. This matter was above politics.

'We might work on that,' Latif said, his teeth flashing. 'But perhaps in the meantime we could allow you to use the green, white and black of an Iraqi national flag and you can vow to cleanse it of the fascist dictatorship that has besmirched it. It hardly matters in these circumstances.'

I agreed to this and made arrangements to meet up with Latif and the others later that night.

'What is the purpose of tonight's meeting?' I asked him.

'We are going to see a man you will be keen to meet.'

'Who?'

'Kalid Fakher al-Takriti.'

At nine o'clock that night I was with Latif, Rafik, Abdullah and Salem outside the home of Kalid Fakher in the Baghdad suburb of al-Khudrah, two kilometres to the west of al-Mansur. Kalid lived alone and I was amazed at the simplicity of the abduction. Abdullah and Salem walked up to his door and knocked while Latif and Rafik stood back and covered them. I stayed in the car. Within two minutes, Kalid was locked in the boot of the car and we left the city, passing through the districts of al-Hamrah, al-Jihad and al-Ta'min, heading south towards al-Hillah. Just beyond Latifia, we took the Karbala fork and crossed the Furat river. Passing the familiar roads to Karbala and al-Najaf, we turned onto the edge of the Shamiya Desert.

We stopped on a deserted stretch of the desert road and Kalid was taken from the boot and dragged onto the sand. He was bound by hand and foot and sat with his back to the car. Abdullah, the youngest of the brothers, was the most passionate during the interrogation that followed. Kalid was beaten without mercy and without remorse. This, after all, was the man who had brutally raped and murdered my wife and mutilated my little children. To an Arab, the blood of family is sacred.

Finally, the man confessed that the order for the murder and the specific treatment given to Amna and the children before they died had come directly from Udai. As Kalid begged for his life, Abdullah took a knife from his belt and sliced his face from mouth to ear. He then passed the knife to Salem, who opened up Kalid's stomach. Rafik took it next, ripped the scalp from the man's head and passed the knife to Latif, who slit Kalid's throat. Finally, the knife was passed to me. As the killer's dying breath sputtered from his gaping mouth, I plunged it deep into his heart. Though this act was utterly foreign to my peace-loving nature, I felt no compunction. Leaving the knife embedded in the corpse, I knelt as if in prayer and called the heavens.

'My dearest Amna,' I intoned. 'My beautiful Nadia. My precious son, Salih Mikhaelef. I am deeply sorry. I swore I would always protect you, but I was not there when you needed me most. Please forgive me.'

Latif embraced me. 'Let us leave this place now, Mikhaelef. We have unfinished business in Baghdad.'

Before we left, Kalid was buried in a shallow grave in the sand. It was after midnight when we returned to the car and took the road back to Baghdad.

The following day, I was back in the presidential palace with Hashim. I had no regrets about the murder of Kalid the previous evening, but the memory of it lay heavy on my mind. I went about my daily routine as best I could, but found it difficult to concentrate. I had never before so much as struck another person. For several weeks afterwards my nightmares about Amna and the children were interspersed with visions of Kalid's terrified face.

The euphoria of 'victory' in the war against Iran had quickly dissipated inside the palace, to be replaced by a tense atmosphere arising from Saddam's infidelities. His extra-marital romances were known to only a handful of people and he went to great lengths to keep them secret. The most prominent at this time was Samira Shahbandar, the ex-wife of the chairman of Iraqi Airways. Saddam's wife, Sajida, would generally turn a blind eye to his indiscretions, but when this affair was leaked and became public knowledge, she exploded in fury.

I discussed the matter with Hashim and was astounded by what he told me.

'Samira is Saddam's second wife,' he volunteered.

'Since when?' I asked, disbelieving.

'He married her discreetly several years ago.'

'Several years ago! How is it I have never heard of this?'

Hashim looked at me as a schoolteacher might look at a child who has asked an impertinent question. 'Why should you have known? It is not your business to know.'

'Perhaps. But you know.'

'I am an officer of the Mukhabarat, attached to the presidential palace. For matters of national security it is my business to know.'

'I am amazed,' I said, shaking my head. 'How does he know her?'

'She once taught in the Khark school where Sajida was the head principle,' Hashim explained. 'I believe they met on a school trip to Takrit which Saddam attended. She has a son by Saddam, called Ali. That is why he married her. The boy must be about seven now.'

I grinned mischievously at Hashim. 'Abu Ali? Saddam's enemies will be delighted.'

'Be careful, Mikhaelef,' Hashim cautioned. 'Some jokes are best left unsaid.'

"Abu Ali" literally meant "the father of Ali", but it is much used in Arabic to indicate a rogue or ne'er-do-well. Islamic law does not prevent a man taking a second wife, or more. However, it is against one of the basic principles of Ba'athism. By taking a second wife, Saddam was thumbing a nose at his own 'religion'.

The fact that this 'affair' had now been widely publicised enraged Udai, who was particularly close to his mother and he took the humiliation personally. He also feared that Saddam's dalliance with Samira could undermine his own position, especially now that the relationship was out in the open. Although angry with his father, he exacted his revenge on the man who organised Saddam's love trysts, Kamil Hannah Jejjo. This was the man also employed as Saddam's personal food-taster, the son of Saddam's cook, Hannah Jejjo.

It happened at the home of Taha Mohedin Marouf, Iraq's sixty-four-year-old Vice-President from the northern Iraqi city of Salimaniya, a man with little or no authority. As a Kurd, his position was purely cosmetic, but he was permitted to play the diplomat at public functions, and on this occasion was hosting an official party in honour of Suzanne Mubarak, wife of the Egyptian president.

His house was situated on Um al-Khanahzir, an island in the middle of the Dijlah, near to the al-Jahdriya Bridge. A drunken Kamil, celebrating the end of the war, was shooting his pistol into the air, a popular pastime recently prohibited by Saddam due to the number of injuries occurring when the spent ammunition returned to earth. Hearing the shooting from across the river in the presidential palace, Saddam issued an order that it be stopped.

Udai Saddam was on his way to the island and intercepted his father's instructions over his car radio. When he arrived, he pushed past Taha Mohedin who tried to intervene, and ordered Kamil to behave. There was no love lost between the pair and when Kamil, made rash by alcohol, responded with abuse, Udai lashed out at him with a *megawar*, a small, tarred stick covered in nails or stones, which he often carried. The blow landed on the man's temple and he fell unconscious. He was rushed to hospital and died there the following morning.

Many versions of what occurred that night circulated among the Baghdad elite, but Hashim, who was there, confirmed that Udai Saddam was not drunk and had not been firing the gun as some accounts suggested.

'He was his usual arrogant self,' Hashim testified, 'and his treatment of Kamil was brutal. But Kamil was drunk, not Udai.'

Even so, Saddam was not at all pleased. Not at the act of murder, but at the loss of a valuable employee. When confronted with the news, he administered a beating to Udai. Sajida tried to intervene on her son's behalf, but she was also beaten by Saddam. The President threw his son into prison where he was left to sulk in solitary confinement for six weeks.

A commission was set up to look into the killing, but its conclusions were foregone from the start. It was headed by Judge Abdullah Wahab Hussein al-Duri, a cousin of Saddam's constitutional successor, Izzat Ibrahim. Jejjo's family were well compensated by Saddam, but his death was recorded as a tragic accident.

When he was released from prison at the end of November, Udai was sent to stay with his half-uncle, Barzan Ibrahim, in Switzerland. I was relieved to see the back of him, but it was a short-lived reprieve. Within days of his arrival, Udai had pulled a gun on a Swiss police officer in a restaurant and was promptly deported back to Iraq. On his return, measures were taken to give him something else to keep him occupied and in due course he was married off to Hawazin, daughter of Izzat Ibrahim al-Duri. Little else changed.

Even Saddam was beginning to acknowledge that Udai was a liability, and it was noticeable that Qusai, who shared his father's calculating ways, was playing a more prominent part in affairs of state. While Saddam was no humanitarian and could be every bit as brutal as Udai, everything he did had a purpose, and therein lay the difference between father and older son. Saddam was not a psychopath, and did nothing without first satisfying himself of the consequences of his actions. The same could not be said for Udai.

Surprisingly, the most open critic of Saddam at this time was Adnan Khairallah Al-Talfah, his wife's brother, who was also his cousin and lifelong friend. The two argued fiercely for several days after Kamil's murder and Saddam was left fuming over Adnan's stance, which was essentially supportive of his sister, Sajida. Adnan was put out that Saddam, by his selfish behaviour, had dishonoured his sister and his family. Saddam, for his part, was deeply wounded by Adnan's verbal assaults, but was soon to learn of matters that would have the most dire consequences for Adnan.

Chapter Eleven

1989
Jumaada al-Awwal 1409 – Jumaada al-Thaany 1410

For all but the first of my ten years at the Karradat Mariam, Iraq had been at war. Now that peace had finally been restored and the threat of invasion was behind us, a relative calm descended upon Baghdad. With fewer official duties to perform, I spent long hours with Hashim in the Dark Room and was more frequently invited to join Saddam in his private study.

There I would sit and dutifully listen to his ramblings, never disputing anything he said and responding to his passionate deliveries in a manner appropriate to my station. I would not claim I enjoyed any kind of a special relationship with Saddam, though he still trusted me and would often share with me his views on the more vital issues of the day. Had I been more of a lion and less like a lamb, I might have been tempted to make an attempt on his life during one of these sessions. Albeit that I had now tasted blood, I had not been transformed into a warrior overnight.

Saddam would discuss many subjects in my presence,

but he became increasingly obsessed with the way he was portrayed in the Western media. There is a general feeling abroad that Saddam is indifferent to the opinions of foreign politicians and journalists. This is not the case. He is a prolific reader of the international press, and some members of his staff are employed solely to scour the world's newspapers and magazines for any mention of his name. He is surprisingly sensitive to any form of criticism, especially from those over whom he has no control.

Much of what is written about him is pure fiction, fabricated by those with their own political agendas to pursue. But even though he is aware of the motive, Saddam flares up irrationally whenever he reads derogatory comments in the foreign media. It was something he never came to terms with in all the years I was with him.

Early in the year, Saddam was passed an article taken from an American magazine which purported to analyse his ambitions in the Middle East. It was, in fact, little more than a vitriolic condemnation of every aspect of his presidency. It examined Iraq's record on human rights and presented Saddam as a psychopathic megalomaniac. I enjoyed seeing him so incensed by what was, after all, mere rhetoric that would receive scant attention elsewhere.

'Why do they write such garbage?' he stormed, pacing his study with the magazine cutting in his hand. 'What is the purpose of it? Explain it to me!'

He thrust the cutting at me and I saw immediately what had really offended him. The article was accompanied by a cartoon in which an excessively obese Saddam, grinning inanely with a gun in his hand, was addressing his terrified ministers gathered around a conference table. Each man had an arm raised as if voting on a proposal.

'Good!' Saddam said in the caption below. 'We are all agreed then. I am still the President!'

Latif was understandably delighted that Saddam was prepared to speak to me so openly. Whenever we met, he would question me at length on Saddam's spoutings and suggested ways I might probe further, without attracting suspicion. He was particularly interested in anything said by or about Udai.

Udai, however, resented my presence at all times and generally refused to discuss even the most mundane affairs of state when I was about. If ever I was present when he entered Saddam's study, he would leave immediately without speaking. Much to his father's amusement.

'Do not mind him, Mikhaelef,' he once said, indulgently. 'He is young and hot-headed.'

On the rare occasions I found myself alone with Udai, there was always an air of tension between us and I had no doubt he would kill me but for his father's patronage. He spoke to me only when absolutely necessary, but he would happily regale his circle of hangers-on with the sordid details of his extramarital affairs when I was within earshot. Despite his outward displeasure over his father's philandering behaviour, it was clear that marriage had done little to curb Udai's own wandering eye. One morning it was passed on to me in a whisper that Udai frequently held love trysts at the apartment of a friend in the Cairo district of Baghdad, close to where I had first met Saddam ten years earlier.

I related this morsel of information to Latif and we discussed how best to use it. We were agreed that this may be his Achilles Heel, an opportunity to remove Udai for good.

'Who escorts him?' Latif asked, when we met one evening to discuss the matter.

'He has two armed guards with him at all times,' I reminded him. 'Fortunately, he is too arrogant to think he needs more.'

'And he is always armed himself?'

'He would feel underdressed without at least one gun to hand. Although Saddam invariably confiscates any weapon he finds on him, I am sure he replaces it within ten minutes.'

Latif stroked his chin as he weighed the risks. 'It is not a problem. We will attack when he is between the sheets,' he pronounced at length.

This "we" included me. It was taken for granted I would be included in the assassination party – terrifying though the prospect was!

Over the next couple of weeks, through my informant who was one of those gossips who just cannot help spreading stories, I kept Latif informed whenever Udai was using the Cairo apartment. After a period of surveillance, Latif was able to verify that the President's son was indeed only ever accompanied by two guards. The pair would stand outside the apartment and chat between themselves as Udai went about his 'business'. He rarely stayed more than an hour.

'And that includes thirty minutes talking about himself and twenty minutes in the shower afterwards,' Latif dryly concluded.

We decided to make our move on Udai's next visit to the apartment. Only a few days later, in my presence, he joked with his guards of the fun he would be having with a new 'conquest' later that evening.

It was necessary to act quickly. I was able to slip away from the palace and inform Latif. We met up at seven o'clock. Latif was accompanied by his brothers and Salem, and the five of us drove to the Cairo apartment block in a car Latif had access to for such a purpose, arriving just after eight. In order to obviate any risk of my being recognised, even in wearing my usual facial props, it was decided, much to my relief, that I should stay in the car and sound the horn if anything untoward developed outside. The other four casually made their way towards the apartment block.

Latif and Rafik entered the block first, their task being to deal with the two guards outside the apartment. Abdullah and Salem, the two would-be assassins, followed behind. So as not to attract undue attention with gunfire, Udai was to be stabbed to death. All of them carried guns though, in case anything went wrong.

Once alone, I could not settle and looked anxiously about for any sign of life, but the area was completely deserted. The minutes passed slowly. After what seemed like an hour I checked my watch and was startled to find that barely five minutes had elapsed since my accomplices set off on their mission.

Suddenly, I was startled by the unmistakable sound of two gunshots, followed a few seconds later by several more. Having never learnt to drive and thinking all four of my friends had been shot, I was tempted to abandon the car and run for my life. Before I could move, the main door to the apartment block crashed open and Latif and Rafik burst onto the street. I quickly reached across and opened both the near-side doors. Latif scrambled behind the wheel and immediately started the engine, as Rafik threw himself onto the back seat. The car screeched away from the kerbside, like the getaway car in a bank robbery.

'What has happened?' I yelled, close to panic. 'Where are Abdullah and Salem?'

'They are dead!' Latif snarled back. Tears were streaming down his cheeks.

I was stunned.

Latif, sobbing and cursing, drove erratically, once nearly overturning the car. Startled pedestrians stepped back sharply as we roared past along Abi Tahleb Street. I looked over my shoulder to see Rafik kneeling on the back seat, gun in hand, peering anxiously through the rear window.

'We are not being followed, Latif!' he shouted. 'Slow down. You are attracting too much attention.'

Latif duly eased his foot from the accelerator and at a more moderate speed swung off the main thoroughfare, and began to thread through a labyrinth of back streets towards the city. Weeping intermittently, he began to relate what had happened.

As expected, Udai's two bodyguards were patrolling the corridor leading to the apartment. Latif and Rafik pretended to be drunk in the hope that the guards would take them to be residents of the building. And indeed, it did not appear that their suspicions were aroused, so that as Latif and Rafik passed the guards, who were watching their antics in some amusement, Latif made to shake the hand of one of them and used his free hand to knife the man in the belly. Rafik, more or less simultaneously, disposed of the other guard in the same manner.

Abdullah and Salem, who had concealed themselves in the stairwell, then came up and smashed down the door. That was when our plan started to unravel. Another guard was seated just inside the apartment with a gun in his lap. Only Allah knows where he came from, but he had of course been alerted by the forced entry. He shot Abdullah through the head the moment he set foot inside. Salem was hit too. He fired back and the guard cried out, but carried on shooting nonetheless, and Salem was hit again. A third shot finished him off and he fell in the doorway. Latif fired blindly into the apartment, covering Rafik while he dragged their fallen comrade into the corridor. But he was beyond saving. As Latif emptied his magazine, he and Rafik, heard Udai shouting from somewhere inside, but they decided that it would be suicidal to press ahead. Flight became the only option.

At that moment, we were approaching the outskirts of the old city and pulled over to the side of the road at Khulafah Square.

'Get out here, Mikhaelef,' he said with urgency. 'You must not be seen with us.'

I opened the door and began to climb out, turning towards Latif as I did so.

'I knew nothing about the third guard,' I said, feeling desperately guilty about the inadequacy of the intelligence I had provided.

'Another time,' he answered, more composed now. 'You must look out for yourself now. I will be in touch.'

The car pulled away and disappeared into the evening traffic.

I was still some distance from my house but decided to walk along the deserted streets for a while to clear my head. I stepped out briskly towards the Abbahsid Palace and turned into Rashid Street, which runs parallel to the east side of the river. As I walked, I was tormented by the fear that Udai might already have telephoned the police headquarters or, worse, ordered the Mukhabarat to set a trap for me. Guilt about the presence of the third guard continued to plague me, though I reminded myself that Latif had had the building watched during the preceding week or so, and Udai had only ever been accompanied by two guards. The mystery of how the third guard got in there was never explained.

Close to the Ahrah Bridge, I picked up a taxi and went home. I had no sooner closed the front door behind me when the telephone rang . It was Udai.

'Ah, Mikhaelef,' he said, as if nothing extraordinary had happened to him that evening. 'I am glad to catch you in.'

'Where else would I be at this time of the evening, Udai?' I asked, praying that this was the first time he had called.

'I really don't know,' he replied, his manner excessively friendly. 'Have you been out?'

'No,' I answered as confidently as I could.

'You were not home twenty minutes ago, Mikhaelef. I called you.'

Fortunately, Udai could not see the anxiety on my face as I strove to keep calm. My heart was fluttering.

'I apologise, Udai, but I drink heavily of a night these days. I must have been asleep and did not hear the telephone. What do you want?'

'Nothing,' he answered, sounding far from convinced by my glib explanation. 'Nothing that cannot wait until to-morrow. I will see you then.'

The following day, I was met in the Dark Room by a noticeably subdued Hashim. He responded to my attempts at conversation in nervous monosyllables and clearly knew something of what had occurred the previous evening. Within minutes of my arrival, Saddam entered in the company of Udai. The latter was smiling, in a smugly secretive fashion that inspired no confidence at all in me.

'Please be seated, Mikhaelef,' Saddam said equably enough. 'We have important matters to discuss.'

He waved a hand at Hashim who immediately left the room without speaking.

'Last night,' Saddam continued as soon as Hashim had closed the door, 'an attempt was made on Udai's life. Two of the would-be assassins were shot dead. Two escaped. One of the dead men was your brother-in-law, Abdullah Pasha al-Rabaka. We are assuming the two men who got away were his brothers, Latif and Rafik.'

As he spoke, Saddam watched me closely, perhaps seeking some giveaway sign in my expression.

'I see,' I said, my mind too frozen with fear to produce a more articulate response.

'You do not seem surprised,' he said.

'I am sorry, Saddam,' I replied, forcing myself to respond more appropriately. 'This is an enormous shock to me. Are you sure the dead man is Abdullah?'

Udai stepped forward, his face reddening. 'Of course we are sure, you imbecile! And we are just as sure that his brothers will soon be dead also. Where are they?'

I looked at him, as if astonished he should expect me to answer the question.

'Why would I know where they are?' I asked, summoning up a burst of indignation. 'If they are not at home, I have no idea where they could be.'

'I have made enquiries,' Udai hissed at me, 'and I know that you were aware of my regular visits to that apartment. You think I am stupid enough to believe it is a coincidence your brother-in-law tried to assassinate me there?'

I did not answer. He turned away from me in frustration. 'Have him arrested, Father. There is a quicker way to deal with this nonsense.'

Saddam had been observing me closely, but it was to Udai he spoke first.

'Leave us, Udai. I wish to talk to Mikhaelef alone.'

Udai was about to protest, but his father looked at him sternly and he realised the futility of doing so. He walked from the room, slamming the door behind him.

'Well, Mikhaelef, what am I to do?'

I looked Saddam in the eye with all the innocence I could muster. 'What do you mean, Saddam?'

He smiled wearily. 'I can think of no other man to whom I have shown such tolerance as I have shown to you. Anybody else I would have thrown in jail long ago. You are, it seems, surrounded by conspirators.'

'I am not responsible for the family of my late wife, Saddam. If what has been said is true, I know nothing of it.'

Saddam nodded and to my amazement said, 'I believe you.'

He stood and walked to the window, looking across the river towards the city.

'Unfortunately, that may no longer be enough. There are few men I can trust in Baghdad and although you have for a long time been one of them, I cannot ignore the fact that you are related to some very dangerous people. I need to be able to justify to myself – and others – why you should continue in my service.'

I remained silent, knowing I was treading dangerous waters.

'I need a demonstration of loyalty, Mikhaelef. You have to do something that will repudiate any suggestion you are not devoted to your President.' He turned towards me. 'What will you do?'

'I can think of nothing,' I replied, as earnestly as I could, 'except to say I have and always will support you.'

'Not enough,' Saddam said, shaking his head and moving away from the window. 'For me, perhaps. For Udai, no.'

He said nothing for a moment, pondering on the task he might set me. Then he smiled. 'Before long, the two fugitives will be found. They will, of course, be sentenced to death.' He looked at me directly before he continued. 'I want you to take part in their execution.'

I went cold with horror at the thought.

'That is impossible!' I blurted out. 'They are my wife's brothers. They . . . I have never fired a gun in my life. I am not capable of killing a man.' Since my participation in the killing of my family's murderer, Kalid Fakher, that was no longer true, but I was not likely to concede the point to Saddam. Instead, I reminded him of my reaction to the execution of Mullah. 'I do not have the stomach for such things. You know how they affect me. I could not do it.'

Saddam sat down in one of the armchairs and invited me to do likewise.

'Since I decided to dedicate my life to my country many years ago,' he said, 'I have had to do many things for which I once thought I might not have the stomach. But I had no choice. During the war, many Iraqis had to do things they thought they could never do, but they too had no choice. Now, Mikhaelef, if you wish to retain my trust, you have no choice.'

He had left me nowhere to hide. I nodded slowly.

Saddam stood up. 'Good, it is settled then.'

He left me alone with my fears and doubts. All I could do was pray to Allah that neither Latif nor Rafik would be found.

Udai was delighted by the decision to appoint me executioner and my greatest fears were realised later in the day when he triumphantly strode into the Dark Room.

'Rafik Pasha has been arrested!'

My heart sank. Rafik's execution would take place whether or not I was able to pull the trigger, but I seriously doubted my ability to save my own skin by taking part in it. I wrestled ceaselessly with my dilemma in the days that followed, but I also had something else to worry about. During his interrogation, Rafik was sure to be violently tortured and there was the very real possibility of his revealing my involvement. It was selfish of me to think of this, but self-preservation is a powerful force.

Indeed the questioning must have been thorough, for Rafik was held in the Mukhabarat prison in the Karada district for the best part of a fortnight. Fortunately for me, he showed rare courage and gave only the names of those unit members already dead or known to the Mukhabarat.

I was expecting to be summoned to the prison for the execution every time the Dark Room door opened, until a furious Saddam burst in one morning.

'Rafik is dead,' he said, barely able to contain his ire.

The most complex emotion of grief and relief swept over me. While I was deeply saddened by Rafik's death, that it should not be by my hand was an enormous release. I did what I could to contain my conflicting feelings.

'There is no need for a performance, Mikhaelef,' said Saddam, more than a little sarcastically. 'I know you are not disappointed.'

'What happened?' I asked.

'Your brother-in-law was being questioned. It seems his interrogator was tormenting him by pulling the trigger of what he thought was an unloaded gun. He was wrong. He shot Rafik Pasha through the back of the head.'

Several weeks went by. Latif remained at large, but I had no means of exchanging messages with him. I began to wonder if he was dead. Until one morning, about two months after the failed attempt on Udai's life, I received a bizarre telephone call.

'Hello, it is Sara,' the female caller said.

'Who?' I asked, not sure I had heard the name correctly.

'Sara!' the voice said again, somewhat petulantly. She spelled it out: 'S-A-R-A.'

'I am sorry,' I answered, thinking it strange that some-body should spell out a name in such a manner. 'You have dialled the wrong number. I know of nobody by that name.'

'Yes, yes,' the voice persisted, 'Sara in al-Mawsil.

'I think you. . .' I began to say, but my caller hung up. Replacing the handset, I put it out of my mind and not until I lay in bed that evening did the possible meaning of it come to me. Sara. S-A-R-A. Salim, Amna, Rafik and Abdullah. Maybe the caller was trying to pass a message from Latif, using the initials of his friend and three siblings. The reference to al-Mawsil could mean Latif was now hiding there. I was far from confident about my reasoning, but it was something to cling to in the absence of any other news.

In May came the news that Saddam's brother-in-law, Adnan Khairallah had been killed in a helicopter crash. The official cause of the crash was given as a sandstorm, but few believed it. Rumour was rife that the machine had been blown out of the sky on Saddam's orders, a method he was using with increasing frequency to dispose of the senior army officers who stood against his authority during the war. It certainly seemed we were losing more helicopters in mysterious circumstances than we ever had to Iranian anti-aircraft fire.

Adnan, it was true, had dared to argue with the President over his public humiliation of Sajida, but even by the ruthless criterion of the house of Saddam that hardly justified his assassination. The truth was more believable. In the first week of the year, Saddam had cancelled a review of the Iraqi army, an annual event, when it was discovered that the conspirators intended to turn their guns on the grandstand in which Saddam and his family would be seated. Adnan, who had conspicuously arranged to be somewhere else on the day, was directly responsible for such security provisions. The reasonable conclusion was that Adnan was involved in a plot to topple Saddam. And indeed it subsequently emerged that Adnan had been in contact with American intelligence agents for that very purpose.

Saddam ordered the wrecked aircraft be brought back to the palace and promised that the country's leading air-crash investigators would be instructed to discover the cause of the 'accident'. To this day, it remains rusted and broken in the palace grounds, and no inquiry findings were ever released.

The issue of demonstrating my loyalty to Saddam seemed to have been temporarily set aside, but I was again reminded of the brutality of the regime shortly after Qusai had decided to divorce his wife, Lamia. Within a few weeks of their separation, I heard of an incident that almost beggared belief. Lamia, who was said to have been distraught over the estrangement, was rumoured to have sought solace with a young man from the district of al-Kindi, close to the Khair river, a tributary of the Dijlah. The relationship was almost certainly a platonic one, but when Udai heard of their meetings, he saw it as a slight on his brother's honour and decided to take action. The young man was dragged from his parent's home and battered by four of Udai's thugs. As if this were not bad enough, Udai instructed one of his accomplices to re-sculp the man's genitals. This imaginative individual sliced the young man's penis from the scrotum to the foreskin and committed other atrocities on his testicles that I cannot bring myself to describe. Yet he still lived. He was left lying in his own blood and vomit, and would have died had his terrified parents not come looking for him. Despite the fact that Lamia was separated from his brother, Udai's message was clear: the women of the al-Takriti family, past or present, were out of bounds.

In June, we were enthralled to read that the first open elections for nearly fifty years had taken place in Poland and the governing Communist Party had been defeated. The regimes of Hungary, East Germany, Czechoslovakia, Bulgaria and Romania would shortly follow suit and before the end of the year, a debate opened on the re-unification of Germany. With the collapse of the Eastern bloc, the threat of a nuclear world war was rapidly receding and the end of the Cold War was in sight. This was a cause of celebration for most people in the West, but possibly a mixed blessing for the United States. Without the ever-present threat of the Soviet Union, how could the US justify its massive armament programme? Its huge defence industry was faced with bankruptcy and the need for a global defender of 'democracy' would soon be no more. As the world's only genuine superpower, America needed a new role and an alternative enemy to focus on. Saddam Hussein's Iraq was quickly identified as a potential candidate.

As nations talked of world peace, it was business as usual in the Middle East. Our old enemies in the West may have been dormant, but the likelihood of another Arab-Israeli war had not diminished at all. Between Israel and Iraq there was much sabre rattling as Saddam sought to impose his will on the region. Emerging victorious from the confrontation with Iran meant Iraq was the nation most Arabs looked to for a military lead and the one Tel Aviv most feared. Saddam was a threat to the status quo and furthermore the US was not prepared to tolerate the world's most vital oil resources being dominated by one man. While Saddam maintained his present course, a confrontation of some sort became increasingly inevitable.

In the end, the way it happened surprised nearly everyone.

Chapter Twelve

1990
Jumaada al-Thaany 1410 – Jumaada al-Thaany 1411

In the early part of the new year, Latif reappeared. I was at home one Friday morning in early January when once again the telephone rang at eleven o'clock. When I answered it, nobody spoke. I hoped with all my heart it was Latif and not somebody using the code on his behalf.

Our meeting was a duplication of that of more than a year earlier, Latif striding past me at the railway station, bound for the same spot by a wall, some ten minutes walk away. Once again, we did not acknowledge each other until Latif's associate passed us and nodded the all-clear.

'It is good to see you again, Mikhaelef,' Latif said then with great warmth. 'I wondered if I ever would.'

'It is a blessing to see you, too, Latif,' I responded, with equal emotion. 'Where have you been?'

'In al-Mawsil,' he replied. 'I tried to get word to you, but—'

'Yes,' I cut in, 'I got the message, but it was so vague I could not be sure what it meant.'

He nodded. 'There was no other way. It is certain your telephone is bugged.'

He related to me how he had escaped from Baghdad in the boot of a car, driven by a sympathetic government official. They were stopped twice but, due to the man's status, allowed to pass without the vehicle being searched. Saddam, no doubt, would be furious if he ever learned how Latif had evaded capture with the connivance of one of his own employees.

'Do you know what happened to Rafik?' I asked, hoping he did. I had no wish to be the bearer of bad tidings.

'Yes,' As he spoke, a spasm of anguish crossed his face. 'I also know of his suffering and the manner of his death. The same fate awaits us both unless we are extremely careful. It is about such things that I need to talk to you.'

Latif had clearly been living under an enormous strain, but his passion and intensity remained undiluted. He struck me as even more resolute and determined than when I had last seen him, on the night his brothers were killed.

'I have lost a sister and two brothers by Saddam's hand,' he continued, clasping his hands so hard the knuckles whitened. 'My life has no other purpose now but to avenge them. I do not care what happens to me, but I will gladly give my life, if in doing so I can relieve Saddam and his sons of theirs. I do not expect you to join with me in this.'

'You forget,' I said sharply, 'my wife and children were murdered also. I hunger for revenge as you do.'

Bold words indeed from a former schoolteacher! Latif tended to have this effect on me.

'I do not forget,' he said, smiling sympathetically. 'But to hear you say such things is music to me.'

He momentarily held his tongue as a young couple ambled past, then brought me up to date with his movements since his return to the capital.

'I have acquired a new identity in the name of Ra'ad Mohammed and have formed another active service unit within the ICP, which is now almost non-existant in Iraq. I am the only person in it whose identity you know and it is better for everyone that we keep it that way. I require your help for a greater purpose, Mikhaelef. The ICP is now part of a coalition. If we succeed in removing Saddam, will you replace him until we have taken control?'

Amna had once asked me the same question and I had derided the notion. Now I agreed without hesitation.

'Good. There is something else we need to discuss. I have to be sure that any attempt made on Saddam's life does not occur when you are in his place. Put a cactus plant in the window of your front bedroom. Whenever you are standing in for Saddam, remove it. If at any time you are unable to do this and are faced by assassins who believe you to be Saddam, shout "cactus". My people will know to abort the mission.' Latif looked at me and laughed. 'If, of course, such an attack is the work of another organisation, your assailants will think you raving mad!'

'They will also presumably proceed to carry out their task,' I said, with some irony.

'This is the risk you run,' Latif agreed.

He had also decided it was time we changed the procedure for making contact with me.

'In future, I will leave a cactus plant by your front door. If you take the plant in, I will know you are in Baghdad and have received the message. Come straight here the following day at noon.'

'Do not arrange to meet me in this way too often, Latif,' I said. 'I may have trouble explaining to visitors why my house is filled with desert plants!'

Latif stood up, laughing again, and as I joined him we embraced.

'It is good you can still make jokes, my friend.' He then held me at arms length. 'We may not meet again, Abu Salih,' he said affectionately, using an Arab term of respect I rarely heard applied to myself. Having been through so much together, we parted with heavy hearts.

I was worried for Latif. After the brutal murders of Amna and the children, and the further loss of his two brothers and close friend, he seemed to me now almost fanatical in his desire to rid the country of Saddam and his like. I, too, had changed, become harder and tougher, though not to anything like the same extent as Latif. I was concerned that his state of mind might cloud his judgement.

Iraq was no place for the foolhardy.

By this time, the United States was mounting a campaign of political and media hostility against Iraq and the duplicity of the policy became apparent following two separate incidents in the early part of the year.

In March, a British-based Iranian journalist, Farzad Barzoft, was executed in Baghdad for spying and Saddam was condemned for it from all corners of the Western world. Protestations of his innocence by Britain were scoffed at by Saddam. In fairness to the President, there was ample proof that the man, arrested in September the previous year as he was about to leave the country, had been a tool of intelligence on a regular basis and Saddam had not the slightest doubt he was disposing of a foreign agent.

Around the same time, a Canadian scientist, Gerald Bull, was murdered in Brussels. He had been working for Iraq for a number of years and Saddam was furious when the news of his death reached the presidential palace. Bull had been one of the world's leading experts in the development of long-range 'superguns' and when the American and Canadian governments had dispensed with his services in the late 1970s, he took his skills to the highest bidder.

There was no outward motive for this killing. He was not robbed, despite the large sum of money – said to be in excess of $20,000 – found on his person. He was, though, clinically shot five times in the head and body, and the assassination bore all the hallmarks of a Mossad death squad. Saddam, certainly, blamed the Israelis and publicly condemned the governments of the West – the same democracies who appeared outraged at the lawful execution of a convicted spy, yet remained mute when a scientist was shot dead on a European street.

During a television broadcast, Saddam sent out a chilling warning to Israel as to what they might expect if they continued to operate against Iraq. He brought the Israeli threat of nuclear war out into the open.

'Israel has threatened to attack us with nuclear weapons!' he thundered. 'By Allah, if they do, we will retaliate. We have enough weapons to start a war which will burn half of Israel with a "double" chemical!' Saddam was referring to the new binary weapon of VX nerve gas.

The only part of the speech generally reported in the West was Saddam's indirect reference to his chemical weapons 'burning half of Israel', the context in which it was set being largely ignored.

Over a period of months, the regional spotlight shifted from Iraq's preoccupation with Israel to its deteriorating relationship with Kuwait. The root of the problem goes back more than a hundred years, to when Britain first tried to isolate Kuwait from the Ottoman empire. When the empire collapsed in 1918, Iraq emerged as a new nation administered by the British, who immediately regarded Kuwait as a separate entity. The borders, though, have never been acknowledged by any Iraqi government. Iraq itself was divided into the three administrative regions of al-Mawsil, Baghdad and al-Basrah and further broken down into eighteen *muhafaza*, or provinces. Kuwait was a province of the al-Basrah region centuries before Iraq ever existed as a nation-state, and it is for that reason Saddam regards it as the 'nineteenth province'.

However, it was economic rather than territorial questions that influenced Iraqi-Kuwaiti relations at this time and negotiations between the two were dominated by four central issues.

Since the end of the war against Iran, Saddam had struggled in vain to revive an exhausted economy. This was primarily due to the artificially low price of oil, Iraq's only significant export commodity and source of income. Kuwait, consistently guilty of exceeding oil production quotas agreed at OPEC summits, had invested heavily in overseas oil-related industries and was thus able to compensate for the loss of export revenue with increased commercial profits abroad; they were, in effect, selling cheaper oil to themselves. By driving the price of oil down, however, they were crippling Iraq's recovery programme and Saddam insisted that the price of oil be restored, by force if necessary.

Secondly, Kuwait had assisted Iraq during the war to the tune of some $14 billion, a considerable sum, but realistic in view of the emirate's vulnerability to an Iranian invasion. Indeed, some referred to it ironically as 'protection money.' In January, Saddam requested a further advance of $10 billion and was furious when Kuwait initially responded by raising the matter of the war loans. Saddam pointed out Kuwait would have been removed from the map had not the Iranians been defeated. He demanded the loans be written off.

Thirdly, Saddam accused Kuwait of stealing more than two billion dollars worth of oil during the war from the Rumalia oilfield, part of which was clearly, by anyone's definition, on the Iraqi side of the border. This they had done by drilling at an angle from their own side. It was particularly galling for Saddam that Kuwait was using Iraqi oil to help cripple the Iraqi economy.

Finally, Saddam had long been pressing for permission to build military bases on the Gulf islands of al-Warba and al-Bubiyan belonging to Kuwait. They had steadfastly refused to give it, even at the height of the war with Iran, no doubt concerned that Iraq, once stationed on the islands, would never leave. Saddam also planned to dredge the channels surrounding the islands in order to construct a harbour, something they probably suspected. A deep-water port in the Gulf would have given Saddam direct and unrestricted access to the open sea for his oil-tankers and allowed him to move his navy, anchored off the coast of Jordan, into home waters.

Despite these contentious issues, the Kuwaiti response to

Saddam's proposals was conciliatory. They were prepared to forget the debt, if not actually write it off, as long as Iraq recognised the border between the two countries. They suggested a further initial loan of $500 million and were prepared to conform to OPEC oil quotas as long as everyone else did. They also had no objection to a substantial rise in the price of oil. To most Arabs, an agreement looked imminent. Alas, in the months that followed matters deteriorated.

It seemed the Kuwaitis wanted to do little more than talk and by the end of July, Saddam's patience ran out. At a summit in Riyadh, he insisted through his Vice-President, Izzat Ibrahim, that the time for words was over and demanded that Kuwait immediately acknowledge their compliance with his demands. Kuwait stalled again and Saddam believed he was being both duped and humiliated. Loss of face to an Arab, no matter how lowly his standing, is intolerable. To Saddam, it was unforgivable.

Convinced the Kuwaitis were being encouraged, even manipulated, by the US, Saddam accused Sheikh Jabir al-Ahmad al-Sabah, the Emir of Kuwait, of arrogantly exploiting Iraq's economic weakness. Ibrahim Gassim al-Bahu, the Kuwaiti ambassador for Iraq, oozed concessions and assurances in Baghdad, but Saddam was beyond propitiation. He suspected Kuwait was determined to antagonise him and had no genuine intention to co-operate or compromise.

When Izzat Ibrahim returned to Baghdad empty-handed, Saddam made ready to invade. His original plan was to seize only the Kuwaiti section of the Rumalia oilfield and the two islands of al-Warba and al-Bubiyan, but he was furious at what he felt was a personal insult to his honour by Sheikh Jaber. He decided in an impulsive rage to annexe the whole of Kuwait. In so doing, he believed he would eliminate most of Iraq's economic problems at a stroke. Over the preceding week, Saddam had moved eight divisions, consisting of some 100,000 men, to the Kuwaiti border. The world believed Saddam was bluffing. They were about to learn he was not.

At two o'clock in the morning, 2 August, Saddam ordered his troops gathered around al-Basrah to cross into Kuwait. Hardly any resistance was met, and within three hours the capital was taken. The Iraqi populace was jubilant. Later in the day, now disguised behind dark glasses and one of the luxuriant false beards issued to me for such occasions, I travelled by road to Kuwait in the company of Hashim and Saddam's cousin, Ali Hassan al-Majid, who was to be the new governor of the Kuwaiti 'province' of Iraq.

During the trip, Ali intrigued me by stating that our 'victory' would be celebrated in Tehran as well as Baghdad. Hashim noted my furrowed brow and explained.

'Ali is referring to a decision by Saddam to repatriate Iranian prisoners of war.'

'The war ended two years ago,' I said, still none the wiser. 'There cannot be more than a handful.'

Ali smiled. 'Oh, a handful of 70,000 or more.'

I was staggered, but Hashim's warning glance advised me not to pursue the matter further. I was intimidated by his mere presence and I was in no doubt he had been instructed by Saddam to show the Kuwaitis the same 'compassion' he had offered the Kurds.

My arrival was not publicised. I was there in case Saddam needed me to make an appearance on his behalf, but as the leaders of most Arab states were on the telephone to Saddam by the hour, his real whereabouts were well known and I was instructed to observe a low profile until further notice.

Sheikh Jaber of Kuwait had been spending the weekend with his family at a coastal resort near al-Ahmadi when the Iraqi tanks rolled in. Once word of the invasion reached him, he made for Ras al-Khafji, thirty kilometres across the Saudi Arabian border, before travelling on to al-Ta'if, near Jiddah, on the al-Bahr al-Ahmar (Red Sea) coast. Failing to capture the Emir irritated Saddam, even though he was already reconciled to the fact that, whatever the military outcome, his tenure of Kuwait was likely to be a temporary one. Saddam began to ponder how he might withdraw with his honour intact.

Many Kuwaitis fled in the dust-trail of the 'royal' family and there were reports of huge sums being transferred in panic to European banks. Saddam received intelligence that close on $10 billion had been moved from the Gulf in the first week of the invasion. Apparently, Europe became so flooded with the Kuwaiti dinar that banks refused to accept it and many wealthy Arabs found themselves temporarily destitute as their credit cards became worthless. Even in Egypt, the dinar slumped to a value some twenty-five times below its pre-invasion rate.

Arriving in Kuwait City, resplendent in beard and dark glasses, I watched through darkened windscreens the jubilant troops and despondent Kuwaiti citizens fraternising uneasily. I was en route to the Se'if Palace, where the Emir used to spend his working day, when we stopped for a moment as an artillery unit crossed our path. Suddenly, all hell broke loose. A truck exploded behind us and lifted our car high into the air. As we fell back to earth, my legs were thrust through the shattered windscreen, and I was badly cut from the waist to the knees. It transpired the bomb had been planted by the Kuwaiti Resistance, a rather disorganised and diffident group, deterred no doubt by the retributions every hostile act engendered; at least five Kuwaiti civilians were executed in retribution for every Iraqi soldier they killed. This particular bomb destroyed several shops and injured several soldiers, two of whom were killed, an act that would guarantee the deaths of at least ten innocent Kuwaitis.

Apart from several deep lacerations on my legs, I was badly shaken but not seriously hurt, although my dark glasses and beard had vanished. Hashim, completely unscathed, put his jacket around my head so I would not be recognised amid the bedlam that followed, and within minutes I was being whisked off to the al-Adid hospital to the south of the city. There I was carried on a stretcher to a private ward and attended by a local doctor, Aref Hassan al-Hamid.

Hashim told Aref I was a close relative of Saddam's and should be treated as if I were the President himself. Aref acknowledged this with a shrug of the shoulders.

'You need not worry,' he said casually. 'I treat all of my patients as if they were al-Qaed al-Muhib.'

There was a hint of flippancy in his tone, but his smile was disarming and I raised a hand to prevent Hashim from stepping in.

'Let the doctor do his job,' I said.

Once he was finished, a nurse cleared away the bloodied swabs and Aref turned to Hashim.

'You can tell the President his cousin is perfectly well, but badly shaken. He needs to rest.'

Hashim nodded. 'For how long?'

'I cannot say exactly. For a few days perhaps.'

Hashim stepped towards me and spoke in an undertone. 'You are as safe here as anywhere. This is not one of the busiest hospitals in Kuwait. A guard will be posted outside your door and I will come and see you every few hours.' He then turned to Aref. 'I have to insist, doctor, that nobody with the exception of yourself and the nurse here, be permitted to enter this room. That means you will have to take turns catching some sleep, but there is no alternative.'

'I understand,' Aref replied. 'It is not a problem. I am here all the time anyway.'

The following day, while checking my wounds, Aref began to chat.

'How long have you been impersonating Saddam?' he asked.

'What are you talking about?' I replied, shaken by the casual candidness of the question.

He shrugged casually. 'It matters nothing to me if you wish to continue with the pretence. I will tell no one. I thought perhaps, in such difficult times, you might want to talk about it.'

He was so confident in his assertion, I could see there was little point in lying to him.

'How did you know?' I asked.

'Why else are you here? You are a cousin of Saddam's and identical to him. And yet I have never heard of your existence. Also, plastic surgery has been done on your nose. It does not take a brilliant mind to deduce that Saddam uses you to impersonate him.'

His logic was so sound. I did not bother to rebut it.

'Are you really related?' he asked.

'No,' I answered. 'I was a teacher in Karbala. Saddam heard about me through my brother-in-law who worked in the Mayor's office in Baghdad.'

'A fortunate day for you, yes?'

'Some might think so.'

Aref glanced up at me. 'But not you?'

'I am an educated man, doctor, but my needs are simple. Working for Saddam has ruined my life beyond my ability to explain it to you. In any case, we should not discuss such things. It is not safe for either of us.'

Conversation was suspended while Aref placed a fresh dressing on my leg, but once he was finished I again felt the desire to unload my burden. In the end, I spoke with Aref at length about my situation and the nature of my recent activities. He was a good listener, but he offered no advice.

The nurse, Sophie Hamed, was an American with the Red Crescent, the Moslem branch of the International Red Cross, and had stayed behind long after most of her compatriots had gone home. Her real name was Safah al-Hamed and, although born in Baghdad, she was raised in New York after her family fled Iraq in February 1963 in the wake of the Ba'athist Revolution. The day after the coup, more than 2,000 citizens of Baghdad were killed in street battles between the Ba'athists and the Communists. Sophie's father was a Communist and, fearing for his family, left Iraq that night. The parallels between Amna and Sophie were not lost on me. I was confident that, as an American, Sophie could be trusted with my secret and I spent many hours discussing with her what options were open to me. She argued that I would be insane to return to Baghdad and should use the present opportunity to make good my escape from the clutches of Saddam and his family.

'You are convinced Udai wants you dead,' she persisted, 'and yet you think your good fortune will last forever.'

'But I have things to do in Baghdad,' I protested. 'My brother-in-law may need me at any time. He has to know where to find me.'

'There must be a way you can communicate with him. If you wish to work against Saddam, there is much you can do outside Iraq.'

To avert undue harassment by Hashim, Aref told him I was more badly shaken than was at first realised and needed more rest. Sophie continued to try and persuade me not to return to Iraq and having finally found some temporary solace from the troubles of my life, I was more than susceptible to her suggestions. To my intense surprise, I was also growing quite fond of her.

As my stay in hospital lengthened, Hashim became ever more restive. On the tenth day he finally insisted I be made fit to be driven back to Baghdad. If I was to make a move in a different direction, therefore, it had to be soon. Aref came to see me and said that if I was ready, he could have me smuggled out of the hospital that night and taken to a house vacated by a fellow doctor and his family, who fled when the Iraqis arrived. From there, arrangements could be made to transport me across the border.

In September, Saddam declared his intention of bombing Israel if the US intervened in Kuwait. This was more than simply a means of striking back at Washington, which most Arabs believe is hand-in-glove with Tel Aviv. Saddam believed the Israelis would not be able to resist the forces compelling them to retaliate and in doing so would change the entire character of the invasion. Once it became an Arab-Israeli conflict, no Arab nation could refuse to stand alongside Saddam.

There was furious diplomatic activity between the region's heads of state looking for an Arab solution to the crisis, but nothing was resolved. After the Iraqi army had failed to capture the Kuwaiti Emir, Saddam had stated he was prepared to order a withdrawal. It proved easier said than done, being beyond the leaders of the Middle East nations to agree on the conditions and manner of it. As days, then weeks passed, Saddam's attitude hardened.

It was four o'clock in the morning when I was woken by Aref to be told I was leaving. The guard outside my room was momentarily distracted by an attractive young nurse who asked for his assistance in lifting a patient who had conveniently 'collapsed' en route to the toilet. Within a minute, I was outside the hospital and climbing into the back of an ambulance. Sophie was there waiting for me.

Fifteen minutes later, we were dropped at a private house in the Bneid al-Gah suburb of the city and told not to venture outside under any circumstances. Food would be delivered to us each day. As soon as arrangements had been made to take us across the border, we would be informed.

The four weeks that followed were among the happiest of my life. I was at first nervous in Sophie's presence, but her American ways soon removed my inhibitions and before long a passion was awoken within me, the intensity of which I had never before experienced. Since Amna's death, I had largely avoided female company, but Sophie was a very attractive woman and I a normal red-blooded man. On our third day in hiding, the inevitable happened.

I was lying on the bed as she treated the wounds on my leg, still occasionally seeping a little blood. She touched me gently as first she cleaned the wound and then applied a new dressing. I cannot recall exactly what happened next, but be it suffice to say that we became lovers. It was as the bursting of a great dam. In the days that followed making love became almost our sole occupation. In between, we related to each other the stories of our lives. I laughed as I had not done since I was a child and enjoyed a sense of fulfilment I had never known before, even with Amna.

Sophie, just turned thirty, was quick to dispel my fears about the gap between our ages.

'You do not look like a man of forty-eight,' she said dismissively, and when I foolishly continued to bemoan the discrepancy, she silenced me with a certain female technique that, being an old-fashioned Arab, I am too embarrassed to set down in words. It was, though, most effective and the matter of age became irrelevant.

Aref occasionally sent messengers to the house, whose only message was that we must be patient. As Iraqi patrols swarmed over every road out of the city, it would take time to organise our escape. With Sophie alongside me, I was happy to wait forever.

We talked of many things, some good, some bad, and it was from Sophie I learned that Saddam was using the bodies of murdered Kuwaitis to help solve Iraq's shortage of organ donors.

'It is unbelievable!' I gasped. 'You must be mistaken.'

'I am not,' she answered quite adamantly. 'Bodies are taken to the hospitals and from their condition it is clear they have been tortured before dying. If a qualified Iraqi is not available, then a local surgeon is forced to remove the vital organs. In the early days of the occupation, some refused. They were then shot dead and had their own organs removed while their bodies were still warm.'

Even after so many years of exposure to the barbarism of Saddam's regime, I could still be sickened by some new revelation.

We were asleep in bed late one afternoon when I was woken suddenly by the sound of the front door crashing in. I sat bolt upright and almost immediately the bedroom door swung open and a half-dozen soldiers stormed in. I did not know if we had been careless or betrayed, but they knew exactly who they were looking for; my likeness to Saddam did not in the least surprise them.

Within minutes we were dressed, dragged from the house and loaded into a car waiting outside. As we were being driven out of the city, I asked the officer who sat between Sophie and myself where we were being taken.

'Baghdad,' he said without looking at me. 'Please do not speak again.'

Five hours later, we entered the prison of the Amn al-Khas in the Hai al-Tashriya district of Baghdad, run by the al-Takriti family. Sophie and I were separated. No farewells were allowed. The last I remember of her before she was marched away was her eyes meeting mine – eyes that shone with defiance yet conveyed her unspoken love for me.

I never expected to see her again.

Chapter Thirteen

1991

Jumaada al-Thaany 1411 – Jumaada al-Thaany 1412

After being totally ignored and near-starved for the best part of three weeks, I was finally dragged from my cell one morning and taken directly to Saddam at the Karradat Mariam. I was convinced the sole purpose of the trip was to give the President the satisfaction of killing me personally. When I was presented before him, I was not disappointed to see that Udai was not among those present. If I was about to die, I would rather do so without his smirking, arrogant face gloating over me.

Apart from Saddam, there were only three other men in the room: Tariq Aziz, Izzat Ibrahim and Taha Yasin. Tariq and Izzat looked as if they would rather be anywhere other than here, but Taha had found himself a seat near a window and was settling down, as if to enjoy the spectacle.

I stood in the middle of the room, unwashed, unfed, and desperately tired. Saddam stepped forward to confront me.

'You are unbelievable!' he screamed, his spittle splashing my cheeks as he unleashed his rage on me. 'I cannot

comprehend what you have done! It is beyond my understanding!'

He turned away and stormed across the room, then
returned to confront me.

'You were nothing when I found you! Nothing! I
plucked you from a life of near poverty. I gave you
everything – money, a beautiful home. Anything you
wanted. I have treated you as my brother. I have stood by
you when even members of my own family said I should be
rid of you. "He is no good, Saddam," they told me, "he
cannot be trusted." But I said: "No. You do not know him
as I do. He is a good man. He is loyal to me." And now,
when the guns of hell are pointing at my head, you
abandon me!'

It mattered not that I was resigned to my fate. I trembled
in the face of his fury, too terrified to reply. I was resigned
to accepting the tongue-lashing and whatever followed it
without protest, without speaking in my defence.

Another quick pace across the room and he was back,
his nose thrust in my face. 'For ten years I have been your
friend. I helped you whenever you had difficulties. If you
ever had a problem, you only had to bring it to me and it
was a problem no more. Tell me if that is not true.'

I said nothing, barely able to raise my head to look at
him.

'Tell me!' he roared.

'It . . . it is true,' I said, still looking at the floor.

'Of course it is true! But you? The one man I thought I
could trust. The one man who is always there when I need
him, who never objects to anything I ask him to do. You
do this to me! At a time when I am surrounded by enemies,
when fellow Arabs I once thought were my friends want to
stab me in the back. You, the one man in Iraq I thought I
could depend upon decides to take a month's holiday to
shag a fucking nurse!'

For a moment, I thought my ears had deceived me. What
was Saddam saying? I was too tired, too weak to think
clearly, but surely I was not mistaken.

Then, softly at first, Saddam started to laugh. The other men in the room looked at each other dubiously, as if they too could not credit what they were hearing. Saddam's laughter grew in volume, and then Taha joined in. Within seconds everyone in the room except myself was laughing near hysterically. I was still too frightened to risk anything more than a rictus of a grin.

'In the name of Allah,' Saddam said, tears in his eyes and still barely able to speak. 'We are so alike it frightens me! Who else, Mikhaelef, but you and I could raise a stiff dick when we are surrounded on all sides by the might of Satan?' He looked towards Tariq. 'What shall I do with him, Tariq? Tell me.'

'I am sure I do not know,' Tariq answered tactfully, probably still unsure whether to defend me or accuse me.

Saddam embraced me.

'It gave me no pleasure to have you locked up, Mikhaelef,' he said, 'but these are difficult times. I had to teach you a lesson. I need your help now more than I ever have in the past. You must resist temptation and address the mighty task Allah has put before us. Please, promise me you will keep your dick in your pants for a while.'

'I am sorry, Saddam,' I replied, relief washing over me. 'It will not happen again.'

'Good, good. Stay close to me, Mikhaelef. I am in need of friends.'

At first, it seemed incredible that Saddam believed I was guilty of nothing more than taking some unauthorised leave, but perhaps he was just giving me the benefit of the doubt. Now that he was in a lighter mood, he was able to share with me his side of the story. Perhaps he really did like me.

'Do you know how I found you?' he asked.

'I have had three weeks to wonder about that,' I answered, regaining some of my confidence. 'I still have no idea.'

'I ordered the Istekhabarat to do a house-to-house search of the city to look for any members of the al-Sabah family who might have been left behind. It seemed unlikely, but it was possible and I was determined to leave no stone unturned trying to find them. Your little love-nest was not due to be covered for another week or so, but a Palestinian in the neighbourhood watched a dog ravage some rubbish you had put out. He saw a large quantity of bloodied dressings and bandages and reported it to the authorities. They were curious enough to watch the house for a couple of days. The rest you can put together yourself.'

Although I did not learn of it until later, one of the reasons for the lightness of Saddam's mood was that he had recently taken a third wife, Nedhal Mohammed al-Hamdani. She was the manager of the Solar Energy Department, a part of the Ministry of Industrialisation. Another blow for the principles of Ba'athism.

I realised it would be stretching my good fortune to raise the subject of Sophie, but I had to know what had become of her. I kept my tone offhand as I phrased the question.

'Are you fond of her?' Saddam said in reply.

I shrugged, suggesting indifference. Then immediately regretted it when he said, 'She need not trouble you again.'

'She is an American,' I reminded him, wondering if she might not already be dead. 'She could be useful.'

'An American?' Saddam was clearly surprised. 'I was told she was an Iraqi.'

'She was born in Baghdad, but her family moved to New York nearly thirty years ago when she was an infant. Once she was arrested, it is hardly surprising she said she was an Iraqi.'

Saddam was silent for a moment. 'Yes,' he said finally. 'This might be useful for propaganda purposes. I will have her brought here and make sure those devils in the CIA know it. An American citizen in the palace will give them something to think about if they decide to attack us.'

Using foreign workers as hostages was a much publicised tactic of Saddam's, and a never-ending stream of statesmen from around the world trekked to Baghdad to negotiate their release. Generally, Saddam was receptive to their appeals as long as they were made with respect and the appropriate dignity. One such emissary was the former British Prime Minister, Edward Heath, who arrived without the blessing of his government to plead for the release of a number of British expatriates, said to be in need of urgent medical attention.

Saddam granted Heath's request and later spoke of him with some admiration.

'He is a brave man to come here without the protection of his government and talk to me the way he did.'

Heath had advised Saddam to vacate Kuwait as a matter of urgency, but did so in a manner the President did not find offensive.

'It is a pity his day has passed,' Saddam added. 'I could negotiate with a man like that.'

A few days later, Sophie was moved into the palace and kept under lock and key and twenty-four hour surveillance in a private chamber. I was anxious to see her, but dared not push my luck with Saddam any further. I thought I might bring up the subject with Hashim, but he was no Mohammed Qutaibi. One morning when Saddam was away from the palace, however, Hashim himself brought up the subject.

'I am surprised you have not spoken of the American woman,' he said, not raising his head from the paper he was reading.

I looked at him, startled. 'Why would I want to do that?'

'Oh, please, Mikhaelef, I am not still taking milk from my mother's breast. You spent four passionate weeks with the woman. You are bound to have feelings for her.'

'That is behind me now.'

'As you please, but Saddam told me this morning he has no objection to you seeing her, providing I accompany you. He is not a man without compassion. You more than anybody should know that.'

I suspected I was being set up for one of Saddam's

practical jokes, but my desire to see Sophie was stronger than my fear of ridicule.

'In that case, yes. I would like to see her.'

Five minutes later, I walked into the chamber where Sophie lay in bed. Hashim came in with me, but stayed by the door and allowed me to approach her alone. Her face was badly bruised, both eyes being blackened and puffy; her lips were cut and swollen and her ear lobes were bandaged and bloody, presumably where her ear-rings had been torn out. A common practice among Saddam's jailers. Speaking in a whisper, she told me she had been raped and beaten many times. When she opened her mouth I saw that her two front teeth were broken off at the root. I crossed her lips gently with my forefinger.

'Say nothing more for now. We will talk again when you are stronger.'

I sat alongside her and stroked her forehead until, heavily sedated, she fell asleep.

As I made my way back to the Dark Room with Hashim, I was deep in thought. Her condition was much worse than I had feared, but there was little more I could do to help her without publicising the depth of our relationship. This, my instinct warned me, would be potentially fatal for us both. Saddam would never tolerate my becoming involved with an American woman, even if she were Iraqi by birth.

'She is not well, Mikhaelef,' Hashim remarked, 'but you can be sure she is being properly looked after – now that Saddam attaches some value to her.'

As the UN deadline for withdrawal from Kuwait neared, people stayed at home and the streets of Baghdad were quiet. Some watched national television and others listened to *Radio Baghdad*, but most Iraqis were tuned into foreign radio stations. Even *Israel Radio* was broadcasting in Arabic. Whatever the station, the message was the same: the crisis was worsening.

Up to the last moment, Tariq, as Foreign Secretary, and

his deputy, Nizar Hamdun, worked ceaselessly towards negotiating a settlement. The air-traffic between Baghdad and Amman, the only foreign airport open to Iraq, consisted almost exclusively of heads of state, politicians and diplomats, casting around for a last-minute solution. The UN had determined that Iraq must withdraw its troops by midnight, 15 January, but that deadline came and went and the Iraqi army remained in Kuwait.

Baghdad awoke on the morning of 16 January to a heavy mist covering the city. Was that why the bombers had not come? Most of the population stayed at home, still listening to the radio for news, staying close to their loved ones, waiting for the bombers. The streets were deserted and, in general, the shops were *mughlug*, closed for the day. Those who ventured out were mostly carrying or queuing for bread. The day dragged slowly, but there was no news. By lunchtime, the few storekeepers who had bothered to open were locking up.

I was late going home, staying on at the palace longer than usual in case of developments. When I finally left, I was surprised that most of the street lighting, although dimmed as it had been for some time, was still operating. There was no blackout.

After eating my evening meal, I spent a couple of hours talking to my mother then went to bed. I lay awake for a while, listening to the sounds of the night. Baghdad was silent and I wondered if the bombers would come. Finally, I fell asleep.

It was two-thirty in the morning when I was woken by the sound of barking dogs. It seemed that every hound in the neighbourhood was yapping and howling. Then, only faintly at first, I picked up the rising drone of aircraft. The sound rose to a crescendo. My house was far enough from the city centre for me feel confident that no bombs would fall in the area, so I was not afraid for myself and my mother. Then came the first explosions as Coalition bombers poured over the city and unleashed their lethal cargoes. The ground shook and the night sky lit up as bright as mid-day. I heard the belated wailing of the air-raid sirens, but they were redundant. Baghdad was awake.

I went out onto the veranda and watched as anti-aircraft fire traced across the sky. There was a brief lull in the bombing and then another wave of aircraft screamed overhead, and the devastation continued. After that they came in waves fifteen minutes apart. After one series of explosions, the city was plunged into darkness and the lights of my own house went out. Looking across the city, I could see some government ministries had been hit and were ablaze, as was the Daw'ra oil refinery. The Iwadhi district, where a large number of light industrial units and office blocks was located, was also on fire. Other sites, critical to Baghdad's ground-to-air defence systems, were being taken out one by one. Then the communications centre, standing tall on the Baghdad skyline, went up in a great orange eruption.

Like every other inhabitant of Baghdad, I was awake for the rest of the night. My mother, woken by the tumult, joined me on the veranda and together we watched our beautiful city reduced to ruins. On reflection, the risk we took in not seeking the sanctuary of the shelters was foolhardy, but we had suffered air-raids during the war with Iran and had become inured to the dangers. We felt compelled to watch the full scale and horror of the destruction taking place before us. My mother wept for those people who lived closer to the main target areas.

'Every bomb,' she said, melodramatically, 'has a child's name on it.'

The air-raids continued through the night and into the morning, though the intervals between them extended to thirty minutes as dawn broke. I left for the palace at seven-thirty. I could see that a number of important targets had been flattened, but many ordinary buildings had been hit too. I passed a jumble of smouldering rubble that used to be a school I had visited several times over the years but, praise Allah, it had clearly been hit before the children arrived for the day. The stadium, underneath which was Saddam's bunker, had not been hit. Nor had the palace. Saddam was sure to claim divine protection. Others suspected the Allies of deliberately avoiding putting Saddam's life at risk. If so, I find it inexplicable.

The raids continued all day and into the next, much of it merely rearranging the rubble. The bombing was far in excess of anything the city had suffered during the war with Iran. At times, the noise was terrifying. On the third night, the telecommunications centre was hit again and totally destroyed. Further damage was done to all means of communications by the Coalition practice of dropping carbon fibres, which attached themselves to electric cables and rendered them useless.

From the bulletins broadcast by foreign radio stations, everybody knew the Americans were boasting to the world how deadly accurate the campaign was. The precision with which strategic targets were being hit was astonishing. Considering the tonnage of bombs being unloaded, the number of civilians killed was negligible.

As the days passed, the bombing continued relentlessly. By the fourth week, everyone's nerves were in shreds. One night during that week, I was still at the palace in the early hours of the morning when I heard a report of a substantial number of civilian casualties in the Suma suburb to the north. This was followed by another report, that an air-raid shelter in the district where I lived was hit. According to the rather confused details, more than 700 people had been in it at the time and at least 400 of them, mostly women and children, were dead.

During this period I had taken to spending the night in the palace and my mother had taken to using PS (Public Shelter) 25, which was only a short walk from my house. I could not telephone home, as the lines had been down since the early days of the bombing, so sought the permission required to leave the palace immediately. Saddam was unavailable. Believing that one of the bombs would have his name on it, he had moved in to a secure bunker beneath the Qudisiyat Stadium on the north side of the Qudisiya motorway, a kilometre from the palace. Instead, I was able to talk to Tariq, who immediately allocated me one of his ministerial chauffeurs to drive me home.

My first call was the house, but my mother was not to be found. Expecting the worst, I instructed the chauffeur to drive to the shelter. Despite having witnessed first-hand the effects of nearly thirty days and nights of constant bombing, I was stunned by the extent of the chaos I encountered in the streets around the shelter. Dozens of dead bodies were laid out on the ground and women were wailing, some looking for their children, some having found them. Smoke was still pouring from the shelter and a frantic but pointless rescue operation was taking place. The shelter had been hit by two 'smart' bombs and most of the dead had been killed instantly. I passed along the line of corpses, looking for my mother. She was not among them, which I thought a blessing. I went among the injured calling her name, before finally joining in the rescue, helping sift through the rubble in search of my mother.

Dawn came and the body count rose, but one end of the shelter was so badly damaged it was going to be days before the true casualty figure would be known. Later in the morning, I tracked down the PS supervisor, Hassan Mohammed al-Janadi. He had been at the heart of the rescue operation for several hours and only agreed to rest when there was not the remotest possibility of finding any more survivors. He was grief-stricken by the disaster and it was difficult to get coherent answers from him.

When I told him my mother's name and asked if he knew her, he stared at my blackened face and matted hair. Even with my face undisguised, for once I was not about to be mistaken for Saddam.

'Naziha?' he said dazedly. 'You are Naziha's son? You work for the government?'

'Yes,' I answered. 'Have you seen her?'

He looked at me with compassion and the answer was in his eyes.

'I need to sit down,' he said, lowering himself slowly to the ground. 'Please, join me here.'

He wiped his face with a rag and ran a hand through his hair. I knew he was searching for the right words to say.

'Naziha has practically been living in the shelter for the past couple of weeks. She always sat in the same place and would often talk about you. Your name is Mikhaelef Ramadan, yes?'

'Yes.'

'There is no easy way to tell you this, Mikhaelef. I am sorry. I am quite certain your mother is dead.'

Hassan explained that she had been seated at the end of the shelter completely flattened by one of the bombs. She would have died instantly. Her body was still buried under tons of masonry, and would not be recovered for at least twenty-four hours.

'Naziha would not have felt a thing, Mikhaelef. It is a small mercy Allah has granted her, but should we not be grateful all the same?'

'Allahu Akbar,' I replied heavily. 'Allah is mighty.'

Wahab took my mother's death badly and cursed our moving from al-Mansur, a district where many of the foreign embassies were located and, consequently, left untouched by the bombing. The Karradat Mariam palace, too, was undamaged. Perhaps the Allies, aware that hostages were being held there, deliberately avoided it. It is inconceivable that it escaped by chance, but whatever the reason I was grateful that it had been spared and Sophie too.

Saddam, ever ready to exploit opportunities to make capital of enemy atrocities, immediately ordered the TV cameras and those members of the foreign media still in Baghdad to visit al-Amiriya. The Americans were insisting the shelter was 'a command and control centre' and therefore a legitimate target, but it was an insulting lie.

It was also significant that most of the city's shelters were deserted in the days following the al-Amiriya bombing. To his credit, Peter Arnett reported this on CNN. He was dismissive of any suggestion that the shelter was anything other than just that. I never met him personally, for obvious reasons, although Saddam had played with the idea of having me stand in as President when he gave Arnett an exclusive TV interview that was broadcast all over the world. To my enormous relief, he decided against it. I doubted my ability to carry it off under the probing lens of a TV camera and the scrutiny of the world.

Those I spoke to who knew Arnett described him as a decent, determined man with perhaps a tendency to be a little self-opinionated. It was in response to a question from Arnett, asking how many doubts he had about a successful military conclusion to the war, that Saddam had answered: 'Not one in a million.'

Regardless of the controversy that may have raged in the West, the bombing continued. Twenty-four civilians were killed in the town of al-Dour and the Holy city of al-Najaf was heavily bombed. Two of the six Dijlah bridges were destroyed, although neither carried much in the way of military traffic. The two largest bridges, to the north and south of the city, were never badly damaged and remained in use.

In mid-February, I was sent back to Kuwait, on standby. Much had changed since my last visit, including the governor. Saddam had recalled his 'cousin', Ali Hassan, to Baghdad and replaced him with Aziz Saleh al-Naumahn, a former governor of my home town, Karbala.

At the time of my arrest in mid-September, the army were in total control, but there was then a degree of discipline and restraint among the soldiers that seemed absent now. Driving through the city to the Se'if Palace, which I never reached on my earlier visit, I saw no fewer than twenty bodies. Some were strung up outside houses, others lay in the streets and gardens. Most of them had clearly been there for several days. The local people ignored them, as if they were an everyday part of the scene.

'Why are the dead left on the street?' I asked . 'Why are they not taken away by their families?'

'It is not permitted,' he said. 'They are bodies of resistance fighters, returned to their neighbourhoods by the Istekhabarat as a deterrent to others.'

The car came to a halt behind a convoy of army trucks and alongside the body of a young man, scarcely more than a boy. His body was propped up in the doorway of a burnt out delicatessen. His chest was punctured by two round holes in his chest. His eyes had been gouged out.

'Resistance?' I asked, nodding in the direction of the stricken body.

'Probably,' he replied. 'His wounds are the handiwork of the Istekhabarat. Do you see the bullet-holes in his body?'

'Yes, of course.'

'They are not bullet-holes. If we were closer you would see they are too small. If we turned him over, there would be no exit wounds. They are drill-holes.'

I grimaced. I should have been inured to such atrocities, yet I still found them hard to stomach.

The car moved on again. We passed more corpses and I noticed that I had not yet seen a female body.

'There are no dead women,' I said. 'Are only men being killed?'

'I think not,' Hashim replied. 'There will be many dead women in Kuwait.'

'Then why do they dump only the bodies of young men?'

'For effect. In any society, it is the young men who are expected to defend it. If the Kuwaitis are shown the mutilated remains of their young warriors, they will be deterred from continuing their rebellion. On the other hand, if the broken bodies of their women are returned to them, their bitterness and resentment inspires them. We are talking of human nature at its basest, but it true nevertheless.'

'Do you approved of this, Hashim?' I asked, taken aback by the matter-of-fact manner of his discourse.

'By Allah, Mikhaelef!' he growled. 'Do you think I am not human? As a man, I am as appalled by what I see as you are. But I am an officer of the Mukhabarat. I have seen such things many times before. I accept them. You do not.'

We came to an intersection and were stopped by traffic lights. Across the road three Iraqi soldiers were removing goods from a large electrical store and loading them into their truck. Within the short time we were held up, several hi-fi systems and video units, and a large television set were taken. The shopkeeper stood beside the entrance, looking forlorn. The goods had clearly not been paid for, but he would know better than to dispute the point.

At the palace, I telephoned the al-Adid hospital and asked for Dr Aref. After being kept on the line for a good twenty minutes, I was eventually informed he had been transferred to either the Mubarak or al-Amiri hospitals. They had never heard of him at the Mubarak, but after another long wait, I was told by the telephonist at the al-Amiri that Dr Aref was indeed employed at the hospital as a general surgeon, but had not been seen for some time.

Wearing sunglasses and beard, I took to walking the streets with Hashim during the day and was dismayed by what I saw. Many of the shops had been looted and closed, and there were far fewer Kuwaitis about than on my previous visit. As neither of us wore uniform, Hashim and I were stopped regularly by Iraqi patrols and on several occasions subjected to abuse. Hashim was invariably able to put a stop to it, using his Mukhabarat identity card to threaten those who did not immediately let us pass with arrest.

During one of these walks, I expressed a wish to visit the al-Amiri hospital.

'What is of interest to you there?' Hashim asked.

'The doctor who treated me at the al-Adid is now working there, but he has disappeared.'

He smiled at me knowingly. 'So you wish to visit the doctor who arranged your private accommodation on your last visit? Perhaps you hope he will be able to do the same again?'

I realised he was teasing me.

At the hospital, we were directed to the office of the chief administrator and Hashim introduced himself as an officer of the Mukhabarat. The man responded predictably by giving us his complete and undivided attention.

Hashim explained that had been injured in an explosion during a previous visit, and went on, 'He was treated at the al-Adid by a young doctor who we have been told is now working here.'

The man, clearly agitated by our presence, was all to anxious to help.

'Yes, yes, that is not unusual. What is his name?'

'Dr Aref Hassan al-Hammed,' I said, speaking for the first time.

He was shaken by the mention of the name. 'But this man is dead. You did not know this?'

The news distressed me, though I was hardly surprised.

'If we had known he was dead, we would not be here asking after him,' Hashim snapped. 'What happened to him?

The administrator was visibly trembling, perhaps expecting to be held responsible for Aref's demise.

'He was arrested with his sister, Rana, by the Istekhabarat and accused of treating wounded members of the Resistance.'

'And was he?' Hashim asked.

'Yes, but he treated everybody. He would no sooner walk past a wounded stranger than he would his own mother.'

'Do you know for certain he is dead?' I asked, hoping he might be locked up somewhere.

'Oh, yes,' the man replied, going visibly pale with the recollection, and literally wringing his hands. 'Three days after he was arrested, his body was returned to his parents' house. He had been shot dead, but his body had been mutilated.'

'In what way?' I asked.

'His eyes were gouged out and both his hands amputated.'

'You saw this for yourself?' Hashim asked.

'Yes. His body was strung up outside his home for several days before his parents were permitted to cut him down. I saw it.'

'Is his sister dead also,' I asked.

The man shrugged. 'I do not know. She was taken to the Qasmah athletic stadium, but I think she was transferred from there to the Ne'if Centre. As far as I know, she is still there, but nobody has heard.'

Once we were outside the hospital, I asked Hashim what he knew of the Ne'if Centre.

'It used to be the Kuwaiti police headquarters, but is now the offices of the Istekhabarat.'

'I would like to go there,' I said.

'What is the point?' Hashim said testily. 'Aref is dead. Besides, of what concern is the fate of two Kuwaiti prisoners-of-war to you?'

I was not really sure. 'He treated me. I feel indebted to him. I have never met his sister, but if there is something I can do for Aref's family, I would like to do it.'

I was, of course, far more indebted to Aref than I could ever acknowledge to Hashim. He had taken on great personal risk when attempting to smuggle me from Saddam's clutches. The least I owed him were some discreet enquiries.

'I cannot allow this, Mikhaelef,' Hashim said adamantly. 'You cannot interfere in such things.'

I was not to be deterred by Hashim's disapproval. 'If you do not come with me, I will go alone.'

Reluctantly, Hashim agreed to escort me on the condition that I let him do the talking.

We found the centre in the shadow of the telecommunications tower that dominates the Kuwait City landscape.

As we approached it, we noticed that a large crane had been placed to one side, and from it hung the dead body of a Kuwaiti soldier. The centre itself, surrounded by a two metre, white wall, consisted of four blocks of office buildings placed around a large courtyard used as a car park. Hashim showed his papers to the guards and, passing rows of stacked sandbags, we entered the compound.

In the main reception building, Hashim asked to see somebody in authority and within a few minutes we were shown into the office of a man in his forties wearing the blue uniform of the Istekhabarat and holding the rank of colonel.

'How can I help you?' he asked politely, indicating two chairs placed before his desk.

In response, Hashim produced his Mukhabarat ID and asked me to remove my beard and glasses. The officer's jaw dropped and he immediately jumped to his feet, stood rigidly to attention and saluted. Before he could speak and further embarrass himself, Hashim told him to relax.

'This man is not Saddam. His name is Hassan Ibrahim al-Takriti, a cousin of our President. The likeness is remarkable, yes?'

Hashim had deliberately given me a name that would sound familiar to the officer. Saddam's family was full of Hassans and Ibrahims and they were all al-Takritis.

'Yes, yes,' the colonel stuttered in reply. 'Remarkable.'

'I am here unofficially,' Hashim went on, imposing his authority while the officer recovered his aplomb. 'But I would be grateful for your assistance. I would like to talk to one of your prisoners. Rana al-Hamid.'

'That is not possible,' the colonel answered nervously, unsure of his ground. 'No one is allowed to see the prisoners.'

'I am sure you are right,' Hashim persisted, 'but I would remind you that I am an officer of the Mukhabarat and a personal aide to the President.'

'The Mukhabarat have no authority here. You know that.'

'Yes, of course, but I am not attempting to give you an order. You are my superior in rank. I am asking for your assistance.'

'Then I am sorry. I cannot give it.'

Hashim stood up. 'Not a problem. When I am back in Baghdad, I will tell the President I was unable to carry out his orders. Come, Hassan, our colonel is a busy man.'

The colonel made a restraining gesture.

'Wait! Do not be so hasty. I am . . . I am sure the rules can be relaxed for al-Qaed al-Muhib. Who is it you want to see, did you say?'

Within minutes we were in what had once been an office, but was now being used as a prison cell. We were left alone with Aref's sister, an attractive young woman in her twenties whose hair had been roughly cut close to her scalp. She was half frightened to death by our appearance and sat in a corner of the room, her face buried in her lap. Only after several minutes coaxing was she prepared to believe we meant her no harm.

'Do you know why are you here?' Hashim asked her.

'Because I am a Kuwaiti,' she replied.

'That is not enough reason to be brought here,' Hashim said, quite sternly. 'You helped your brother treat members of the Resistance and did not report it.'

'They say I am in the Resistance, but they know very well it is a lie. My brother was arrested for treating sick Kuwaitis. Afterwards, they raided our house and I was arrested because I was there. I am here for their entertainment.' She nodded her head in the direction of the door. 'They come here and beat me. Then they rape me.'

'You have been raped?' Hashim asked, showing a rare compassion.

'Many times. But women do not have to be brought here to be raped. It is going on everywhere. Women are raped in their own homes, in front of their husbands. Then they are forced to watch as their husbands are tortured and murdered. Most of the women who are arrested are taken to the Qasmah athletic stadium. They are using that as a female prison. The swimming pool there has been converted into a huge body pit.'

'How do you know this?' I said.

'I have been there,' she said. 'When I was first arrested I was taken to the Qasmah. Then they brought me here for interrogation. There are fewer women here, so I was raped more often. If I resist, they torture me.'

'How?' Hashim asked.

'Many ways.' She pointed to an electric fan atached to the ceiling. 'They hung me naked from the fan by my hair, before it was cut, with my hands tied behind my back. They switched the fan on so that I revolved slowly around the room. Another time they wrapped one end of a length of cable around the fan and tied the other end around my breasts. They tried to lift me off the floor by my breasts. Fortunately, they are quite small and the cable kept slipping off.'

The young woman, stripped of her dignity, began to cry softly. 'I know women who have had their breasts cut off. Once they do that, it is the end. They have no use for us after that. Soon they will do this to me. I have been raped more times than I can remember, but they come to me less often now that I have the disease. There is fresh meat in the marketplace. When this happens, the only sport left to them for such as me is mutilation.'

It seemed to me that, much as we sympathised with her plight, there was nothing we could do to alleviate it. But Hashim surprised me when we returned to the colonel before leaving.

'That woman is innocent of any charges of conspiracy against Iraq,' he said firmly.

'They are all innocent,' the officer replied, and would have yawned if Hashim had been of lesser status. 'If you believe them, that is.'

Hashim would not be deflected. 'When I return to the presidential palace in Baghdad, I will tell Saddam you are holding an innocent woman here. I know the President. He will telephone you personally and ask if what I say is true.

It would be better for you if you can say that she was found to be innocent and has been released.'

The colonel looked distinctly unimpressed by Hashim's implied threats, but had enough wit about him not to call his bluff.

'I will look into her case personally,' he said. 'If she is innocent, she will be released.'

Once we were back in the street, I looked at Hashim with considerable admiration.

'I am impressed. And a little surprised. Do you think he will release her?'

'Probably. He has nothing to gain by holding her any longer and, in his own mind at least, much to lose if he does not.'

'Do you really intend to report it to the President?' I asked.

Hashim regarded me with a patronising smile. 'Your innocence is amusing, Mikhaelef. To be honest, I believe that Saddam is indifferent to innocent Kuwaiti women being treated this way. But during such times, he is not about to tell his security services to go around making jokes with the local populace. He needs the Mukhabarat, the Amn al-Khas and the Istekhabarat to be greatly feared. He would regard events here as being an unfortunate consequence of what has to be done.' His eyes narrowed, a sign he was about to become deadly earnest. 'I must ask you to tell nobody what you have seen and heard here today.'

I agreed without hesitation. 'Of course, but why did you go to such lengths to help her?'

'Because I am a fool, perhaps, who listens too much to the romantic notions of an incurable idealist.' His eyes sparkled mischievously. 'If I am to be honest with you, I also enjoy a little sport with our friends in the Istekhabarat.'

My respect and indeed liking for Hashim increased tenfold.

Following a visit to Moscow by Tariq, Saddam

announced the progressive withdrawal of troops from Kuwait. President Bush, by this time determined to have his war, insisted the process be completed within a week. Saddam rejected this as impractical and on 23 February, as good as his word, Bush launched the ground war against the Iraqi occupying forces. As Saddam prepared the Iraqi people for *Um Alma Arik*, the Mother of all Battles, at least 5,000 Kuwaiti civilians, perhaps many more, were already dead.

As Coalition troops poured across the Saudi border, it was clear that the end of the occupation was days rather than weeks away. Three days after the ground war started, Saddam ordered a complete unconditional evacuation of Iraqi forces from Kuwait.

The presidential office had ensured that Hashim received notice of the withdrawal before the general order was given out, and within twenty minutes of receiving it we were heading north on the Kuwait to al-Basrah motorway. And not a moment too soon. Stopping in al-Basrah to stretch our legs, we heard reports that the evacuation was turning into a rout.

The six-lane motorway behind us was heavily congested with our retreating army when the US air force arrived over Mutlah Ridge, near az-Zubayr, and attacked with rockets and cluster bombs for several hours. In desperation, many vehicles drove off the road and tried to pass the carnage by driving on the sand, only to be blown up by the hidden, impenetrable system of landmines laid by the Iraqi army in the build up to the invasion. For a stretch of five kilometres, the road was strewn with the remains of tanks, trucks, and an assortment of commandeered vehicles. Thousands of Iraqi soldiers died, many burned alive in their vehicles. As the Coalition army swept north across the Shamiya Desert, the Baghdad road was cut off and those not already dead surrendered with little resistance.

Although the Gulf War was clearly lost, Saddam remained in power and *Baghdad Radio* broadcast claims of a 'glorious victory'. This assertion was ridiculed in the West, for the Iraqi army had been comprehensively defeated. As if to underline the fact, Coalition aircraft flew over Baghdad on the first Sunday following the ceasefire, breaking the sound barrier on five occasions.

To many Arabs, Iraq deserved praise for standing against 'The Great Satan', but although the nation had survived, at least 90,000 Iraqis were killed during the Gulf War. Although fewer than 1,000 of these people were civilians, even those Arabs who opposed the rule of Saddam felt no inclination to celebrate a Coalition victory. Condemnation of the in the Middle East was as universal as it had ever been.

Although the figures were never released in the national press, as many as 170,000 Iraqi soldiers were taken prisoner of war. In contrast, only about sixty members of the Coalition forces, mostly airmen shot down over Baghdad, were captured. Within days of the war ending, they were released. I also learned that Ian Richter, the British businessman jailed for illegal dealings with Samir Mohammed in 1986, was allowed to return home, having served just five years of his twenty year sentence.

President Bush announced to the world that the Coalition had done its job and insisted that Iraqis themselves eject their 'evil dictator'. Sectarian fighting had started in al-Basrah, a full month before the ground offensive began and, by the time I passed through the city on the way back from Kuwait, government authority was in retreat. The revolt quickly spread to other cities in the south, including al-Najaf, Nasiriya, Kut and my home town of Karbala.

In the north, the story was the same. The cities of Sulaimaniya, Kirkuk, Arbil, Amadiya and Tuz fell to the Kurdish rebels as a huge popular uprising swept the region. Louis was able to confirm that American and British special forces were active in the area, inciting insurrection. Amid the mutinous euphoria, the Kurds began a process of formulating their own independent state, believing Saddam was as good as overthrown.

At the peak of the rebellion, fourteen of the eighteen provinces of Iraq were outside of Saddam's control, the exceptions being Baghdad, Mawsil, Deyala and Romadi. The world waited for Saddam to fall, but he was busy re-deploying his forces. Suspecting the ground war might be fought on the streets of Baghdad as well as Kuwait, Saddam had held back more than twenty Republican Guard divisions around central Iraq. Substantial numbers had also been withdrawn from Kuwait and southern Iraq prior to the commencement of the ground war. Once they were mobilised, the retribution was merciless.

In the north, Sulaimaniya, Kirkuk and Tuz were re-covered by Saddam's forces and were accompanied by mass executions and expulsions. People fleeing the towns were attacked by helicopters using napalm. Troops raided the hospitals in search of wounded peshmerga rebels. Those they found, they threw through the windows, finish-ing off any who survived the fall with a bullet to the brain. Innocent women and children were also butchered. In Kirkuk, fifty women and thirty children were murdered at the Saddam Hussein Hospital, some having their throats slit as they lay in their beds. Indiscriminate artillery fire poured into the towns, killing thousands. Tens of thousands were physically and brutally evicted from their homes, which were then destroyed. The persecuted Kurds fled across the mountains to Turkey and Iran and harrow-ing television pictures of the massive exodus that followed flashed around the world. As many as 20,000 Kurds were killed.

Even this, however, did not compare with the horrors that took place in the south. In suppressing the uprising, Saddam's forces sought to eliminate huge sections of the Shi'a community. Tanks were emblazoned with the slogan: 'No more Shi'a'. As well as the mass executions, people were killed in their homes. Women were gang-raped then killed. Any area was deemed a potential haven of Shi'a rebels, and women and children were tortured until they revealed the location of their menfolk. In al-Basrah, children were forced inside petroleum-soaked tyres which were lit and sent rolling along the street.

Once the rebellion had been routed, Saddam's forces began destroying the mosques and cultural institutions of the Shi'a. The holy shrines of al-Najaf and Karbala were looted and defaced. Shi'a clergyman and religious scholars were arrested and executed. The total number of people murdered during this period is incalculable, but has been *conservatively* estimated to be in excess of 400,000 men, women and children. Despite the fact that such a scale of genocide had not been witnessed since the Holocaust of the second world war, the victorious UN forces of Operation Desert Storm stood back.

General Hassan Ali al-Hakim, Commander of the Iraqi Air Force, had approached the Americans and proffered his willingness to take part in moves to topple Saddam. He asked that his helicopter gunships, grounded since the end of the war, be allowed to fly in the south to move medical and military supplies between Baghdad and al-Basrah. This, he told them, would enable him to gather his forces against Saddam. The Americans agreed.

In reality, al-Hakim had been sent by Saddam. Once the UN allowed the Iraqi helicopters into the air, over 200 in number, they bombed and gunned the people of southern Iraq from Baghdad to the Kuwaiti border. This was followed by missile attacks and ground-force offensives. In Baghdad, the predominantly Shi'a districts of al-Saura and al-Shulah were attacked without mercy. My father's home town, al-Kadhimia, on the northern perimeter of the city was devastated by rocket fire.

The rebellion in the south had been a spontaneous reaction of the people against Saddam in the wake of the Gulf War, but it was without co-ordinated leadership. Once Saddam unleashed the horrors of his armoury upon them, they were all but wiped out. When the Americans woke up to the duplicity of al-Hakim, they immediately imposed a No Fly Zone, but by then it was too late. By the end of March, the rebellion was over in southern Iraq and Saddam's victory was complete.

In the north, enormous international publicity was given to the plight of 600,000 Kurds crowding onto the mountains, where the UN established a Safe Haven. In March, the Americans imposed another No Fly Zone and the Kurds were able to declare a Liberation Zone (LZ), which survives to this day. The area is a crescent shape in the north and east, following the borders with Turkey and Iran from Zakhu in the north to al-Salaimaniya in the east. In April, the Kurds gained control of Arbil, but there has been stalemate since. Saddam suffers the existence of the LZ only because he has no choice. Both his ground and aerial forces are prevented from entering the zone. He vows, however, to return one day.

In May, the recently-formed United Nations Special Commission (UNSCOM) for decommissioning all non-conventional weaponry within Iraq, paid the first of its myriad visits to Baghdad. The UN had passed Resolution 687, which re-established Kuwaiti sovereignty and demanded the dismantling of Iraq's weapons of mass destruction (WMDs) and UNSCOM officials arrived to regulate and enforce it.

Rolf Ekeus, chairman of UNSCOM, was to oversee the removal of 'all chemical and biological and all stocks of agents and all related subsystems,' in addition to 'all ballistic missiles with a range greater than 150 kilometres'. He was further ordered to ensure that Iraq could not 'acquire or develop nuclear weapons'. His brief certainly represented the most wide-ranging inspection programme ever imposed on a member nation of the UN, and Iraq was given just forty-five days to make all WMDs, and their locations, available to UNSCOM. Saddam argued that the time scale was unrealistic. What he really meant was that he could not relocate missiles to where the inspectors would not find them, or bury VX warheads in the Iraqi sand within a mere six-and-a-half weeks.

Eventually, the UN was provided with a 'complete'

list of the specified weaponry. Few officials believed it. Saddam designated five nerve gas producing factories and five depots where bombs and shells fitted with chemical warheads were stored. All had been destroyed by Coalition bombing during the war. Saddam also listed substantial stockpiles of chemical weapons: 6,620 chemically fitted shells for 122mm artillery, hundreds of tons of various nerve gas products and 134 missiles with chemical warheads. The UN, assisted by American satellite intelligence, returned to Saddam insisting on a more comprehensive list, but in the event, few further particulars were forthcoming.

By July, Bush was talking in terms of a resumption of aerial bombing if Iraq did not co-operate, but no real progress was made until September when information, which Saddam assumed had been given to the CIA by an Iraqi defector, was passed on to the UN. A few days later, UNSCOM officials converged on the Social Insurance Department of the Ministry of Labour in Khulani Square and seized a large number of files. As they left the building, they were detained and five days passed, after government officials had catalogued the files, before they were permitted to take them away.

By this time, the Americans were in the process of extinguishing the 700 Kuwaiti oil wells torched by Iraq in the last days of the war. The UN passed Resolution 706 which permitted the sale of $1.6 billion of Iraqi oil, to be spent under UN supervision on humanitarian aid for Iraqi people. The revenue from any oil exports beyond this was subject to considerable deductions to pay for war reparations, including the cost of reopening the oil wells, and the UNSCOM monitoring process. Saddam demanded that reparations be suspended for five years and wanted the permitted oil revenue raised to $65 billion per annum, rising to $214 billion in five years when reparations could commence. Anything less, he maintained, would ruin the Iraqi economy beyond repair. The UN were unmoved and Iraqi oil stayed in the ground.

UNSCOM then reported that Iraq's stock of chemical

weapons was far more abundant than the UN had realised and would take at least two years to destroy. The sanctions imposed on Iraq after the invasion of Kuwait were not lifted during this period. Notwithstanding my hostility to Saddam, it angered me that the ordinary people of Iraq, especially children and the aged, would have to suffer and die as a consequence of the UN's inability to impose its will on Saddam.

On my return home, a cactus plant awaited me at the front door and the following day I met up with Latif. I told him about Sophie. Although I had been married to his sister, he was pleased to hear I had found somebody else and promised he would do whatever he could to have her freed.

'We need to communicate in a more covert way, though, Mikhaelef,' he added. 'It is too great a risk that we arrange to meet in the open, as we do.'

I suggested using public telephones, but Latif dismissed the idea.

'We can never be sure which telephones are not tapped. Do you have a friend living outside Baghdad you could trust? Somebody you could visit who would not attract suspicion?'

'Yes,' I answered promptly. 'In my home town of Karbala. But I would be reluctant to involve him in anything of this nature.'

'Only you need know his identity. If he will help, give him this telephone number. Ask him to call the number once a week and ask if there is a message for . . .'

Latif hesitated, thinking of an appropriate name to use.

'The cactus?' I suggested.

'No. I like the idea and perhaps we can use that for another purpose, but it is too obviously a code. We will simply call you "a friend from Karbala". Tell him never to telephone you unless he has received a message stating I need to see you. The next evening, come here at sunset. You will be collected and brought to me. We will change the pick-up point each time we meet.'

He then returned to the subject of Sophie.

'In the next few days, a package will be delivered to your home. It will contain a phial, the contents of which you must empty into a drink to give to her on your next meeting. It will give her the symptoms of food poisoning, but the dose is fairly harmless. She will recover quite quickly.'

'What is it?' I asked.

'Salmonella paratyphoid.'

'Paratyphoid?' I said, alarmed. 'That could kill her!'

'Not in such a minute dose, but it will be enough to have her transferred to a hospital. From there we will find it much easier to arrange her escape. Do not worry, Mikhaelef. We have used it many times.'

The plan worked to perfection. Three days after I had laced her drink, Sophie broke out in a rash of rose-coloured spots and complained of severe headaches and diarrhoea. She was admitted to the Saddam Hussein General Hospital as an ordinary patient and within twenty-four hours Latif and a friend walked her out with ridiculous ease. I met up with them at the friend's apartment and was allowed to spend one precious night with my beloved; she was to be smuggled over the border into Saudi Arabia the following day.

She would soon recover from the mild paratyphoid infection, but the psychological damage caused by the brutality of her ordeal at the hands of the Mukhabarat was not so easy to eradicate. She would need expert help and much patience. In the immediate aftermath of her decampment from the hospital though, she was surprisingly coherent, and as we lay side-by-side on the narrow bed, she talked freely, unloading the horror of her experience.

'I was transferred from the prison in Hai al-Tashriya to the Mukhabarat's al-Hahkimiya prison on 52nd Street, opposite the Passport Office. Do you know it, Mikhaelef?'

Indeed I did. This was the same place I had been imprisoned for two miserable days four years earlier.

'It is a huge, dark place,' Sophie continued. 'I was taken to one of the lower floors and placed in a small cell with about fifty other women and some children. I was bound and blindfolded, as was everyone else. We could hear the screams of those being tortured in nearby cells and the ranting of the torturers. When the interrogators were exhausted from their work they would play tapes of people screaming. There was no end to it. They played the tapes all night.'

I had no desire to hear this but refrained from saying so. I assumed it was good therapy for Sophie to talk about it, so I squeezed her hand and murmured words of comfort in her ear.

'In the morning,' she went on, 'a guard took me from the cell to be interviewed. I cannot describe the terror of it. In the room there were two other women already there, with four guards standing around. Both of the women were naked. One was lying curled on the floor, barely conscious. The other was seated on a wooden chair, crying. The woman on the floor was perhaps in her thirties, but the other woman was no more than a girl, perhaps sixteen or seventeen.

Sophie closed her eyes, the dreadful reality of it all burned into her memory. Small beads of sweat ran from her forehead to her cheeks.

'I was told to raise my arms and did so, but almost immediately I was punched in my right breast. As I stumbled backwards, I was punched by another guard in the kidneys and fell to the floor onto my hands and knees. I was kicked several times, then they dragged me to my feet and stood me by the wall. One of the guards came over to me and called me "an American whore and a piece of shit". He spat in my face.

'The woman on the floor was thrown onto a table on her back like a piece of meat for carving. A wire was clamped to her right nipple and she was given electric shocks for perhaps two minutes. She was then raped, but I don't think she really knew what was going on. When the guard had finished, she was rolled off the table back onto the floor. The rapist left the room laughing and another guard took his place. The teenage girl was then made to stand up and was dragged to the wall opposite where I was standing. One of the guards leaned back against the wall and pushed her down onto her hands and knees. While she was forced to perform oral sex, another guard raped her from behind. Then it was my turn.'

She stopped talking for a moment and took some water from the cup I had passed her.

'I was told that because I was American they had some special services for me to perform. They said they had heard all about American women. I was told to undress. When I showed reluctance, I was slapped or punched. Once I was naked, I was laid out on the table on my back and tied to it by my wrists and ankles. One of the guards raped me while the other three urinated on my face. When he was finished, my feet were untied and I was turned over. I was then buggered by each of the other three guards in turn. When they were finished, they told me to get dressed. As I struggled to my feet, I noticed the teenager was already dressed and she was helping the other woman with her clothes. We were taken back to the cell, but nobody there spoke to us. For any woman, such treatment is the ultimate degradation, but for Moslem women it is worse. They do not feel anger, only deep shame and disgrace.'

Sophie began to weep softly. I felt she wept for the women who were with her as much as she did for herself.

'This kind of treatment went on every day. One time I was in that room with a mother and her twelve-year-old daughter. They each had to watch as the other was raped. A baby boy was burnt with cigarette butts until his mother betrayed the whereabouts of her husband. There were things that happened in there, Mikhaelef, that I am not capable of repeating to you, but I know that I would kill myself rather than go back.'

'Do not say such things, my love,' I soothed.

She looked up at me with fire in her eyes.

'If they find me, I will kill myself.' I had no doubt she meant what she said.

She finally fell into a fitful sleep and although I held and caressed her, she woke up frequently during the night, screaming and sweating. In the morning, we delayed our parting for as long as we could and promised to meet up again as soon as I could leave Iraq. Two days later, she was smuggled over the Saudi border and taken in by Communist Party members in Riyadh.

Once again we were separated. We were not destined to be re-united for six long, lonely years.

Chapter Fourteen

1992
Jumaada al-Thaany 1412 – Rajab 1413

In the weeks that followed, I lived in dread that I would be connected with Sophie's escape. I went to the palace each day expecting at any moment to be hauled away to prison, torture and a miserable lingering death. When, after a month, nothing had happened to me, I wondered if I was deliberately being left at large in the hope that I would lead the authorities to my associates. I also recalled the way Adnan Khairallah was killed and whenever I climbed into a vehicle I was terrified it would blow up. My paranoia deepened and the risk of being killed when standing in for Saddam faded into insignificance by comparison.

During these days of uncertainty, I swung from a state of staunch resilience to one of quivering dread. At times I was consumed with the desire to avenge Amna and the children, but the cold truth was that it was against my nature. I lacked courage, but I did have nerve. If I berate myself for jumping at shadows and the ease with which Saddam was able to intimidate me, I know of few men who could have behaved normally in the face of the mental pressures I had to endure. Latif recognised this, I am sure. He was always reluctant to actively involve me in his conspiracies, but he never disowned me.

Often I wondered whether Hashim was aware of my treason. Of late he had been less communicative than usual, which was an indication that I was out of favour with Saddam and he wished to distance himself from me. I had grown fond of Hashim over the years and, though we were never as close as I had been with Mohammed Qutaibi, a friendship had developed between us that I valued. His reticence worried me and I could bear it no longer.

'Something is bothering you, Hashim,' I prompted. 'What is it?'

'Nothing,' he replied, not meeting my eyes. 'I am fine.'

'You are not fine. I know you well enough.'

He did not immediately respond and I feared the worst.

'I received a telephone call last night,' he said finally. 'It was bad news.'

I was taking everything personally by now and instantly assumed I was the subject of the information he had received.

'Bad news?' I asked with great trepidation.

'My father is dying,' he stated flatly.

The relief that swept over me was shaming, engendered as it was by Hashim's misfortune. Naturally, I felt sorry for him, well remembering the pain of my own father's demise, but I was indeed glad not to be the cause of his dolour.

'My sister called to say he has only days to live,' he went on. 'I will be travelling home later today.'

Home for Hashim was al-Musayib, a small town I knew quite well, as it was only twenty-five kilometres from Karbala.

'I am sorry to make you speak of it, Hashim,' I said. 'It was clumsy of me. I grieve for you.'

'Not at all, my friend,' he said, standing and walking towards me. 'You have reminded me there is something I wished to ask you before I leave.'

The 'something' was a provisional invitation to his father's funeral. Much to my surprise as I had never met his father or any members of his family. There was no obvious reason for me to attend.

I made a token protest. 'Surely my presence would be an unwelcome distraction. A man who so closely resembles the President might disrupt the quiet dignity of the service.'

'I would like you to come,' Hashim responded keenly. 'My father was very proud that his eldest son worked in the presidential palace, but I think few of his friends believed him. It would mean a lot to my mother if she saw you there. Nobody need know you are Mikhaelef Ramadan.'

'You wish me to come as Saddam?' I said, startled. 'I am afraid it is not as easy as that, Hashim. I can only impersonate the President on his authority. If I were to be seen attending your father's funeral when Saddam was known to be elsewhere, it could have serious repercussions.'

'Perhaps you could ask him. He might have no objections.'

It occurred to me I could use the funeral as an opportunity to see Abdullah Yunis in Karbala with Saddam's blessing. Accordingly, I arranged to see Saddam later in the day. He was in the company of several ministers and inclined to be receptive. He readily agreed to my attending the funeral and then travelling on to Karbala as him.

'It is appropriate,' he said, to the approving nods of his sycophantic cabinet, 'for the President to be seen attending the funerals of ordinary citizens who suffer the privations imposed upon us by our enemies. However, you should be incognito when you go to Karbala.'

Despite the world view of Saddam as a man prone to uncontrollable, violent outbursts, I always found him remarkably consistent in his behaviour towards others. He has a mood and a style to suit each occasion. Being introverted by nature, it is only when speaking in public that the real fire in his belly flares up.

When in the company of foreign statesmen, Saddam is always subdued and pensive, his expression brooding. Some of the more eloquent observers have likened his demeanour to that of a stalking tiger, a view it suits him to cultivate.

In the company of his own ministers and staff, Saddam is more open, more expansive. He is generally quite amicable and of good humour, but he maintains a hint of enough menace to command respect. He rarely resorts to ranting. The occasion I was lambasted for 'disappearing' in Kuwait was the only occasion he ever lost his temper in my presence.

Two days after my talk with Hashim, I arrived at the palace in the morning to be told that his father had died in the early hours and I was to leave for al-Musayib immediately.

Turning up at the home of Hashim's parents, with an entourage appropriate to my supposed status, I was welcomed by his mother and numerous sisters. They made an enormous fuss of my presence, despite being naturally quite devastated by their loss, and spoke of the 'great honour' to the memory of Hashim's father. Apparently his death had been unexpected until he fell ill a few days ago, and his loss was therefore all the more devastating.

The men of the family were washing down the body at the mosque half-a-kilometre from the house and I was told to be at the *mejehna*, the cemetery, for eleven o'clock. It is traditional in Arab countries for the dead to be buried on the day they die, but generally the women of the family do not attend the burial. At the *mejehna*, Hashim, with his brothers and uncles, was already there and I kept a respectful distance with my escort while Hashim's father, wrapped in white linen sheets, was lowered into the ground, his head directed south, towards Makkah. I wondered if any of those present were Hashim's friends in the Mukhabarat, but there was no way of telling. They are trained to go unnoticed.

I returned to the house and the family who, in true Arab

tradition, would be in mourning for a full Hijri year. After a few minutes, Hashim pulled me away from his grief-stricken mother to another room where we sat alone. His sister brought us tea and left us together.

'My father's death is painful,' Hashim said, after a few moments.

'I know how you feel, Hashim,' I replied. 'My own father died seventeen years ago, but we were very close. I miss him still.'

Hashim was understandably subdued, but I sensed he had pulled me to one side for a purpose. There were matters he could discuss with me that he could share with no one else. Even his brothers knew little of his life in the Mukhabarat.

'My father was a proud, decent man. It troubles me that he will now be aware of the many things I have done.'

'What have you done, Hashim?'

'I am an officer of the Mukhabarat, Mikhaelef. I have done many things that dishonour me and the memory of my father.'

'I doubt you can shock me,' I said truthfully. 'If it eases your burden, I am prepared to listen.'

'I would not know where to begin,' he admitted. 'For instance, there was an occasion some eight or nine years ago, about a year before I was transferred to the palace. I was with a Mukhabarat unit responsible for the interrogation of two Kurds when we were looking for the perpetrators of an attempt on Saddam's life. We had no idea if the two men were responsible, but we had reliable information that they could tell us who was. I was with one of the men when he was tied flat to a board and slowly immersed into a bath of sulphuric acid.'

I knew only too well what effect such an experience could have on a man, but it surprised me to hear that a hardened member of the Mukhabarat like Hashim had not recovered from it.

'As his feet, then his legs disappeared,' Hashim continued, 'it was all we could do to understand his gabbling, but I swear he told us everything. He screamed out the names of several conspirators, but it did him no good. When the acid reached his genitals, the rope was lowered more slowly, to be sure he was not withholding anything. In the end, he passed out before he died.'

I sensed that Hashim had never spoken of this incident before. It made me aware of how deeply he was moved by his father's passing. The loss of my own father had affected me too in ways that surprised me. The desolation and sense of loss had overwhelmed me for several weeks, and for the best part of a year I was completely unable to adjust to his absence from my life. I became excessively self-critical and to this day I carry the guilt of never having provided him with a grandson in his lifetime. Although nothing in my past approached Hashim's demons, I was nevertheless able to empathise with the soul-searching process he was going through. I tried to reassure him.

'How many times have you told me the means justify the ends?' I reminded him.

'That is easy to say, Mikhaelef. I feel my father looks down on me with contempt. I can feel it – here.' He thumped his chest.

'What will you do? You can hardly leave the Mukhabarat.'

'No. I would be suspected of a thousand conspiracies. I do not know what I will do.'

I believed his remorse was genuine, but I forbore to utter the platitudes that would ease his burden. In a sense, I felt that for him to suffer a little, and repent his sins, would not be such a bad thing. Perhaps also, I might be able to further his repentance.

'We will talk of this again, Hashim,' I said. 'It is possible I can help you ease your conscience. For now, return to your family. I have to go to Karbala.'

I had called Abdullah earlier in the day. When I arrived, we embraced and kissed each other on both cheeks. My visit coincided with my fiftieth birthday, a fact I had kept to myself. To my surprise and embarrassment, the occasion had not been forgotten by Abdullah, and he made a great fuss. His son Sa'dun's birthday was the day before mine and thus his birthday always reminded Abdullah of mine. Sa'dun had been dead seven years, but his loss had taken its toll on Abdullah and his wife. They had both aged considerably.

Alone with Abdullah that evening, I briefly related to him much of what had happened since we had last met, then quickly came to the object of my visit.

'What do you think of Saddam Hussein?' I enquired of him.

'What kind of a question is that, Miklef?' Abdullah answered smiling. 'I think he is wonderful!'

The whiff of sarcasm in his voice encouraged me to proceed.

'I have to tell you something, Abdullah, that is in the strictest confidence. You must never repeat what I am about to say to you.'

'You insult me if you think I would ever betray your confidence, Miklef.'

I nodded in acknowledgement of this rebuke and said, 'For some years now I have been working against Saddam.'

'In the name of Allah!' Abdullah exclaimed, utterly taken aback. 'It is not true!'

'It is true. I am working with people whose sole purpose in life is to assassinate Saddam. Obviously, I cannot reveal to you who they are.'

'Of course, but your brothers-in-law must be among them, Miklef. They are the only names you could give me I would recognise.'

I sighed with exasperation. Obviously Abdullah was better equipped for the game of espionage than I was, though his astuteness did not really surprise me. Some years earlier he had voiced his suspicions of the al-Rabaka family.

'Of the al-Rabaka brothers, only Latif is still alive. You must come to your own conclusions as to why, Abdullah.'

He was quick to reassure me. 'Your worries are groundless. Your secret is safe. I am no disciple of Saddam Hussein.' He pondered for a moment, before asking, 'Why are you telling me this now? You must have a reason.'

I hesitated before answering. 'I need someone who can act as a messenger for me. There is more than an element of risk involved and I will never mention it again if you feel you cannot or should not help. Nor,' I added wryly, 'will I blame you.'

'What do you mean – a messenger? What would you want me to do?'

'I would give you a telephone number to call once a week. You would ask if there is a message for your friend in Karbala. If there is no message, you do nothing and call again a week later. If they say there is a message, you say nothing and hang up. You then call me and talk as we have done in the past. Give me no details. If you only call me when there is a message, I will know that I have to be at a certain place the following day.'

'That is all?' he said, as if he had been expecting something much more demanding.

'That is all. It is best if that remains the full extent of your knowledge. And be assured, I will be the only person who knows who you are by name.'

'I will do it, Miklef, but you worry me. Are you sure you wish to be involved in this?'

'I am sure, Abdullah. It is for Amna and the children.'

He stared at me, then dropped his eyes. Now he understood.

A few days later, I was alone with Saddam in his study when he finally raised the subject of Sophie's escape. He had been railing bitterly against what he saw as America's manipulation of UN policy when he stopped suddenly in mid-flow.

'Whatever happened to that American woman?' he fired at me, a severe frown on his face.

'Which American woman?' I said ingenuously, knowing quite well he was referring to Sophie.

'The one you shacked-up with in Kuwait. She was brought here. Where is she now?'

Was it possible he had never been informed of her escape? I hardly dared to hope.

'I have no idea, Saddam,' I answered. 'The last I heard of her she was very ill and rushed to hospital.'

Saddam genuinely seemed to have no recollection of the incident.

'What was wrong with her?'

'I do not know. She had a mysterious illness and was taken for treatment.'

'Did she die?'

'Perhaps, Saddam. Would you like me to make enquiries?'

He raised his eyebrows with indifference. To Saddam, it was a matter to which he attached little weight.

'No, there is no need. It is of no consequence.'

From that day the subject was never raised again. It did cause me to wonder what could have happened to the normally impeccable system of security that exists around Saddam, but I came to no firm conclusions. As Sophie had been held in the palace, she was not the direct responsibility of any of the security services. When she disappeared from hospital, those responsible may have been too frightened to report it. During the weeks following the end of the Gulf War, the hospitals were inundated with casualties, and administration must have been chaotic. Alternatively, perhaps Latif had paid for silence. Whatever the circumstances, it was a stroke of luck for which I was grateful.

One amusing episode during this otherwise unamusing period occurred after Tariq Aziz came to see me one morning as I sat with Hashim. He raised the subject of my sister's husband, Akram. I saw little of Akram, which was no loss, and I rarely spoke of him, so it intrigued me when Tariq brought up his name. Tariq had relinquished his position as foreign minister, but he was still very much in favour and remained one of Saddam's staunchest ministers.

Akram had contrived to attach himself to Tariq shortly
after my appointment as Saddam's understudy and had
steadfastly stayed with him ever since. His position as safe
as it could be, inasmuch as any position was safe as long as
Saddam remained in charge.

'How close are you to Akram Salem?' Tariq asked me,
unconcerned by Hashim's presence.

'I seldom see him, Tariq,' I answered. 'But he is my
brother-in-law, so I know him fairly well. Why?'

'Oh, it is nothing really, but I thought perhaps you could
talk to him for me.'

The idea was captivating, though I kept a straight face.
Tariq was not Saddam, but it was still wise to tread with
caution in his presence.

'I do not think he would listen to me,' I said, without
regret. 'But perhaps if you explain to me what you wish me
to talk to him about . . .'

Tariq seemed have some difficulty with this.

'Well,' he said at length, 'I do not think anybody could
question your brother-in-law's loyalty, but in a way that is
the problem. At times, he is . . . well, too loyal. Too
everything, if you understand my meaning.'

I smiled encouragingly. I well understood that Tariq was
testing the water with me and in that respect I was able to
put his mind at rest.

'I understand perfectly what you are saying, Tariq.
Personally, I find his company trying and do my best to
avoid him. Feel free to talk frankly about him. I will not be
offended and it will go no further.'

He appeared relieved. 'At times, I wonder who is the
deputy prime minister – Akram or me. He is exceptionally
arrogant. I do not wish to be rid of him, as I know he is
married to your sister and he does have some uses, but I
must find a way to keep him quiet. He has too much to say
and it is rarely worth listening to.'

'I will speak to him, Tariq.'

Once Tariq had left, I joked with Hashim and we
agreed to have some fun at Akram's expense. I sent word

for him to come and see me in the Dark Room and an hour later he turned up in his usual forthright and impatient manner.

'What is it you wish to see me about, Mikhaelef,' he said abruptly. 'I am very busy.'

It was Hashim who stood up to greet him.

'Please sit down, Akram. I asked Mikhaelef to send for you.'

Akram knew Hashim was an officer of the Mukhabarat. His loftiness evaporated as he sat down meekly.

'You will no doubt agree,' Hashim said, 'that the security of our President is always our foremost consideration.'

'But, of course,' Akram replied, in all innocence.

'Well, it has been brought to my attention that a government official formerly with the foreign office is working for the Americans.'

'What?' Akram blurted. He could not have been more astonished had Hashim told him American Marines were in the grounds of the palace.

'Personally, I do not believe it,' Hashim went on. 'Nevertheless, it must be investigated. This intelligence has been passed on to me because I spend so much time here at the palace.'

He paused and stood before Akram, looking forbidding, as befit an officer of the Mukhabarat. It was a superb piece of play acting.

'I would like your co-operation, Akram Salem. I need someone who I know I can trust implicitly. I believe I can trust you.'

'Of course!' Akram gushed. 'Of course!'

'Good. The person we are looking for is said to be excessively confident in his manner. He has too much to say and is unpleasantly self-opinionated, always giving advice, always right. Do you know of such a person, Akram?'

He made a show of pondering, an exaggerated frown creasing his brow. Finally, he shook his head.

'No, Hashim,' he said, with a nervous grin. 'I can think of nobody.'

'It is of no importance,' Hashim said. 'But I would appreciate your vigilance. If you come across such a person, you must let me know.'

Akram nodded frantically.

The one potential flaw in the game we played was that Hashim might be pestered by Akram whenever somebody raised their voice in his presence, in an effort to ingratiate himself and divert suspicion. Hashim had anticipated this.

'Please only come back to me if you have something worth looking at,' Hashim told him in an earnest voice. 'I will be displeased if you send me chasing after a succession of people who prove to be completely innocent.'

Akram left and we laughed for several minutes afterwards.

'I am grateful,' Hashim said, 'that it is you who is so like the President and not your brother-in-law.'

I telephoned Tariq a few days later and asked him if Akram's behaviour had improved.

'I do not know what you said to him, Mikhaelef,' he said, followed by a small chuckle, 'but it has worked to perfection. Akram has been as quiet as a mouse!'

During the year several attempts were made on the life of Saddam. As I was now seldom in contact with Latif, I was never sure which of them were at his instigation. Following the war, the number of illicit weapons on the streets had increased and the incidence of gun attacks increased in proportion. This encouraged me to be especially careful that whenever I stood in for the Saddam, the cactus came out of the window. It was a system that continued to serve me well.

Saddam was not injured in any of the three attempts on his life, though he was lucky to survive them all. Once, when he was being driven along Palestine Street in Baghdad, a genuine road traffic accident just ahead brought the presidential motorcade to a halt. Any such incidents are viewed with deep suspicion by Saddam's security guards and the motorcade immediately went into reverse. The ambush party were actually laying in wait some two hundred metres further along the road. They opened fire on the rapidly receding vehicles, but the distance was too great for accuracy. Two bodyguards were killed and several more wounded; the President escaped unscathed.

Another attempted ambush occurred a few weeks later and failed due to one of the assailants losing his nerve and opening fire before Saddam's car was properly in the target area. Saddam lost another bodyguard, but they are as replaceable as fleas.

The third attempt took place in al-Basrah and was almost certainly the work of the al-Da'wa, the Shi'a resistance group. Saddam was visiting the Ba'ath party offices and was preparing to leave when a bomb exploded in the entrance. Three men and a woman were killed and more than twenty people injured, but Saddam, of course, survived. One of the dead men was reported as having a passing resemblance to Saddam, and it is quite possible he was one of the establishment of ten or twelve doubles. Although I never stood in for Saddam in Kuwait, the idea of having doubles in different places had appealed to him, and it is possible the dead man was placed in al-Basrah with that in mind.

Iraq having been so comprehensively routed by the allied forces the previous year it was both a surprise and a relief to Saddam that the UN, or more pointedly the US, did not interfere with the country's internal problems. Now and again Saddam would send for me for the sole purpose of airing his views on the Western world in general and the US in particular. He seemed to enjoy using me as a kind of sounding board, though to get a word in edgewise was quite a challenge.

One afternoon I entered his study to find him on the telephone, speaking, it transpired, to Tariq Aziz. He was smiling broadly and as he listened his smile was transformed into a storm of laughter. On replacing the handset, he did not hesitate to give me the details.

The story was that Tariq had just returned from the Abu Ghraib prison. A delegation from the UN had demanded to see the conditions there, and Tariq was happy to oblige them personally. Of course, he escorted them around the criminal block, not the "Re-education" complex where dissidents are kept. Inside, a number of prisoners began to jeer at them. Within a minute, hundreds of convicts were hissing and booing at the delegation.

'Can you imagine it?' Saddam clapped his hands in delight. 'How I wish I had been there!'

Such was Saddam's elation, he sent notification through to the prison governor that every prisoner who took part in the special 'welcome committee' should have their sentence halved.

He was ever scathing in his criticism of the UN Security Council. He believed the UN was criminally inconsistent in the implementation of its resolutions and had succumbed to US pressure when authorising the 'liberation' of Kuwait.

'The US have no interest in the welfare of a nation's people,' he complained. 'If they did, they would not continue to enforce the sanctions which are killing ordinary Iraqis every day. They declared war on Iraq, because we were too strong. No other reason.' He pounded the desk. Pens rattled. 'Israel has many times been the subject of UN Security Council resolutions demanding their withdrawal from the Golan Heights of Syria, the West Bank of Palestine and southern Lebanon. Those damned Jews have ignored them all and the UN has done nothing about it.'

It was a subject that invariably inflamed his passion. Once launched, he would talk in this way for hours.

His view was that the US policy has always been exclusively one of self-interest. That in order to control the price of Middle East oil, they aim to ensure that no single Arab government totally dominates the region. During the

'80–88 war, they supported Iran and then Iraq and then Iran again. It was a standing joke in those days, Saddam reminded me. 'Whose side is America on?' one would ask. 'Who is losing?' was the reply. The US will not support a dominant Arab nation. They opposed Iraq last year because they would not tolerate Saddam having control of the rich Kuwaiti oilfields. They have long opposed the Kurds, because a united, independent Kurdistan would be the richest country in the Middle East. They oppose the Shi'a because they would form an Islamic empire with Iran. They oppose the Communists for no other reason than that they are Communists. Saddam guffawed when he made this last point.

'The Americans want division in the Middle East,' he declaimed angrily, and went on to pontificate about a united Arab world. I agreed with him that the US would never permit it. He maintained that even if every Arab nation democratically voted for it, they would go to war before they let it happen. Now that Iraq had been defeated and its capacity to wage war destroyed, the USA was content. Better a subdued Saddam than a rising Kurdish or Shi'a nation. Sometimes, I too feel the Americans are not interested in words like freedom and equality. They pay lip service to the rights of man, yet in reality they seek only power and profit.

Despite my hostility towards and anathema of Saddam and his terror-based regime, I had much sympathy for his laments. It may be seen by many as a serious distortion of history, yet his assessment of the motives of the US was shared by many Iraqis and non-Iraqis, even moderates.

Chapter Fifteen

1993
Rajab 1413 – Rajab 1414

The arguments between Saddam and Ekeus continued. Whenever Saddam accused the UN of effectively killing the people of Iraq with the ongoing sanctions, Ekeus referred him to UNSC Resolution 706, passed in August 1991, which permitted Iraq to export a limited quantity of oil in return for the supply of 'humanitarian goods'.

This invariably sent Saddam into a frenzy.

On one occasion, I was with Saddam and Tariq when the Deputy Prime Minister was relating the gist of what had been discussed with Ekeus earlier in the day. Saddam rarely attended such discussions personally.

'Do they think I am stupid?' he roared. 'As well as destroy the people of Iraq, they wish to confiscate our sovereignty. The quantity of oil they permit us to export is barely sufficient to pay the war reparations they imposed on us! The people of Iraq will receive nothing. Is that reported in the so-called Free Press of the West? I do not think so!'

Saddam's criticism was essentially correct. The UN

Compensation Commission had, through Resolution 692, demanded that war reparations be deducted from any overseas profits made on Iraqi oil exports. In addition, the full operational costs of UNSCOM had to be met by Iraq. The meagre balance would allow the Iraqi chancellor precious little for the purchase of humanitarian goods.

For all that, Saddam, his family and favoured cronies had been able to circumvent the sanctions from the date of their introduction. The roads from Jordan, Turkey and Syria were cluttered with black market traffic carrying contraband en route for Saddam's palaces and government offices. Udai and Hussein Kamil, in particular, were making a fortune from sanctions-busting.

The effects on the common people of Iraq, though, were truly serious. It was mooted that the dire state of the Iraqi economy and the consequences being suffered by the population were causing a great deal of soul searching among many members of the UN.

The greatest stumbling block was the argument presented by the United States, and Britain, that any easing of sanctions would permit Saddam to recommence his armament programme and again threaten the peace of the region. Russia and France were the two member nations most in support of lifting sanctions. Russia, with its own economic crisis to worry about, was owed $11 billion dollars by Iraq and had no hope of recovering any part of it until Iraq was permitted to re-enter the trade arena. France had a huge interest in both the oil and conventional arms industries of Iraq. The US, on the other hand, was not suffering at all: indeed, the successful conclusion of the Gulf War had led to the development of lucrative trade relationships with the states of the lower Gulf. Clearly, the priorities of member nations were at odds, and equally clearly, those of the USA would prevail.

The cold reality for Iraq was that thirty years of staggering economic growth from the end of the second world war to the outbreak of the Iran-Iraq war had been virtually wiped out. The Achilles heel in the economy was its excessive dependence on oil revenue. When Iran had attacked our oil installations, the GDP went into immediate decline. By 1980, military expenditure was already nearly 40% of GDP, a 600% increase in just five years, and rose to nearer 70% before the war with Iran ended. After the Gulf War, output was shrinking rapidly towards single billion dollar figures.

The effects of two costly wars and ongoing sanctions were reaching into all corners of Iraqi society. The people directed their anger towards the US and, to a lesser degree, Britain, these two being the major obstacles in any moves to have the sanctions lifted. Whenever speaking in public, Saddam blamed all of the country's ills on the 'The Great Satan', and Stars and Stripes were burned in the streets throughout Iraq during emotional demonstrations. Saddam's reputation was largely restored. He was once again, at least to the watching World, the people's champion. Even I was impressed, though not deceived; nor deflected from my long term object of aiding his downfall.

Saddam was keen to exploit this renewed acclaim, and in June I was ordered to go on a number of visits to children's hospitals in his place. One such trip took me to the al-Mansur hospital in Baghdad and I was horrified by what I saw.

I was met at the hospital by a Dr Sa'dun al-Thakafi, a senior orthopaedic surgeon, who took me first to the children's cancer ward. Passing the children's beds, it seemed to me a great many more children were present than on my previous visits and I brought this up with Dr Sa'dun.

'Yes, Your Excellency', he said sadly. 'There has been a considerable increase in the cases of cancer and leukaemia in the children. We can treat few of them successfully.'

'Why not?' I asked. On such occasions Saddam displays great compassion, mostly contrived. In my case, no acting was necessary; I was greatly affected by what I saw and at that moment was ready to blame the UN, the US, and most of the rest of the world. In such situations, outrage came naturally to me.

'We have neither the medication nor the means to administer it, Your Excellency,' the doctor explained, with due deference. 'What little we have is occasionally supplemented by small voluntary organisations from the West who are sympathetic to our plight, but they risk prison sentences in their own countries by bringing it in. What they are able to supply us is gone within days.'

I was curious to hear to what the doctor attributed the increase in the number of cancer cases.

'We have performed countless autopsies on children over the past two years, Your Excellency. The vast majority have one condition in common – their lungs are infected by thousands of minute carbon fibres. We know now the Allies were dropping carbon fibres during the raids in order to cripple the communications systems. These same carbon fibres have, it seems, been damaging the lungs of our children. It cannot be a coincidence. There are also other symptoms of which we cannot yet determine the cause.' The doctor hesitated. 'With respect, Your Excellency, these details have all been passed on to your office.'

'Yes, of course,' I said hastily. 'It had slipped my mind. I have many matters to remember. What are the figures?'

'Since the war, the number of cases of cancer and leukaemia in children between six and fifteen-years-old has increased fourfold.'

'It is that bad?' I asked, genuinely shocked by the scale of the tragedy.

'Yes,' he replied in a lacklustre voice. 'But in the under-fives the number of cases has gone up sevenfold.'

I was aghast. I knew of the Coalition practice of dropping carbon fibres, which caused communication systems to fail without any outward signs of damage. But I was horrified to learn that the technique gave rise to such a lethal by-product.

A disturbing number of children were also being hospitalised with malnutrition, and it was such youngsters whom we visited next. In urban areas, before the introduction of sanctions and the war that followed, cases of malnutrition among the young were practically unknown. Now, as we entered the ward, the sight that greeted me took my breath away. The ward was occupied by as many as thirty emaciated children, most of them bedridden and very poorly. A few of them were supine and appeared barely conscious. Others were sitting up, but their pinched, sullen faces in which their eyes seemed so huge, were evidence of their desperate plight.

'How many children do you have in this condition?' I asked.

'Here? Several hundred. But this scene is repeated in every hospital and clinic throughout the country. There are many thousands. We estimate that up to one third of our children are suffering from life-threatening food shortages, but only the emergency cases are permitted to enter hospital.'

In other words, the ones who were dying.

'These children are all here because of a lack of food?' I asked the doctor.

'The great majority, yes,' he replied. 'Their immune systems are weak, so they have little resistance to any virus or form of infection. They are suffering from a variety of ailments which we do not have the drugs to treat, but they have all been starving to death.'

As I passed the foot of each bed, I stopped to talk to those I thought were capable of responding. One little girl sat on the edge of her bed, staring listlessly at the floor. Her arms and legs were thin as sticks, and her gaunt face was an abject picture of misery. I stepped forward and sat on the bed alongside her.

'How old are you?' I asked, in my best bedside voice.

'Six,' she replied, almost inaudibly.

'Where are your parents?'

'My mummy is at home, but my daddy was killed in the war.'

She looked up at me briefly, but if she recognised me as her President, it was not reflected in her expression.

'What is your name?'

'Nadia,' she said.

'Nadia?' The name produced in me a wave of grief I found difficult to contain. I glanced over my shoulder to be sure that no one was within earshot. 'I once had a little girl called Nadia,' I whispered.

'Is she dead?' she asked, with the innocent tactlessness of the very young.

'Yes,' I said.

'Did you love her?'

'Yes, I loved her very much.'

She nodded. 'Soon I will be dead. When I see her in heaven, I will tell her that her daddy loves her.'

My eyes blurred with tears and words failed me. I touched her shoulder and tried to tell her that she would not die and that soon she would be well again. But the sentiments stuck in my throat. I kissed her on the forehead and went to rejoin Sa'dun, who was bending over a prostrate child on the other side of the ward.

It was not until I had left the ward that I had my emotions sufficiently under control to be able to speak again. I turned to the Sa'dun 'If that little girl was your daughter, where would you send her?'

He seemed both touched and surprised that I had been so deeply affected.

'Please, Your Excellency, she is receiving the best attention we can give her. But our facilities—'

I raised a hand. 'I understand your problem, doctor. No criticism of the standard of care was implied. I am sure you are doing everything in your power. I, too, wish more could be done. But answer my question. Where would you send her?'

'I do not know,' he answered sincerely. 'I suppose I would look for a private clinic, but they are expensive. It would—'

I interrupted him again. 'Then please do me the courtesy of finding such a clinic for that child. The cost of the treatment is irrelevant. Send the bill to me.'

This was an act of great rashness on my part. It was impossible to predict how Saddam would react, but I hoped that he would indulge me this once. In any case, if I had to pay for the treatment myself, I would do so.

We visited several more wards, where the same heartbreaking scenes awaited me, but I lacked the courage to talk to any more of the children. I could not save them all.

'What other problems are you having here?' I asked Sa'dun.

'Almost every medical problem that exists. Routine ailments such as duodenal ulcers are becoming fatal because we do not have the drugs to treat them. Operations on gall bladders are on the increase because of the lack of antibiotics. There has even been a sharp rise in traffic accidents because vehicles are not being properly serviced or repaired. The casualty ward is stretched beyond its ability to cope.'

Such is the corollary of defeat in war.

Although I had seen many indications of just how wretched life was becoming for the Iraqi people, I had spent little time in the city's poorer quarters and was unaware of the extent of the suffering. My reaction on leaving the hospital was to resolve to do all I could to help. I said as much to Hashim during the drive back to the palace.

'And what exactly will you do, Mikhaelef?' he asked, his tone revealing a deep scepticism. 'The hospitals of the entire country, not just Baghdad, require an infusion of capital beyond the ability of any one man to raise. If Saddam himself invested his entire wealth into our health system, it would do little more than scratch the surface. What the United States is doing to punish Iraq is a crime that will embarrass their own historians in the future. It is their shame, but our tragedy.'

Maintaining any kind of contact with Sophie was difficult and would have been impossible without Latif and Abdullaha's assistance. I had been told early in the year that she was now in New York and I was relieved to hear it. On the few occasions I met Latif, I handed him a letter for her, and now and again I would receive one in return, despite the risks. A letter falling into the wrong hands would have been my death warrant. I had no idea how the letters travelled between Baghdad and New York, but assumed Latif had a contact within one of the few embassies remaining in Baghdad.

Considering that she been through the most dreadful ordeal, her letters encouraged me to believe she was making a steady recovery. It was nearly two years since I had seen her and although I missed her badly, I was consoled by the fact that she was safe and as well as could be hoped. Her endearments were as warm as ever, encouraging me to hope that her love for me had not dwindled.

I heard from Abdullah less often, but following one of his calls I travelled incognito into the city the following evening. Having arrived a good half-an-hour before sunset, I strolled to and fro, trying as best I could not to look conspicuous. I waited patiently, but my anxiety grew as time passed. Finally, after waiting for over two hours, I went home. I was sure I had remembered the arrangements correctly and was worried that something serious had happened.

Abdullah was not due to call the contact number again for another week and if Latif and his fellow-freedom fighters had been arrested, and it seemed likely they had, I had several things to worry about. Who else would Latif have told of my existence? Would my part in their operations be revealed? Latif was using the name of Ra'ad Mohammed, but a false identity was no protection. The Mukhabarat are experts at the art of extracting the truth. Even if I was not linked to him, I did not doubt that Saddam would revive my appointment as Latif's executioner. It was a chilling prospect.

I heard nothing until Abdullah called again, the following week. After exchanging some small talk for a few minutes, he found a way of telling me what had happened when he called the contact number.

'I telephoned my brother today,' he said, making it sound like a passing remark.

I knew that Abdullah had several sisters, but was an only son.

'In fact,' he continued, 'I rang him several times, but there was no answer. Do you not think that strange, Miklef?'

'Perhaps,' I answered. 'Maybe he is busy today. Keep trying.'

Once again, I was concerned that serious misfortune had befallen Latif. Several weeks passed and Abdullah's telephone calls revealed nothing further. He called the contact number each week, but it was never answered. On his latest attempt, the line was disconnected. I dared not make any enquiries through official channels, but I began to fear that Latif and his accomplices might be dead – until a conversation with Hashim led me to believe otherwise. Since his father's death, Hashim and I had grown much closer, though I had not pressed him on his revelations of shame. If he wished to reopen the subject, he would do so when he was ready.

On the day of the conversation referred to, I had not seen him all morning when he finally came into the Dark Room.

'It is good of you to come in today,' I noted with gentle sarcasm. 'We can share some tea before we go home.'

Hashim smiled, but clearly had his mind on higher things.

'I have come from the Abu Ghraib prison,' he said soberly. 'I was asked to question a prisoner who the Mukhabarat believe was involved in an assassination attempt on the President some months ago. As I was a witness to the incident, they wished me to furnish them with some details. I was present for the interrogation.'

'What happened?'

Hashim looked up at me. 'It was not pleasant,

Mikhaelef. You will recall the conversation we had when my father died?'

'Of course,' I answered.

'Then I will not lie to you. I have been party to such interrogations before. I have done things to people of which I am deeply ashamed. But I did believe in what I saw was the greater good. I have never, though, enjoyed it as some . . . as some of my fellow officers appear to.'

The death of his father had dramatically changed Hashim's view of life. This was his first participation in the questioning of a prisoner since the funeral, and he seemed decidedly uncomfortable with it.

I nodded but said nothing.

'The man who was being questioned was guilty, I am sure of that. But he showed a courage that has affected me profoundly. Only a man with the deepest and most sincere beliefs could stand up to the horrors he was put through and not break down.'

'Is he dead?' I asked.

'No,' Hashim answered, breathing quite deeply. 'He has information the Mukhabarat need. They will kill him eventually, but not for some time yet.'

'What is his name?' I asked as casually as I could.

'His name?' Hashim replied, puzzled. 'Why does his name matter?'

'It does not,' I quickly responded. 'But he is a real person. He has a family.'

'Well, yes. I am sure he has, but I do not know his name. He did say something, though, that amused most of those present, but I have no idea what he meant by it. He was being held in a chair and one of the guards was sliding pins beneath his finger nails. His arms and face were covered in cigarette burns and he had been badly beaten from his head to the soles of his feet. He was barely conscious, but a fire of defiance, of . . . of dignity still burned with in him. Even with all my experience I have rarely seen the likes of it.'

'What did he say, Hashim?' I asked, wishing to be spared any further detail of the torture the poor man had endured.

Hashim looked at me thoughtfully, perhaps wondering what motive lay behind my questions.

'He was being asked what his organisation was called and who was its leader. One of the officers spat in his face and asked him who they would have put in Saddam's place had the assassination attempt been successful. The man responded to the officer with a fortitude that had to be admired. "We will replace him with a cactus!" he said.'

My ears pricked up. 'That is a strange thing to say,' I kept my voice neutral. 'What do you think he meant?'

Again, the contemplative look from Hashim.

'We do not yet know. But I am sure my colleagues will find out . . . eventually.'

Chapter Sixteen

1994
Rajab 1414 – Rajab 1415

I was desperate to do something to help Latif. I felt sure he would soon be dead (with or without my unwilling participation), but though I cudgelled my unresponsive brain, I could not conceive a plan that had the remotest hope of being successful. Hashim was still occasionally called to take part in the interrogations of the man I was sure must be Latif, and I fleetingly considered enlisting his aid, but decided the risk was too great. His disillusionment was with himself rather than the regime and I doubted he would entertain any action that succoured an enemy of Saddam.

I was resigned to my helplessness, when Hashim brought me news that both confirmed the man arrested a couple of months earlier was definitely Latif and presented me with an unexpected opportunity to engineer his escape.

'Do you remember the prisoner I told you of a few weeks ago?' Hashim asked me one afternoon. 'The one whose spirit so impressed me?'

My immediate impression was that Hashim was about to tell me Latif was dead.

'The one who would replace Saddam with a cactus?' I replied.

'Yes, the same. I saw him this morning. He has been moved from the Abu Ghraib to the Mukhabarat's own prison in al-Mansur.'

Though obviously relieved to learn that Latif was still alive, I wondered why Hashim had brought up the subject.

'So?' I prompted.

'He has been interrogated for several weeks now, but they have not broken him. He is weak, but remains as defiant as the day they brought him in. He is a remarkable man.'

It was on the tip of my tongue to reply 'I know,' but I was not yet ready to commit suicide.

'If they cannot break him,' I said instead, 'then I am surprised they have not killed him.'

'He will not be killed until he is no longer able to talk.'

'How long will that take?' I asked, feeling desperately sorry for Latif.

'How long is a walk in the desert, Mikhaelef? I have no idea, but I think not much longer now. He is being transferred to Samarah.'

My blood ran cold at the mention of Samarah. The memory of the acid-bath execution of Mullah al-Barzinji was still vivid. The thought that Latif might soon go through the same horror sickened me.

'He will be dead within an hour of arriving there,' I predicted, unable to fully conceal the dread I felt. ' When is he going?'

'Tomorrow. He is being taken there with six other prisoners, all Kurds.' Hashim stared at me. 'You have heard of Samarah?' he said, sounding surprised. 'It is not a regular prison.'

'I have been there,' I replied, and told Hashim of my experience in the company of Udai.

'Then you can guess the fate that awaits Ra'ad Moham-med,' Hashim said.

'Who?' I asked sharply, my ears picking up at the mention of Latif's alias.

'Oh, that is his name. We know nothing else about him except that he is a Communist and he was involved in conspiracies against Saddam.'

Here at last was definite confirmation that the prisoner to whom Hashim referred was Latif.

In recent weeks, Hashim had taken to driving me home. He lived only three kilometres away from my house and, as our friendship deepened, he would frequently permit my usual chauffeur to leave early. That night, on arriving at my front door, I invited him inside for the first time. The events of the day were clearly troubling him, and I judged him to be in need of further company. He accepted with alacrity.

We talked generally for a few minutes, but the conversa-tion soon turned to Latif's interrogation.

'I love my country,' Hashim said. 'I thought I would do anything for Iraq, but I could not endure what Ra'ad Mohammed has endured. How can a man feel so passion-ately about something that he is prepared to suffer the most degrading agonies to protect it? Where does such fortitude come from, Mikhaelef?'

'Faith, Hashim,' I answered softly.

'Faith?' Hashim exclaimed. 'He is a Communist! He has no faith.'

'His Communism is his faith. He is prepared to dedicate his life, even sacrifice his life to the cause in which he believes. It is a faith no more mysterious than Islamism or Christianity. Some would say less so.'

'Perhaps,' Hashim acknowledged. 'But I am sure he is driven by a greater force. Such passion does not come from reading books. It comes from life. This man has a rare story to tell. I know it.'

'And yet,' I said, without emotion, 'tomorrow he will be dead.'

Hashim hung his head. I looked at him and wondered if maybe he was ready to change his allegiance. Had he undergone such a transformation in the past few months that he might even be prepared to help me save Latif? I longed to press him further, but the ever-present possibility that the house was bugged led me to take precautions first.

'Let us talk outside, Hashim. I need some air.'

He agreed readily enough. Once we were in the garden, seated on one of the benches, I immediately resumed the offensive.

'Do you think this man Ra'ad Mohammed deserves to die, Hashim? After all, he did attempt to assassinate Saddam. If he were free, he would try again. Do you not think he should die for that?'

A barely perceptible shake of the head was Hashim's only response.

'We both know that tomorrow Ra'ad Mohammed will be slowly immersed into a vat of sulphuric acid. The torment he has suffered since his arrest will be nothing compared to what he must now endure before he dies. Is that the way it should be?' I paused ever so briefly before putting to him the one thing he did not want to hear. 'Would your father approve, Hashim?'

He turned on me sharply, his eyes glazed with tears. 'In the name of Allah! What do you want me to say, Mikhaelef? Should the man die in agony? No, he should not! Is it right that a man of such courage should be dissolved alive? No, it is not!' He got up and paced the terrace, waving his arms in remonstration. 'But what can I do? I can do nothing. I could no sooner save Ra'ad Mohammed than I could part the al-Bahr al-Ahmar!'

I remained calmly seated. The moment was ripe.

'The point, Hashim, is . . . would you help him if you could?'

'Of course I would! I admire him more than I can put into words. I would gladly help him if I could. But I cannot!'

'You can,' I said softly.

Hashim suddenly stopped still and regarded me with suspicion. 'What are you talking about?'

I had gone too far now to turn back. If I had misjudged Hashim, I would pay with my life. I had no choice but to go on.

'Sit down, Hashim.' I pointed to the bench beside me. He sat down slowly, not taking his eyes off me.

'What are you talking about, Mikhaelef?' he said again.

I drew in a deep breath. 'The real name of the man we are talking about is not Ra'ad Mohammed.'

I felt Hashim's gaze burning into me.

'Explain,' he said.

My heart was thumping away in my breast like a pneumatic tamp as I prepared to speak. I was about to place my life in Hashim's hands.

'His real name is Latif Pasha al-Rabaka.'

Hashim stared. 'How do you know this?'

'He is my brother-in-law.'

At first Hashim said nothing. Then he nodded very slowly.

'Yes, the al-Rabaka brothers. I remember reading about them in your file in Salman Pak. Was Latif not the eldest?'

'Yes. The youngest, Abdullah, was killed when attempting to assassinate Udai. The other brother, Rafik, was shot dead in the al-Karada prison some weeks later.'

'And you, Mikhaelef?' Hashim asked, having now recovered some of his composure. 'Are you one of them?'

'No,' I answered cautiously, still unsure of where his true loyalties lay. 'Not exactly. But we share some common ground.'

'Which is?'

'I have said enough for now, Hashim. It is your turn. You say you would do something to help Latif if you could. You have also told me of the great shame you have borne since your father's death. Perhaps this is an opportunity to redeem yourself in his eyes. Do you wish to take it?'

He did not reply. For a minute of more he sat lost in his

thoughts. I did not disturb them. He had to decide unaided how far he was prepared to go. If Hashim reneged, I was in serious trouble and Latif would die.

Finally, he stood up and said, 'What is it you wish me to do?'

My relief was tangible. I moved towards him and we embraced, a little stiffly on his part.

'Thank you, Hashim. I will not forget this.'

Within an hour, we were driving north out of Baghdad and heading for Arbil. As Latif was to be transferred to Samarah in the company of six Kurds, Hashim and I agreed that we should seek the assistance of the peshmerga. My original plan was to head for the area I had been held in when kidnapped and comb the place until we found them. Hashim dismissed the idea as ridiculous.

'We will go to Arbil. When you speak with the peshmerga, you do so on their terms. What is the name of the Kurdish leader you met with Tariq Aziz about ten years ago?'

'You know about that?' I exclaimed. 'You must have been about fifteen then.'

'It is in your file, Mikhaelef. What is his name?'

'Mohammed Mahmoud al-Khoshnawi.'

'Right then. We will go the headquarters of the Patriotic Union of Kurdistan in Arbil and ask for this Mohammed Mahmoud.'

It was at this time impossible to drive directly to Arbil, which was inside the Liberated Zone. Instead, Hashim drove to the house of a man in Baghdad who acted as a smuggler between Saddam's Iraq and the north. He was regularly used by the Mukhabarat when they needed to travel between the two zones. Having been paid by Hashim, he provided us with a route to Arbil along which we could travel unmolested.

The PUK are the legitimate, political wing of the Kurdish opposition, but only the innocent believe they have no contact with the peshmerga rebels.

'It will be late by the time we get there, Hashim.'

He grinned wolfishly. 'They are rebels too, Mikhaelef. The night-time is their friend. Somebody will be there if we knock loudly enough.'

As we drove, I gave Hashim an edited account of my relationship with Latif and how, following the murders of my wife and children, I had contributed in a modest way towards expediting Saddam's demise. He asked me many questions and I answered them as honestly as I could. I needed Hashim's unconditional co-operation and if he was merely playing a game, I had signed my own death warrant already.

Four hours later, we crossed into the LZ near the city of Aski Kalk and arrived in Arbil within an another hour. Hashim made straight for the PUK headquarters.

'You know where it is?' I said, surprised.

'Please, Mikhaelef. I am an officer of the Mukhabarat. I am expected to know such things.'

When we pulled up outside a low, concrete building, I was surprised to see the door standing open. We walked brazenly in, to be met by some sort of official. I removed my false beard and he gasped in astonishment as he 'recognised' my face, a familiar reaction.

'Please, relax,' I said, making calming motions. 'I am not Saddam Hussein.'

The man did anything but relax. He called out over his shoulder, 'Ahmad! Ahmad! Come quickly!'

Another, younger man appeared; he too was taken aback by my presence.

'Please!' I implored. 'Listen to me carefully. I am not Saddam Hussein.'

The two men, standing rigidly still and quite terrified, stared at me wide-eyed.

'Neither this gentleman here nor myself are armed,' I continued, speaking rapidly. 'We come as friends. I have important information for Mohammed Mahmoud al-Khoshnawi. You must tell him to come here immediately.'

'What kind of game is this?' the younger man, suddenly

finding his wits, demanded harshly. 'Who are you if you are not Saddam?'

'I will explain to Mohammed. Please tell him to come now.'

Neither of the two men moved. I tried again.

'Place the two of us in a secure room. Lock us up! Put armed guards on the door, if you must. Do whatever you have to do, but bring Mohammed here now.'

The younger man finally sprang into action.

'Please come this way,' he said, and we followed him along a short corridor at the end of which he opened a door and showed us into a small room, empty of furnishings. Without a word, he closed the door behind us and turned the lock. We both sat down on the hard floor and waited.

Two hours passed before Mohammed arrived. I had been formulating a short speech in my mind, to remind him of our previous meeting. I need not have bothered. As soon as he came into the room, his face lit up in recognition.

'Ah, the man who would be Saddam! I wondered if it might be you.' He embraced me and kissed me on both cheeks. I was completely unprepared for such a welcome.

'You knew I was not Saddam?' I asked, somewhat nonplussed.

'It was an impressive performance and when we first met I suspected nothing. Then, as I reflected, a few things unsettled me. That was why I asked you to share a drink. By the time you left, I knew. You do not have Saddam's bottomless eyes and you talked too much . . . even when you were sober! Saddam is always irritatingly quiet in such meetings. He would also never have agreed to see me alone. You have done well to survive such employment for so long. Finally, your ears are not the same.'

'My ears?'

'Yes. They are not so very different, but yours are slightly smaller and stick out a little more.' He chuckled at my discomfiture. 'I am very observant.'

Back in the beginning, my ears had been discussed, but it

is a part of the anatomy that is not easily altered and the dissimilarity was not thought to be noticeable. Clearly we were mistaken!

'What shall I call you?' Mohammed said.

'Mikhaelef.'

'You are a Christian?'

'No.' It was a question I was once asked quite regularly. 'My maternal grandmother was a Christian. It was her father's name.'

'Do you know that the father of Tariq Aziz was also called Mikhaelef?' Mohammed asked.

'Yes, it was mentioned to me once.'

'And who is this?' Mohammed nodded towards Hashim.

'This is Hashim Mushir. He is my friend.'

'And Saddam has no idea you are here this evening?'

'Of course not,' I replied, thinking it a stupid question.

Mohammed turned to Hashim with an engaging grin.

'It is intriguing that a man who has for many years successfully impersonated Saddam Hussein should suddenly arrive here with important information for me. That he should do so in the company of an officer of the Mukhabarat intrigues me further. Let us go somewhere more comfortable and you can tell me why you are here.'

How he deduced Hashim was of the Mukhabarat was a mystery that he did not volunteer to elucidate.

We accompanied him to a small office. He sat behind a desk that was really a table covered in documents, and we occupied stools that, to judge from their condition, had seen long and arduous service. I told him my story from its beginning in 1979. I spoke without break for the best part of an hour, during which Mohammed did not interrupt, except to occasionally ask for some clarification. I finished with the transfer of prisoners taking place the next day. In return for the details of the transportation, I explained that I wished him to organise Latif's rescue.

'There will be Kurds in this convoy?' he asked.

'Yes, perhaps six.'

'Then we will help,' he said. 'The enemy of my enemy is my friend.'

'You trust us?' Hashim said, wonderingly.

'We have made enquiries. There is a risk that you are setting a trap for us, but we are willing to take it. In any case, we will take certain precautions, you may be sure of that.'

Mohammed promised me he would have a band of peshmerga rebels stationed on the Samarah road near the Ruins of Opis at dawn. He gave me a number to call and asked me to obtain as much detail as I could about the timing of the transfer.

'Whatever information you can provide us with will be sent on to the ambush party.'

It was five o'clock in the morning when Hashim and I finally arrived back in Baghdad in a state of near-exhaustion, especially Hashim who had done all the driving. We went straight to the al-Karada prison, but in order not to complicate matters, I remained in the car. Hashim was gone for less than twenty minutes and came back with the basic information we needed.

'Were they not reluctant to tell you anything?' I asked.

'I showed my Mukhabarat credentials and said I wished to interview the prisoner Ra'ad Mohammed later today. I was told it was not possible as he was being transferred to Samarah and leaving at noon.'

'They were not curious as to why you were roaming around at this time of the morning?'

'No,' he answered, glancing towards the prison as we drove away. 'In there, day is as night and night as day.'

I shuddered inwardly at the graphic description of the hell within that place.

We went to the fourteen-storey al-Rashid Hotel, a couple of kilometres away on Yahfah Street, over the road from the Haleb Square entrance to Zowrah Park. The hotel was built in 1982 in a tasteful blend of ancient and modern architectural styles. Four huge chandeliers adorned the foyer where long, ornate glass doors led to the gardens. In the sparsely furnished but elegant lobby, a line of tele-phones hung on the wall opposite the reception desk. From there I rang the number Mohammed had given me and passed on the limited intelligence we had obtained. I was instructed to call back that night.

I spent an uneventful, but anxious day with Hashim in the palace. We rested as best we could and that evening went again to the al-Rashid Hotel.

'I am enquiring after my brother-in-law,' I announced, when my call was answered.

'Your brother-in-law is unwell,' I was told, 'but he is in good hands. The operation was a complete success.'

'Thank you,' I said.

I replaced the receiver. Latif was safe. There was a lump in my throat. When I returned to the car, Hashim knew from my face that the tidings were good.

'Now you can talk to your father in your prayers, Hashim,' I said, eternally grateful for the help he had given me. 'He will be proud of you.'

A week later, Hashim drove me to Arbil again and there I was briefly reunited with Latif. He had been cruelly tortured and was seriously ill, but there was every prospect he would recover. The Kurds were looking after him and promised to do so until he was well enough to leave. I urged him to be in no hurry to return to his old ways.

In the past three or four years, I had seen little of Udai, largely due to his being based in the luxuriant offices of the International Olympic Committee, of which he was the Director or the editorial offices of the *Babel* newspaper, of which he was the publisher and editor. Saddam had been tiring of Udai's erratic and irrational behaviour for some while and I suspected that his younger son, Qusai, far more like his father in mood and manner, was being groomed as Saddam's heir. He was certainly in his father's company far more frequently than Udai.

I also heard that Udai had recently been seen in the company of a well-known Iraqi singer by the name of

Baidah, but I was sceptical about the relationship. It was common knowledge that Udai spent a great deal of time cruising the streets of Baghdad, picking up women. Many of them came from respectable families and were beaten if they did not submit. But Udai was also fond of prostitutes. One of his close friends, Ali Mohammed, was a 'pimp' and Udai saw to it that this provided him with another lucrative source of income.

I saw Udai for the first time in several months when he arrived at the palace during the last week of the Gregorian year. I nodded respectfully as we passed in a corridor close to the Saddam's study, not wishing to engage him unless it was absolutely necessary to do so. To my surprise, he stopped in his tracks and snapped at me, 'You are a dead man, Mikhaelef Ramadan! I care not what my father says. Let him weep over your treacherous body. One day I will personally kill you!'

I scuttled off down the corridor without replying. Why he should talk to me in this manner after so long, I had no idea, but I took the warning seriously. It seemed I was as much reviled by him as I had ever been. From other Government employees friendly to me, I had heard that he remained convinced I was involved in the attempt on his life at the apartment in the Cairo district, five years earlier. If this was true, it was perhaps unsurprising that he wished to see me dead. His threats served to remind me that, unless Saddam and his sons were ousted, I must one day leave Iraq.

Chapter Seventeen

1995
Rajab 1415 – Sha'baan 1416

With Hashim now as deeply incriminated as I was myself, I was able to confide in him about Udai's renewed threat and he agreed I had good reason to fear the man. Over the past five years, as Udai's indiscriminate acts of violence had made him a liability, he had been discreetly placed where he could do the least damage: running the IOC, managing the international football team, producing a newspaper for the Iraqi youth. With Qusai having discreetly assumed the mantle of heir apparent, Udai seemed to be making an all-out effort to reclaim his inheritance and once again he became a frequent visitor to Saddam's offices at the Karradat Marion palace. Regrettably, this occasioned a revival of his vituperative campaign against me. Hashim understood it more readily than I did.

'When did he first demonstrate his dislike for you?' he asked, as we sat in my garden one afternoon in the Spring, on my day off; it was one of the few private places where we felt able to talk freely. Even Hashim was ignorant of whether listening devices were installed in my home. Like me, though, he assumed the worst.

'The first time we met,' I answered, 'when he was fifteen. He said I had the eyes of a coward.'

'Has he ever been pleasant to you?'

'Only in sarcasm.'

'Then it is not personal,' Hashim said, in all apparent seriousness.

'Not personal?' My laugher was derisive. 'He has threatened to kill me, but it is not personal? I am much reassured.'

'You misunderstand me. Udai's problem with you is that you are so like his father. However insolent he is towards Saddam, there is no doubt that he idolises him. He sees you as a threat.'

'That I find hard to believe.'

'But you are a threat! You have told me yourself you are prepared to impersonate Saddam in the period after a *coup d'etat*.'

'Udai does not know that. I hope.'

'He is not a fool. He recognises the dangers of having somebody looking so like Saddam in the privileged position you hold. You have also given him good reason to suspect you over the years. For all that we might both justifiably condemn Udai, he is right to suspect that you present a serious danger to the presidency. Fortunately for you, nobody else in the palace is listening to him. I myself never suspected a thing and I have been by your side nearly every day for the past ten years.'

I considered Hashim's assessment of Udai and had to agree that, however justified I was in so intensely loathing him, his suspicion of me was well-founded; Saddam was indeed wrong to trust me.

'I have to leave Iraq,' I said finally.

'Yes, you do,' he agreed. 'How, is the question.'

'Iraq's borders are lost in the desert. If I am driven across the Ash-Sham (Syrian Desert), I can walk into Syria, Jordan or Saudi Arabia.'

'Perhaps, but what would happen then?' Hashim asked. 'How do you think the governments of those countries would react if a man who is identical to Saddam, but claims not to be him, calmly walks across their borders one afternoon. You might be murdered. You would certainly be arrested. Would you be granted political asylum? Would you be returned to Iraq? Would they not suspect you are the real Saddam who has left an impersonator behind in Baghdad? Whether you tell the truth or lies, they will not believe you.'

I could not dispute Hashim's prognosis. 'What do you suggest?' I asked.

'It would be better to present your case and make your arrangements from this side of the border before you cross over.'

'How will I do that?'

Hashim shrugged. 'I have no idea.'

We discussed the matter at length, but no ready solutions occurred to us. Nor was he willing to consider accompanying me.

'It is different for you, Mikhaelef,' he said, sighing deeply. 'Your disappearance will put pressure on me here. For a while, I may be suspected of complicity, but I will come through it. If I were to admit my guilt by coming with you, Saddam would find ways to punish me. I have a large family here. You do not.'

Not any longer, at any rate, I thought bitterly.

I spent the next few weeks trying to figure out how I might successfully flee the country, the necessity of which was reinforced whenever I came across Udai. He would treat me to a manic smile when our eyes met, usually followed by the drawing of a finger across his throat. I began to fear my days were numbered.

Bereft of ideas for my escape, I was becoming resigned to my fate when an UNSCOM delegation arrived in Baghdad in November and an unexpected opportunity arose. They had declared that although there had been a far greater number of chemical weapons in Iraq than had previously been supposed, they believed that they were now more or less destroyed. When, in August, the US flatly refused to consider the lifting of sanctions, Saddam was exasperated. In November, he was further incensed when the UN held that the two no-fly zones imposed after the war must remain in place. It was, he declared, obvious that the US would never agree to the lifting of sanctions, no matter what concessions Iraq made.

The delegation arrived in Baghdad to pour oil on troubled waters, but Saddam, predictably, declined to meet them. On this occasion, there was some advance speculation that he might be prepared to make an exception, but I learned the reality of his plans when Tariq came to see me.

Saddam, he confided, had no intention of meeting anybody, but instructed me to make an appearance on his behalf as a political gesture. Tariq said I was to drive with him to his offices and wait in a private room next door to where the talks were taking place. I would be called in when needed. My brief was to say nothing and simply nod my head when Tariq indicated that I should. Such reticent behaviour would be quite typical of Saddam in those circumstances.

I accompanied Tariq and was left alone in a room next to where the delegation was assembled. I sat down and nervously awaited possibly the most demanding test of my abilities to impersonate Saddam that I had yet encountered. As I listened to the bustle of the traffic outside, the thought crossed my mind that if only I could make contact with one of the delegation members, I might be able to let them know of my existence and my desire to leave Iraq. I did not expect to be left unchaperoned with anyone from UNSCOM and, even if I were, the building was sure to be infested with microphones. I was nervously waiting to be summoned when the door opened and Akram entered, laden with an armful of overcoats. I could not resist teasing him.

'I see you have a task of enormous responsibility to perform here, Akram. You are the cloakroom attendant!'

Akram, as ever, was not amused by my attempt at humour. 'Very funny, Mikhaelef,' he said coldly. 'I am actually returning to the conference room this moment to sit with Tariq.'

'Oh, yes,' I persisted. 'You must be close at hand for when our respected visitors require refreshment.'

Akram dumped the coats, which presumably belonged to members of the delegation, on the desk before me, and left in a huff. An inspiration came to me. I looked in the drawers of the desk for pen and paper and quickly scribbled a note. I could write only in Arabic, but felt sure that UNSCOM would have interpreters among its personnel.

The note read: 'The man you saw today was not Saddam Hussein. I have been employed as his double since 1979. My life is now threatened and I need to leave Iraq. I will be at the railway station clock tower at nine o'clock this evening, and again on the next two evenings if necessary. Please have somebody who speaks Arabic meet me there. He will be approached by a bearded man who will say "Baghdad is not the place it once was". Your agent should follow that man.'

I signed the note 'Cactus'.

I rummaged swiftly through the coats, but not surprisingly, could find no means of identifying which coat belonged to whom, except that each bore tailors' labels in the Roman alphabet. I chose one of the coats at random and placed the note in the inside pocket. Surely, I thought, the coat's owner must find it by the day after tomorrow at the latest.

An hour passed without my being called. When the door finally opened, it was Akram again, but this time in the company of Tariq. Akram picked up the coats and left the room as Tariq spoke to me.

'I am sorry, Mikhaelef. Your presence here has proved to be unnecessary. I will see you are returned to the palace immediately.'

My initial reaction was severe disappointment. Having

not appeared before the delegation, the first part of my note would now make no sense. Nevertheless, I hoped it would still cause enough curiosity to be taken seriously. I could do nothing but wait and hope.

That night Hashim dropped me off by the clock tower, heavily disguised in beard, glasses and *kefiya*, a cotton head-dress. Parking the car, he kept me under surveillance from a distance. Two men, both obviously European, were standing at the base of the tower, laden with cameras and tourist maps. One was quite tall and athletic-looking and at a guess about thirty years of age. The other man was shorter, heavier of build, and quite a bit older. Both wore conservatively-tailored suits. They were making an effort to appear casual – so much so that, even to my untrained eye, they could only be agents.

As I approached them, they visibly tensed. Perhaps they feared a trap had been set. This sudden thought made me wonder if we were being watched by other, unseen eyes. If so, I just hoped none of them belonged to representatives of the Mukhabarat.

'Baghdad is not the place it once was,' I greeted, with what I hoped was a friendly smile, not too similar to that of Saddam. Neither man spoke, but the older one nodded as I turned away and headed for Zowrah Park. On coming to the wall, I sat down and they joined me, sandwiching me between them. I supposed this was some kind of standard procedure, though to passersby it would seem a little odd. Hashim had followed on foot. Now he came over as if surprised to see me.

'Good evening, Mikhaelef,' he said cheerfully. 'How are you?'

As we embraced, he whispered in my ear. 'You are being trailed by two men,' he said. 'But they are both Europeans, probably colleagues of these two. I am leaving now. Be brief, Mikhaelef. This is an insane risk you are taking.'

Once Hashim had gone, I turned to the older of the two men, who was seated on my left, and spoke in Arabic.

'We were followed by two men. Are they with you?'

'Yes,' the man replied in the same language. 'Although you can see no one, there are four people watching us.' His Arabic was more than adequate, his accent pointing to tutelage by an Egyptian.

'I am impressed.' I looked about, but could see nobody who appeared remotely interested in us. 'Where are you from?'

'London,' the older man said, in plain English.

'British Intelligence?'

'In a manner of speaking,' he answered. 'Did you write the note?'

'Yes. Can you help me?'

'What do you want?' The younger man said, speaking for the first time.

'Although you cannot see it under this beard, I resemble Saddam Hussein very closely. I work for him as a double and have done so for more than fifteen years.'

The younger man nodded, looking away from me as he spoke. 'We are aware Hussein uses doubles,' he said, using Saddam's patronymic as a surname in the mistaken fashion of many Westerners.

'I am prepared to give you information,' I said, 'that may help you to arrange the assassination of Saddam and members of his government. But there are conditions.'

The two men glanced at each other, but their faces revealed neither scepticism nor acknowledgement.

'Which are?' the older man asked.

'His sons, Udai and Qusai, must be killed also. If either or both of them were to win the power struggle that would follow Saddam's death, Iraq would be no better than it is now. You think it is a dangerous place? It is the Garden of Eden compared to what it would be if ever Udai were to become President.'

'Anything else?'

'Yes. I want to be taken out of Iraq at the earliest opportunity and given the financial assistance to set up a new life, preferably outside of the Middle East.'

'You will understand,' the older man said, 'we do not

have the authority to agree to your proposal. We will be here again tomorrow with an answer.'

With that, they both stood and walked away. I felt deflated. I had expected them to be excited by the prospect of an informant in the court of Saddam Hussein.

The following night, only the older man came; he was already sitting on the wall when I arrived fifteen minutes early.

'We cannot help you,' he said, the instant I hopped up on the wall beside him.

'Why not?' I was amazed that they would turn down such an opportunity. 'What I tell you is the truth. I could be invaluable to you.'

'We do not doubt it. But I have been instructed to tell you we cannot accommodate your proposals. We suggest you try the Americans.'

He promised to pass on my offer to them and suggested I be at the same place each night until they turned up, starting the day after tomorrow. I had no choice but to accept his consolation proposal.

'If they don't show within seven days from now, you can take it they are not coming.'

Two days later, Hashim dropped me off at the same spot, with a parting warning to treat with circumspection all my American contact – if indeed one came – told me.

'The Americans are even less to be trusted than the British,' he said lugubriously.

I was making a laborious performance out of tying my shoelaces, when I was joined by a short man, perhaps in his late thirties, with his blond hair cut short. His skin was tanned, but he looked more Slavic or even Russian than American. Because of this I was immediately suspicious.

'Baghdad is not the place it used to be,' he said casually in Arabic, as he lounged against the wall and lit a long filter-tipped cigarette. His accent partially reassured me, having quite a strong American inflexion.

'Are you CIA?' I asked, coming straight to the point.

'Never mind who I am.' He jerked his head in the direction of the lake. 'Let's walk.'

We walked in the direction of the Monument to the Unknown Soldier, looking like a tilted flying saucer in the south-east corner of the park.

'Do you know what I can offer you?' I said to him, after a brief silence.

'We have been told.'

'Do you know what I want?'

'We have been told,' he said again. His voice was almost robotic.

'And?'

The answer was not exactly what I wanted to hear. 'We have no problem with your conditions, only the timing,' he said. 'We are not interested in Saddam's assassination. You will have to earn your passage out of Iraq a little differently.'

'What do you mean?' I asked.

'We think Saddam's assassination would cause a civil war in Iraq. Who would seize power? Maybe the Shi'a, maybe the Kurds, maybe even one of Saddam's sons. You yourself described quite eloquently to our British friends what would happen here if Udai Hussein became President.'

'Udai Saddam,' I corrected him.

The American frowned at me.

'His name is Udai Saddam,' I went on. 'An Arab's second name is his father's forename. Saddam's father was called Hussein. Hence, Saddam Hussein. Udai's father is Saddam. Therefore, Udai Saddam.'

I was surprised that the Americans had not inculcated the structure of Arab genealogy.

'No matter,' he said with a shrug before he carried on. 'Maybe nobody would take overall control. Perhaps the country would break up into three parts: The Sunni Moslems in central Iraq, the Shi'a in the south and the Kurds in the north. Who knows? But such an outcome is not desirable to the United States Government.'

'Then what do you want me to do?'

'Nothing. Just stay where you are.'

What he said bore out much of what Hashim had been arguing for some time. The Americans were worried that if the Kurds came out on top, they would push for the establishment of a national state. As their territory encroaches on Syria, Turkey, Iran and Azerbaijan and includes some of the world's richest oilfields, their ascendancy would without doubt spark off another war. If the Shi'a seized power, there was a serious risk that they would align themselves with Iran and seek to fulfil the late Khomeini's dream of a Shi'a Moslem empire. Again, the US could not tolerate such a situation. It depressed me to hear the Americans were not committed to natural justice in the Middle East, but I was not particularly surprised. They were interested only in the balance of power and its effect on the availability and price of oil.

'You used the name "cactus",' he said, smiling. 'We can live with that. My name is Louis Wolff. You can use either.'

'I will use Louis,' I said.

'Fine. We need to know your real name.'

'Mikhaelef.'

'Your full name.'

I was reluctant to tell him, but was in too deep for reservations. 'Mikhaelef Ramadan Abu Salih al-Kadhimi,' I said.

'Jesus Christ,' he said in English, laughing, before reverting back to Arabic. 'Maybe you could write that down for me.'

Louis told me that his nameless employers were quite exited about the possibility of having a spy inside the presidential palace and, having so far been unsuccessful in penetrating Saddam's inner-sanctum, I was beyond their wildest dreams. He gave me no brief. Anything I heard or saw regarding Saddam's plans, views, moods and relationships were of potential interest.

'Hell!' Louis said, 'we want you to tell us what time of the day Saddam takes a shit!'

If I was prepared to assist, they would agree to all my conditions and in time pull me out of the country.

'What do you mean "in time"?' I said, suspiciously.

'Maybe a year.'

'That is too long. I will not survive a year.'

'That is the offer. It is for you to decide. We have no use for you unless you are inside the palace.'

I told him I needed forty-eight hours to consider the options, but in reality I was not in a position to reject his proposition. The Americans wanted me to stay in Iraq and spy for them, a prospect fraught with danger. On the other hand, if I refused to co-operate, I would have to stay in Iraq anyway.

When I next met up with Louis two days later, I agreed to go along with his proposal, on condition they would carry regular correspondence between myself and Sophie. A week later, he brought me a letter clearly in Sophie's hand. I was relieved to read that she was financially secure and in receipt of the medical and psychological help she needed.

With the letter Louis handed me $5,000 in cash.

'I am not short of money,' I said sharply, more than a little affronted that he believed I might be motivated by profit.

'No insult to your integrity is implied,' he assured me. 'But hard currency is an invaluable tool of the trade for a man in a dangerous situation. Take it.'

He was right, of course. The dollar is a far more potent currency than the dinar on the Iraqi black market. It could prove invaluable to me in an emergency.

The intervals between my being summoned to stand-in for Saddam were gradually becoming more extended, though I read nothing into this. It was during the war with Iran when I had been busiest, which was logical, and ever since I had been used only sporadically for public appearances in Baghdad and, occasionally, elsewhere. I would frequently go two or three months without an official duty. During these interludes I would sit and read or talk to Hashim in the Dark Room, both of us careful to keep away from potentially incriminating topics. My duties were far from onerous. Apart from Udai, who popped up from time to time to renew his threats, boredom was my only enemy.

One morning, we were disturbed by gunfire coming from the other side of the river near Abi Nuw'ahs Street in the vicinity of the Sheraton Hotel. The story emerged that an attempt had been made to ambush the presidential convey as it was approaching the Jumhuriya Bridge, on its return from Kirkuk, where Saddam had been meeting senior officers of the 1st Army Corps. The car in which Saddam should have been travelling was destroyed and its four occupants killed, but Saddam had decided to fly back to Baghdad and had been safely at his desk for more than two hours when the attack took place. Just one more example of the protection accorded him by Allah, according to the inevitable propaganda that came in the wake of the incident.

A few days later, I was informed by Louis that Shi'a fanatics had been responsible, one of whom had died of his wounds. Another three were captured, and from Hashim I learned they were tortured and killed before the day was out.

I knew nothing of the assassination attempt before it took place. Even so, Udai accused me of enjoying spectacular good fortune when next I encountered him on my way from Saddam's study.

'Why is it that these assassination attempts never take place when you are standing in for Saddam?' he said. 'In future, I will ensure you are given no notice of when my father requires you. Let us see how soon your luck runs out.'

It was shortly after this latest threat that I became aware my telephone was tapped. For many years I had assumed that all my calls were monitored and consequently exercised caution whenever using the telephone. Since Latif's arrest, Abdullah no longer assisted me in any way, but he still occasionally called, concerned about my welfare. After one such call, I replaced the receiver and picked it up again immediately to call Hashim and ask him if he could pick me up half-an-hour earlier the next day as I wished to visit the graves of Amna, Nadia and Salih. Several 'clicks' sounded on the line and it was a full ten seconds before I had a dialling tone. This was something new in my experience and I had no doubt what it meant. I could only guess who had ordered it, but Udai was the logical instigator.

It was not only my worries regarding Udai that made the palace a disagreeable working environment. Of late, an atmosphere of constant tension had pervaded the place, most of which could be attributed to Udai's relationship with his brother-in-law, Hussein Kamil al-Majid. The pair of them were amassing a fortune through sanction-busting and it was rumoured they were increasingly treading on each others' toes. This ought to have made them kindred spirits. But no, they could frequently be heard arguing. Hussein, with good reason, I believed, suspected Udai was plotting to kill him and members of his family.

It would have come as no surprise to hear one day that Hussein Kamil had mysteriously disappeared or been killed, but I was not expecting the news I did receive from Hashim when he collected me one morning in early August.

'The al-Majid brothers have gone,' he announced, as soon as I climbed into his car.

'What do you mean "gone"?' I asked.

'They have defected!'

I was stunned. 'Where have they gone?'

'Jordan. They have taken Raghd and Rana and the children with them. Their brother-in-law, Izzedine, also.'

'Saddam will take this badly,' I said, still trying to grasp the implications of the news. In fact, Saddam would be angry beyond words that his two daughters had been taken from him. 'He trusted few men as much as Hussein Kamil.'

'Yes, but to make matters worse, there is a strong rumour they have taken $85 million with them.'

I gasped. 'In the name of Allah! Udai will be insane with fury. He has been calling Hussein a thief for months.' It seemed he was right, and further evidence of his ability to sniff out treason.

In addition to their own personal, considerable wealth, Hussein Kamil, as head of security and director of military industry, controlled the budget for Iraq's build-up of nuclear, biological and chemical weapons. The amount to which he had access in covert overseas bank accounts was beyond calculation. For Udai, the theft of the money was a personal insult, but for Saddam it was possibly the greatest personal blow of his life. Apart from the pain of losing his daughters and grandchildren, and their apparent disloyalty, it was said that he had placed more trust in Hussein Kamil than in anyone else outside of his two sons.

'I remember a conversation I had with Mohammed Qutaibi many years ago,' I said to Hashim. 'It was at the time Barzan Ibrahim was arrested and put under house-arrest.'

'Yes,' Hashim replied. 'I think I remember my father saying something about that.'

'Mohammed said that Saddam would regret the day he decided to place his faith in Hussein Kamil. I disagreed, but Mohammed has been proved correct.'

At the palace, nothing else was being discussed. It soon became clear that Saddam was making it his absolute priority to get the families and the money back.

Chapter Eighteen

1996
Sha'baan 1416 – Sha'baan 1417

Acting as an informant on a full-time basis did not come naturally to me, even though all I did was gather the information I picked up during the course of my regular duties. I was not prepared to take part in any illicit activities within the palace walls and rejected the suggestion that I should read (and photograph) documents left in Saddam's study on the rare occasions I was alone there.

Once or twice a month I met Louis and passed on the gist of what Saddam had been saying and doing over the previous few weeks. To commit this intelligence to paper would have been too risky, therefore I relied on my memory, which has been known to fail me. Still, I did my best. In any case, most of the information I provided was trivia, but I was able to furnish him with the occasional nugget.

One such gem fell into my lap one Jumhah (Friday) in late January after I had been summoned to Saddam's study. I knocked on the door and was called to enter. As I opened the door, I caught the word 'anthrax'. Naturally, I kept a poker face. Saddam was in the company of Ali Hassan and it was he who had spoken the name of the dreaded virus. As I came to stand before Saddam's desk, Ali got up to leave.

'For the present,' Saddam said to him, on his way out, 'we will leave it at the Kan'an site. Let me know what develops.'

Kan'an was a small settlement about fifty kilometres north-east of Baghdad, near the town of Ba'qubah. In due course, I let Louis know what I had overheard, and a couple of weeks later, the UNSCOM inspectors demanded access to 'suspected stores of anthrax in the vicinity of Kan'an'. Saddam was astounded by the quality of their intelligence.

It was particularly damaging for him. UNSCOM was coming to the conclusion that the whereabouts of many of Iraq's chemical and biological weapons sites were not yet known to their inspectors. Their scepticism hardened following this success and by May talks between the two sides broke down completely.

In a bid to stimulate a resumption, the UN passed Resolution 986, which increased the amount of oil Iraq was permitted to export for the purchase of humanitarian aid to $2 billion per annum. Iraq appeared to accept the deal. Oil was pumped into Turkish pipelines in readiness for export, but the bickering over fine detail continued and the oil went no further.

During the evening of the day of the UNSCOM demand, I was at home with Hashim. He told me of Saddam's ranting earlier in the day.

'I have never seen him so angry,' he said. 'He demanded from Ali a list of people who had knowledge of the site, but he will make little progress with that. Apart from the sixty-odd army officers, biologists, electronics engineers and administrators employed there, there are still more in the palace who know of its existence. There must be more than a hundred names on the list, but Saddam says he is determined that every step be taken to uncover the informant in our midst.'

'Is my name on it?' I asked, trying to keep the anxiety from my voice.

Hashim shook his head, but immediately realised the implication of what I was saying. 'No, but why should it be? You have a low security rating. Such information could not come your way.'

'There is no reason why my name should be on the list,' I agreed, deciding I would keep my complicity from Hashim. 'I am just being paranoid.'

He accepted my explanation and the subject was dropped.

The strain of spying on one of the world's most corrupt and vicious dynasties was beginning to weigh on me, and I felt sure I was heading for a breakdown. I was increasingly plagued with severe headaches and suffering from a deep depression. Sometimes Hashim commented on my moodiness. He tended to attribute this to my frustrated wish to flee Iraq and worries about Udai. Accordingly, he tried to be something of a father confessor, in much the same way as I had counselled him after his father's death.

I also relayed to Louis the problems I was having. His response was reassuring – up to a point.

'You may suspect we are playing you along,' he said, 'and that we have no intention of pulling you out. This is not the case, I promise you. If you were discovered, we would not merely lose a valuable source of intelligence, but other people who think as you do will be discouraged from working with us. Rest assured, Mikhaelef, you will be taken to the States in the near future, where you will be reunited with your Sophie. Naturally, you will be debriefed, but not until you feel up to it. I promised we will pull you out soon.'

One day in February, I was 'on call' in the Dark Room with Hashim when the telephone rang. Hashim answered and it transpired he was talking to a friend and fellow Mukhabarat officer at Salman Pak. From the one side of the dialogue I was able to hear, it was evident that something notable had happened.

Hashim replaced the receiver. 'You will not believe it, Mikhaelef. It is incredible!'

'What has happened?' I asked, wondering who had been killed now.

'Hussein Kamil al-Majid and his brother, Saddam, are coming back to Baghdad!'

If they were coming back of their own free will, it was indeed an incredible development.

'Is it the Mukhabarat?' I asked. 'Have they been kid-napped in Amman?'

'I do not think so. The story is they have struck a deal with Saddam. If they bring back his daughters, his grand-children and the money, they will be pardoned.'

'What? And they believe that? They will be arrested the moment they are on Iraqi soil. I know Saddam. When are they due back?'

'Today, it seems.'

'There must be more to this,' I said. 'Neither of the two brothers is so naive as to believe Saddam would pardon them.'

'Apparently, they do believe it. Though their brother-in-law, Izzedine, seems to be more circumspect. I am told he is staying on in Jordan.'

Hussein Kamil had met with many of the opposition groups in exile when he was in Jordan. In doing so, he exacerbated the original crime. Although nothing formal was ever announced, reports from the Western media, claimed he intended to form his own anti-Saddam organisation. Saddam was aware of this, just as he was aware that Hussein Kamil had met with Rolf Ekeus in Amman and alleged the existence of an Iraqi agent within UNSCOM. The spy was a Syrian interpreter and his betrayal and consequent removal angered Saddam beyond words.

For the two brothers now to repent their actions and

be seduced into returning to Iraq was beyond my comprehension.

I heard from Hashim that the brothers had been ostracised by Iraqis abroad. As former henchmen of Saddam's, they were despised by exiled Kurds and Shi'a Moslems, who were not prepared to accept them as a legitimate enemies of the regime. Hashim wondered if they saw a return to Iraq as the only way to recover their status. This did not seem very likely to me. What use is status when you are dead? Alternatively, their father, Kamil Hassan al-Majid, and sister were both still in Baghdad and, though I do not know it for a fact, they may have been used as a means of blackmail, threatening to kill them if the brothers did not return.

Another theory, not without credence, was that their arrogance was their undoing. They had made plans to go to Syria, but King Hussein had made it clear that although the brothers were free to leave, he could not permit them to take Saddam's daughters and grandchildren with them. With nowhere to go, they looked backed to Iraq. They may have believed that, as Saddam's sons-in-law, they would be immune from harm. Saddam Kamil was behaving strangely in exile and both brothers were believed to suffering from severe depression. Perhaps they simply wanted to believe in Saddam's integrity.

Whatever the motivation, the brothers duly arrived with their wives and children in Iraq later that day, although, I learned later, they had taken the precaution of leaving the money behind, thereby reducing some of the value of their return to the fold.

They were met by Udai at the Trebil checkpoint on the Iraqi-Jordanian border. Udai took his sisters and the children directly to Baghdad by helicopter and left the brothers to drive to Takrit alone. Although Udai had been offensive and slapped Hussein Kamil when he tried to prevent him taking his wife, the brothers remained convinced that Saddam would not kill them.

The following day, they decided to go Baghdad and seek

an audience with Saddam. They travelled to the al-Saidia district, less than three kilometres from my house, to the home of their sister, Izzadine's wife. There they were joined by their father, Kamil Hassan al-Majid. That night, the brothers were summoned to Saddam's palace.

When they arrived, Saddam was in the company of a judge and ordered both of them to divorce his daughters there and then. They refused, believing their status as the President's sons-in-law was crucial to their survival. Saddam dismissed them and they returned to their sister's house.

The following day, Saddam gave unequivocal orders to Ali Hassan: 'Bring me the heads of the Majid brothers!' Ali's part in what followed says as much about the man as anything could. He, too, is a Mashid. The two brothers are his nephews and their father, Kamil Hassan al-Majid, his own brother. Yet he carried out Saddam's orders with perverted zeal.

He led a force of al-Majid and al-Takriti family members to Saidia and surrounded the property. Inside were the two brothers, their father, sister and her two children, but nobody was allowed to leave the house. As the day unfolded, other people living in the area were evacuated and late in the afternoon, Udai and Qusai arrived to follow events.

Once darkness fell, Ali's men attacked.

The brothers resisted fiercely, but were unable to defend the house against the missiles being fired through the doors and windows. When Ali's men burst into the building, a furious gun-battle broke out during which Hussein Kamil and two of the assailants were killed. Also dead were Hussein's father, his sister and her two children, a twelve-year-old boy and an eight-year-old girl. Saddam Kalim, wounded in the leg, was dragged outside where his body was blown apart by an RPG7 anti-tank missile. There was little left of the younger brother to take back to Saddam, but Ali went back into the house and decapitated the corpse of his nephew Hussein. The head was presented to

Saddam within an hour. He and his sons denied any connection with the murders, but it did not go unnoticed that Udai attended the funerals of one of the assassins the following day.

When I heard the news the following morning, I was shocked, but most definitely not surprised. Officially, the two brothers were reported to have returned to Iraq consumed with guilt and remorse for their crimes. As a final gesture of repentance, they had returned the President's family to their homeland before both committing suicide. Another popular version was that their family had been so shamed by their defection, that they had quarrelled and begun shooting at each other. All nonsense, but Saddam appropriately expressed his deep regret at the loss of his two sons-in-law.

Raghd and Rana were devastated, particularly Rana, who was known to be very much in love with her husband. They were taken to al-Ouja palace in Takrit where they lived with their children but they both refused to meet with either Udai or their father, whom they were convinced had sanctioned the murders. Rana was close to a complete nervous and mental breakdown. Raghd became so openly critical of her father in front of her children that Saddam had them taken from her.

Four months after the killings, Rana gave birth to a baby girl, whom she poignantly called Dhikra, meaning 'Memory'. There were concerns aired that she had become so withdrawn she might never fully recover. Whatever explanation the women had been given, I know they felt deeply betrayed by their father.

On my next meeting with Louis, I communicated my knowledge of the affair, though it was largely second-hand. He turned out to be almost as well-informed as I was. I learned from him that the CIA had warned the al-Majid brothers they would be killed if they went back to Iraq.

'I have important news for you, Mikhaelef,' Louis proclaimed, once the subject of the al-Majids had been exhausted. 'Sophie is back in Kuwait.'

I was immediately filled with alarm. 'How can that be? It is not safe.'

'It is her own decision. She is working as a medical officer for an American oil company.'

'Why did you let her go?'

'You must understand, she is an American citizen and free to do as she chooses. We cannot live her life for her. She was quite adamant. She still misses you badly. You should be flattered she still wants to be with you. She seems to think that being in Kuwait, being nearer to you, she will miss you less. It is called female logic.'

It was now five years since our parting, but I was as fond of her as ever. The idea of her being so close to Iraq made me uneasy.

Louis then gave me the name of a man, Nadhim, who belonged to an underground movement in Baghdad and informed me I would be contacted by him. Although the US did not want Saddam assassinated, they were well aware it could happen anyway, irrespective of their preferences.

'If Saddam is murdered it is imperative that Udai does not seize power,' Louis said. 'You stated your desire to have Udai removed. This may provide you with an opportunity to bring it about.'

I met with Nadhim. He was a man in his twenties, a Sunni Moslem and member of *al-Nahedha*, 'the Resurgence'. This group of determined young people had vowed to rid Iraq of the "Takriti vermin" and, disillusioned by the failure of the opposition Coalition parties to formulate a cohesive stance against Saddam, they had put their political differences to one side. They include Sunni and Shi'a Moslems, Kurds and senior army officers among their ranks.

I told Nadhim of Latif's plan to use me after Saddam's murder. He smiled. He knew all about me.

'Latif is one of us,' he said. 'Although he is our only Communist, our small organisation is largely his initiative. After he recovered from his ordeal, he spent a great deal of time with the Kurds. He was able to persuade Mohammed that an elite all-party group should be formed, whose sole preoccupation is removing the current regime by whatever means are necessary.'

It was obvious that Nadhim held Latif in the highest regard, for he spoke of him fondly.

'It is not possible for Latif to circulate in Baghdad at present. He is wanted for treason under two separate identities. He has, however, asked that you work with me as you once did with him.'

My innate caution made me question this statement.

'How do I know what you say is true?'

Nadhim tutted. 'Latif said you would be suspicious. He told me of the codename you dreamt up: "Cactus".'

'Louis could have given you that name. He is aware of it.'

Nadhim reflected for a moment. 'He told me you are a gentle man, who wishes no harm to any living thing. But he also told me how one night that was not the case. To prove my credentials, he said I should mention the name Kalid Fakher al-Takriti. You know Latif would only give such details to someone he could trust with his life.'

Significantly, Latif had not revealed this information to anyone, even when tortured by the Mukhabarat.

I nodded. 'That is proof enough.'

'An attempt will be made to assassinate Udai,' Nadhim then went on to tell me, 'when he is presenting honours degrees at the Mustansirriyah University in two days time.'

'I remember another assassination attempt taking place there,' I said. 'It must have been around 1980, I think.'

'Was it successful?'

'No. The target was Tariq Aziz.'

Before parting from Nadhim, I told him how the name 'Cactus' had come about and we discussed how I might let him know when I was standing in for Saddam. As Udai had threatened to ensure I was given no notice of such appearances, the Cactus routine would not work.

'When I began working for Saddam, my first tutor noticed that I had a habit of scratching my right ear when

I was nervous. I had never noticed it before and it has never been picked up since. I do not do it now, but if you see Saddam scratching his right ear, it is me you are looking at.'

Nadhim was dubious about this as a means of identifying myself. He pointed out that Saddam might well be troubled by an itchy right ear at the wrong moment. In the end, though, we decided it would have to do.

At the eleventh hour, I was instructed to accompany Udai at the university presentation, but I was to be in disguise; Saddam and Udai seldom appeared together in public at such functions. We drove there, thankfully, in separate cars and as I climbed out, I was scratching my ear furiously. The awards ceremony was being held in a large hall in the main building. As we entered, shots rang out. I immediately threw myself to the ground.

The shooting lasted for perhaps thirty seconds. When it was over, two of the would-be assassins escaped, but three were dead. Udai, much to my dismay, was still very much alive. I did not know if Nadhim was one of the dead men, but Udai was furious with his guards for failing to take any of the assassination squad alive. Now he would be deprived of the fun of interrogating them, though the bodies were sure to be mutilated before they were released for burial. Udai had to vent his frustration somehow.

Two days later, I met up with Nadhim. He had indeed been a member of the assassination party and had advised his associates to abandon the attack when he saw a man scratching his ear as if his life depended on it, which of course it did. His words went unheeded and though he had escaped, he had paid dearly. One of the dead men was his youngest brother, and he was taking it badly.

Udai sensed that, whether by chance or design, I led a charmed life. Accordingly, he requested permission from his father to have me escort him, as often as possible, when he appeared in public. It was for this reason that a heavily bearded man was seen so much in the company of Udai around this time.

I reminded Udai that an attempt had been made on his life at the university notwithstanding my presence.

'Yes,' he conceded. 'But it did not go unnoticed that the firing seemed to be directed at myself and the guards returning fire from my car, rather than those shooting by your side. A little strange, yes?'

I made no comment. Udai was far too observant for my liking.

'In future,' he said, 'you will escort me whenever I request it, unless you have prior obligations to Saddam.'

This assumption on Udai's part that I was hand-in-glove with every assassination attempt that took place was unnerving. Hashim was quick to point out that I should be grateful.

'If Udai is so convinced you are an enemy of the state, then under normal circumstances I would have said your days are numbered. However, despite his bluster, he is clearly a frightened man. Now he has a use for you and you must look on this as a stay of execution. Make the most of it. Your good fortune will not last forever, Mikhaelef.'

I was warned by Nadhim that another attempt would be made on Udai's life and as I was currently almost his constant companion, my presence would not be a deterrent.

'If you hear shooting, Mikhaelef, just dive to the ground. Scratching your ear will not save you. Also, it is unlikely I will be able to give you any notice of an attack.'

For the next three days, I lived in dread of being called by Udai. When finally the summons came, he told me he would be spending the Thursday (Khamis) evening at the Hunting Club in al-Mansur, alongside the racetrack and close to the apartment I lived in when I first came to Baghdad. Udai wanted me by his side and I was told to wear my disguise.

We had not been long at the club when Udai indicated to me we were leaving. Without alerting his guards, we left the club and went to Udai's car. I knew very well what he was up to. He wanted to cruise the streets looking for young women. He was notorious for this in Baghdad and most women did their best to avoid him if they recognised the car. Having found someone to his liking (*her* liking did not enter into the discussion), Udai would then make his way to the Mansur Miliyah Hotel, between the Sinak and Ahrahr bridges on Haifah Street, or the Palestine Meridian across the river on Abi Nuw'as Street.

We drove away from the club in Udai's Porsche at breakneck speed just before eight o'clock. Udai raced through the gears, accelerating without thought for the conditions. Fast driving was one of the joys of his life and he would not miss this opportunity to terrify me – not to mention other drivers and pedestrians. After a kilometre, we screeched to a halt at the traffic lights at Mansur Street and began to turn right in the direction of the city centre, just opposite the Russian Embassy and a police station. The road here provides Udai with a straight track in excess of three kilometres and he usually makes the most of it. What he could not have known was that he was driving his car for the last time.

Before Udai had completed his turn, another car raced across our path and skidded to a stop in front of us. An immaculate Toyota pick-up then suddenly appeared from a side street and blocked us in from behind. Three armed men emerged from each car, their lower faces covered by scarves. The three in the Toyota moved away from us and covered the area of attack. The others opened fire purposefully on Udai. All hell broke loose.

Udai went for the gun he always carried, but was too slow. He was shot four times within a matter of seconds and slumped forward across the steering wheel. I was sure I would be mistaken for one of Udai's guards and fully expected to be the gunmen's next target.

At that moment, a third car roared into the bloody scene, driven by one of Saddam's guards. No doubt he noticed his master's absence and was trying to do his job. The gunmen raised their weapons and fired on the car. The windscreen shattered and the car veered off the road and bounced off a low wall, before rolling over on its side.

One of the gunmen came up to Udai's car. Although the lower part of his face was covered by a scarf, the twinkle in his eyes told me this was Latif. He fired at the motionless Udai.

'For Salem!' he roared, and fired again. His shot struck Udai in the shoulder, half turning him so that his back was presented to Latif, if it was he. 'For Rafik and Abdullah!'

Latif was now close enough to reach inside the car. He nodded to me, the twinkle even more noticeable now.

'For Nadia and Salih,' he shouted, almost joyfully, as he pumped a bullet into Udai's back. Udai jolted with the impact, but he was now either dead or unconscious.

'For Amna!' Latif leaned inside the car and placed the muzzle of the gun against the back of Udai's head and said, his voice now low, almost a whisper, 'For Iraq.'

He squeezed the trigger but the chamber was empty. He swore under his breath then spun round as the guard, scrambling from the wreckage of his car, began to shoot. The other two gunmen, one of whom I took to be Nadhim, were quick to react and two shots rendered him *hors de combat*.

Latif looked at me as he reloaded. 'We have waited a long time for this day, Mikhaelef,' he said with jubilation.

His accomplices had already regained their car and were revving the engine. Latif saluted me with his gun and hurried away. A squeal of tyres and they were gone.

I looked at Udai's stricken body. Despite escaping the final bullet to the head, he had been hit too often to survive. I was convinced that even if he still lived, he would not last long.

At the conclusion of the gun battle, nothing happened for some minutes. People in the vicinity had raced for cover when the firing started and they seemed reluctant to leave it.

After a few minutes, a lone policeman emerged from the

station and called for assistance on his handset. Soon afterwards, police vehicles and cars began to pour into the area, sirens bleating, lights pulsating. Udai was loaded into one of the cars and rushed to the Ibn Siena Hospital. Despite my protestations that I was unharmed, I followed him a few minutes later.

Saddam was at the hospital within ten minutes, anxiously pacing outside the operating theatre as surgeons tried desperately to save his son's life. I estimated that he had been shot more than twenty times. Saddam confronted the Amn al-Khass officer, Ali Mohammed, who was in charge of the security around Udai. He made it clear the man's life, too, hung by a thread.

'If my son dies,' he roared at the terrified officer, 'you will die one minute later!'

The medical staff had higher priorities than my shattered nerves and I was soon discharged. I fully expected Udai to die and not until Hashim came to see me at home later that night did I learn that he was on the critical list, but still clinging tenuously to life. Over the next few days, conflicting reports filtered back from the hospital about his condition. Finally though, it was confirmed that not only would he live, but he had recovered to the point where he was talking lucidly and receiving visitors. It seemed that he had inherited his father's luck.

Then more details became known. It was stated in a news bulletin that he would be permanently crippled. In all, he had been shot many times. His left knee was shattered and the two bullets Latif had put into his back had lodged against his spine. He was paralysed from the waist down and the doubts were expressed that he would ever walk again. Surgeons could not agree on whether or not the spinal cord was severed. They were also reluctant to operate. With the facilities available to them, there was a distinct possibility they would do more damage than had already been done, and to fail would be to incur the wrath of Saddam. Not an outcome to be risked lightly.

Latif had come closer to killing Udai than any assassin

before him. Yet, the hard truth was that he had failed. Henceforth, Udai would be under round-the-clock protection. It was unlikely that another opportunity would occur for a long time to come, if ever.

Chapter Nineteen

1997
Sha'baan 1417 – Ramadan 1418

In the weeks following the assassination attempt, I was questioned at length by officers of the Mukhabarat, but provided no details that might incriminate Latif or Nadhim. They had no reason to suspect me of complicity, therefore the interrogation was benign. Early in the year, about a month after the attack took place, Saddam came to quiz me personally in the Dark Room. He looked drawn and tired. Frequently, he stretched his limbs as if to rid them of stiffness. However much of an encumbrance Udai had become, Saddam had clearly suffered great trauma as a result of his eldest son's brush with death. As he sat down, Hashim prepared to leave.

'No, stay,' Saddam said. 'I have nothing to discuss with my friend Mikhaelef, that you should not hear.' He turned to me. 'It is a great relief to me that you are unharmed, but as initial enquiries into the attack have produced no suspects, I would like to hear first hand what you may have seen.'

'Of course, Saddam,' I replied. Although I had half-expected this meeting for some time, I felt uneasy now that the moment had arrived.

'As you know, the bodyguard who arrived at the scene of the shooting is still in a coma,' Saddam said. 'We do not know if he will survive. Apart from what little Udai recalls, you are the only eye-witness.'

'That is correct,' I confirmed. I did not elaborate. Weary as Saddam appeared, it was not beyond him to lure me into a careless mistake.

'Udai has said there were three gunmen and you have corroborated that. We have also spoken to the doctor who was the first person on the scene. He was returning home to al-Adel having been working at the Yarmuk Hospital. He saw little of what happened, but says as he approached one of the gunmen was firing at Udai and shouting.'

'I recall him saying, "For Iraq",' I replied a little vaguely, hoping not to be pressed on this critical point. As I waited for his next question, I noticed an involuntary trembling of Saddam's hands. In the twenty years I had been close to him, shared many of his trials and tribulations, I had never noticed this phenomenon.

'Nothing else?'

I shook my head. 'I have no recollection of anything else, Saddam. But I had my mind on other things. It was a terrifying experience.'

'Of course, my friend.' Saddam sighed, his expression lugubrious. 'But I have to ask.'

He stood up abruptly, nodded to Hashim, and left. Hashim and I exchanged glances; he made a spread hands gesture. Saddam had seemed to accept my version of the incident, so I was reasonably sanguine that I had heard the last of the matter. I did not know at that time I had already said enough to fully incriminate myself in it.

'The President has taken this badly,' Hashim observed. 'I have never seen him so deflated.'

I grunted in agreement. Saddam was clearly stressed by recent events, but I only had to recall the grief inflicted on the lives of so many fathers whose sons had been savagely and brutally murdered at the hand of Saddam or his son, to dispel any compassion I might otherwise have felt for him. My part in the plot caused me no remorse.

I also thought of the rumours circulating in Baghdad that Saddam had ordered the shooting himself. According to the gossip, Saddam had ordered the assassins to fire low so as not to kill Udai, whom he wanted to teach a lesson. Although I knew the truth, anybody spending any time with the President would know that he had nothing to do with it.

Udai's shattered knee deteriorated and the doctors were not sure they could save the leg. He had flatly rejected amputation, but if gangrene set in, the decision would no longer be his to make. Shortly after the shooting, surgeons had been flown in from France, but they had refused to attempt the removal of the bullets close to his spine. As if to prove that his virility and strength were unimpaired, Udai had taken another wife – Najah Ali Hassan, the sixteen-year-old daughter of his father's 'cousin'. There is much speculation about whether or not Udai has ever been physically capable of consumating the marriage.

After his release from hospital in a wheelchair, he spent a few days with his girlfriend, Baidah's, at his al-Amiriya apartment. Subsequently, he was moved to the family compound at al-Jahdriya where he could be given full medical care and attention.

Saddam approached medical institutions all over the world in his quest for a top surgeon to operate on Udai's spinal injuries. After the refusal of the French, nearly everybody else said 'no'. The governments of both France and Spain, generally receptive to humanitarian appeals from Iraq, were diplomatically persuaded by some of their NATO allies to decline requests to admit Udai into their countries for treatment. A small number of doctors from the former German Democratic Republic were financially indebted to Saddam, and they duly arrived to operate on Udai's knee. As it turned out, even using sophisticated technology there was little they could do. If Udai ever recovered the use of his legs at all, he would be permanently crippled by his shattered knee. Even today, at the time of concluding this memoir, I am told that a possibility remains that the leg will have to be amputated from the thigh.

Despite being bound to a wheelchair, Udai's acts of violence worsened as he made some semblance of a recovery. In June, he flew into a rage and shot dead Kamil Mahmoud Sabah al-Jenabi, one of his guards. Kamil was a native of Takrit and a distant cousin of my good friend, Mohammed Qatasi. His family were told he had been murdered in the al-Dora district, where Udai has a farm, and that the murderer was still being sought. Shades of Amna's murder, I thought.

A month later, travelling into the city from his farm, Udai's eyes fell on a young woman by the name of Asil Salman al-Mansuri. He took an immediate fancy to her and instructed his guards to have her brought to al-Jahdriya. The terrified woman was subjected to a frenzied sexual ordeal during which Udai tried repeatedly to rape her, though how this could have been accomplished in his debilitated physical condition was not clear. In any event, although she was eventually overcome, he failed to consummate the act because of the impotence brought on by his injuries. In a fit of rage, he shot her dead. The woman came from a Christian family and they were threatened with their lives if they dared make public what had happened. As compensation for their loss they were given $700, a motor car and a 'pension' of $150 a month.

Saddam was the only person who had any control over Udai, but he was becoming increasingly disturbed by his son's insane behaviour. Little progress had been made in the investigation into the attempted murder of Udai and if I was disappointed that he had survived, I had the consolation that our paths rarely intersected these days.

In early October, I was summoned to Saddam's study. As I entered, I was surprised by the pleased look on his face. It was months since I had seen him so elated.

He greeted me warmly and asked after my health, encouraging signs.

'Sit down, Mikhaelef, my good friend, sit down. It is a beautiful morning, is it not?'

Indeed, the sun was shining and birdsong drifted through the open windows.

'It is, Saddam,' I replied. 'Quite beautiful.'

He beamed at me; I smiled cautiously back. 'You look pleased today. You have received good news, perhaps?'

Normally I would not venture such a personal enquiry, but when Saddam was in high spirits, he would forgive almost any infraction.

'Good news?' he exclaimed. 'Ha! I have received excellent news, my friend. The best news possible!'

I wondered what it could be. I was sure he would soon enlighten me.

He came around his desk and stooped over me, looking me full in the face. His dark, almost black eyes, seemed to penetrate my innermost thoughts.

'Can I trust you, my friend?' he said in a subdued tone. 'Are you really my loyal friend and ally?'

I had long ago learned the art of lying with a poker face.

'How can you ask me such a thing, Saddam? I have risked my life for you. Many times.'

'This is true, this is true. Very well. I am going to take you into my confidence, but first you must swear never to repeat beyond the walls of this room what I am about to tell you.'

Haltingly, I vowed never to speak of what he was about to tell me.

He went back behind his desk and unlocked the top right-hand drawer. From it he drew a bulky, leather-bound dossier, many pages thick. He subsided into his throne-like chair.

'Do not fear that I am going to read all of this to you,' he said with a chortle, tapping the dossier. 'A few pages will suffice. After that, you will know why this is the most important day in my life. In the life of Iraq!'

His hands once again showed that uncharacteristic tremble as he opened the dossier. Was this the early sign of some deep-seated disease, such as Alzheimer's? Or was it my imagination in conjunction with wishful thinking. Whichever it was, his brain seemed unimpaired as he began to quote from the opening page of the tome before him.

That evening, I talked to Hashim about the project that Saddam had been unable to resist boasting to me about. It transpired that Hashim was already aware of the broad principles, but had had no idea it was at such an advanced state. I decided not to pass the information to Louis for now. It was too big, too devastating for any one person to be entrusted with. I needed to think.

Weeks passed. I continued to report to Louis, feeding him mostly superficial intelligence of the day-to-day events within the palace. Not once I did not so much as hint at Saddam's project. My quandary remained unresolved.

Early in December, I spent an hour with Saddam in the Dark Room, going over the itinerary for the next few weeks. I was to substitute for him at several ceremonies and, as always, he wished to satisfy himself that I was word perfect. His mood was buoyant and animated.

'You look tired, my friend,' he said, quite cheerfully, a few minutes into our meeting. 'Are you not sleeping well?'

'I have not slept well for many years now, Saddam,' I replied. 'I am a simple man from Karbala. What has happened to me since we first met has taken its toll. I do not possess your resilience.'

'Yes, it is a fact. The people of Iraq may adore their President, but they do not know how many sacrifices must be made to lead this great nation.'

He eyed me with, I felt, a certain compassion.

'Perhaps I can suggest something which may lift you,' he went on. 'It is impossible to stem the ravages of ageing, but there are ways now where the process can be slowed. You will remember in 1980 you received some plastic surgery to your face.'

'Yes, of course, Saddam,' I replied, wondering what he

was leading up to. In the past ten years we had aged slightly differently, but our physical features remained as identical as a surgeon's knife could make them.

'I have recently asked Qusai to look into the possibility of bringing in some surgical equipment that will be of use to us both,' he said. 'Have you heard of liposuction?'

'I have, Saddam,' I replied, realising at once what he was about to suggest. 'But I have to confess I know almost nothing about it.'

'It is a simple process whereby a tube is inserted into different parts of the body and surplus fat is sucked away by vacuum. It is a much quicker process than dieting and has a particular use in our case. You may have noticed that your waistline has thickened more than mine and yet I seem to accumulate more weight here.' Saddam tapped the back of his hand under his chin. 'With liposuction, we can ensure that both our body weight and excess fat distribution remains very much the same. What do you think?'

Why he might have imagined that the idea of submitting to such a disgusting process would 'lift' me, was beyond my comprehension. On the contrary, I was nauseated by it. To object, though, would have been futile. 'When will this equipment be here?' I asked resignedly.

'Quite soon, I believe,' Saddam said. 'Qusai is trying to locate a supplier now. We face so many restrictions, it is not likely we would be permitted to import it legally as necessary medical equipment, but in the end we may have no choice but to try that route. We will see how Qusai gets on first. How do you feel about it?'

'I have no objection,' I lied.

Satisfied with my response, Saddam clapped his hands and departed. As I watched him leave the room, I was not to know that I would never see him again.

The following evening, I heard a car pulling up in the driveway of my house near midnight. I looked out of the window to see Hashim walking up the driveway. He had never before called in person at so late an hour and I wondered what it could be that he could not have telephoned. As I opened the door, he raised a finger to his lips before I could speak and beckoned me to join him in the car, which I did. As I slammed the door shut, he drove away in a great hurry.

'The guard who has been in a coma since the shooting is now talking,' he said urgently. 'You are incredibly lucky I heard of this so quickly. Apparently, he did not lose consciousness until after Udai was hit. He remembers Latif firing. Of more importance to you, Mikhaelef, he remembers what he was shouting.'

My heart froze. 'He remembers names?'

'Yes. Amna, Abdullah, Salem, Nadia and Saleh. Saddam will realise the gunman was Latif, but that in itself does not incriminate you. He has known of your brother-in-law's obsession with killing Udai for some time and has never blamed you. But this time he asked you the names he was shouting. You said you did not know. Your time is up, Mikhaelef. You have to go now.'

Once I had recovered from the initial shock, it was a relief to know that at last I would be leaving Iraq, that the decision had been made for me.

Hashim then told me that Nadhim, who had only narrowly escaped on the day of the shooting, had been arrested by the Mukhabarat. The other five 'would-be' assassins were out of the country.

'You can be sure that if Saddam has not yet been informed of what the guard has said, he will at any time. I fear that your friend Nadhim is in for a rough ride. If I am somehow able to get word to him that you are safe, it means he will be able to reveal what he knows about you without going to hell and back first. It will not save him, but it may mean the end will be a little less agonising.'

'Where shall I go?' I said. I admit, with some shame, to thinking more of my own immediate predicament than the one confronting Nadhim.

'You have to leave Baghdad without a moment's delay,' Hashim said firmly. 'That much is certain. How do you contact the American in emergencies?'

'I have a telephone number.'

'Good. We will leave the city first. Then call him. Arrange to meet him somewhere in the north.'

We stopped at Khan al-Mashahida, sixty kilometres outside the city, and I called Louis, telling him what had happened.

'You were right to leave Baghdad straight away,' he said. 'We now have to get you out of Iraq as quickly as possible. Your days as an agent are over.'

I was not disappointed to hear it.

He gave me an address in al-Mawsil, which I cannot reveal, and told me he would meet me there the following morning. After clearing it with Louis, I then telephoned the number Mohammed had given me and gave word where I was heading.

During the drive to al-Mawsil, I once again brought up the subject of Hashim leaving Iraq with me.

'You will be in great danger once my defection is known,' I pointed out to him.

He did not dispute it, but reiterated his other considerations. 'I cannot leave my family to face the consequences of fleeing Iraq for my own safety. I am still an officer of the Mukhabarat, Mikhaelef. Potentially, I can cause the regime enormous embarrassment by revealing to the Western media all I know. I could tell the UN Commission on Human Rights of incidents that would induce nightmares.'

I nodded. 'I have seen some of those things too.'

'Yes, Mikhaelef, but only as an occasional observer. You may not be believed. You may be seen as having your own agenda to pursue. I took part in these horrors. In revealing all I know, I have to face demons of my own. I cannot go. If I am suspected of having assisting you, then I must face those consequences. I cannot allow my family to be punished for what I have done.'

It occurred to me that Hashim, for all the ignominy of his background, was a very brave man.

'If you are arrested, what makes you think your family will be safe?'

This was a dilemma with which Hashim had wrestled before. 'I am in too deep. I cannot cover every angle, but on balance I will endanger my family more if I leave.'

'Then you must take your family with you.'

'That is easy to say, Mikhaelef. It would take time and an organisation. I have neither.'

'Once I am out of Iraq, I can make the arrangements for you and your family to follow me.'

Hashim would not be persuaded, but agreed that I should organise somewhere for his family to flee if ever he were arrested.

We arrived at the apartment in al-Mawsil just as the rim of sun was peeking over the Zaghrous mountains. Louis was already there, as was Mohammed. A man and woman also present were, I assumed, the inhabitants of the apartment.

Hashim stayed only long enough to be sure I was in safe hands before announcing his departure.

'I will have to go straight to your house as if to pick you up as normal,' he explained. 'Your disappearance will not be well received.'

This was a considerable understatement. I embraced Hashim and thanked him.

'Be careful,' I warned him. 'These are dangerous times.'

'They have always been dangerous times. You watch out for yourself, Mikhaelef. I will be fine.'

'I will send a message when I am safe. I will find a way.'

When Hashim had gone, I sat with Louis and Mohammed to discuss the next move. A knock at the door had Louis on his feet, gun drawn. The woman went to answer it.

'Put your gun away,' Mohammed said to Louis. 'This is someone Mikhaelef will be very pleased to see.'

As I looked towards the door, in walked Latif. I was overjoyed to see him and amazed at how well he looked. Apart from seeing him briefly during the attempt on Udai's life the previous December, we had not been together for three years. I jumped to my feet, and we embraced heartily.

'It is good to see you, Mikhaelef,' he said, a broad smile breaking across his face. 'You stubborn old dog!'

As we stood grinning foolishly at each other, I asked him how he came to be here.

'I am coming with you. At least part of the way.'

'I am surprised. I thought you would never leave Iraq.'

'I am too well known to the authorities now. I am a liability to my own friends. Anybody who helps me is placing themselves in great danger. There is much work to be done outside Iraq.'

We returned to the subject of our escape from Iraq. Mohammed suggested our best hope of crossing the border was at the Military Coalition Centre (MCC), a large air base and office complex in the Liberated Zone at Zakhu. The best way to pass into the LZ was over the mountains north of al-Mawsil.

'We have an old saying: "The Kurds have no friends but the mountains." '

Louis agreed with his suggestion, and proposed that we enter Turkey where we would be met by the Americans and taken to Inkjerlik, a US air base, 700 kilometres to the west in south-west Turkey.'

The following morning, we drove north towards Duhok, making our way over the mountains and into the Liberated Zone on foot. With us was Mohammed Mahmoud and a formidable escort of twenty armed peshmerga, but they were not needed. We entered the LZ near the town and were collected by a fleet of PUK vehicles. From there we were driven into Zahu.

Arriving at the enormous MCC, we pulled over and climbed out of the car. Mohammed came over to me and shook my hand.

'Good luck, Mikhaelef,' he said with genuine feeling. 'I hope your life will be a little quieter now.'

Before I could reply, I caught sight of Louis emerging from the WCC entrance. He beckoned both Latif and myself to hurry.

'Thank you for your help, Mohammed,' I said finally.

We embraced and I walked away towards Louis. Latif, too, made his brief farewells and as we entered the WCC, we both stole glances over our shoulder. Our thoughts were surely the same: that never again would we stand on Iraqi soil.

Despite the agonies he had suffered, Latif felt no relief at leaving Iraq. He had dedicated his life to making his homeland a better place and to a man like him, departure was defeat.

'Will we ever go back, Mikhaelef?' he mused.

'Only Allah knows,' I replied.

With that, we entered the complex and boarded a Sikorsky helicopter without markings. From there we were flown 700 kilometres west to the US air base at Inkjerlik in south-west Turkey, the largest of its kind in the Middle East. Iraq was quite suddenly a long way behind me.

Epilogue

Waiting for me was Sophie.

We had not seen each other for six years and the joy of our re-union proved too much for her, who openly wept onto my shoulder as we held each other tightly. Through her tears, she playfully complemented me on my beard, and was relieved to find it was not permanently affixed to my chin. It was truly wonderful to see her again. Many was the time during those six interminable years when I had resigned myself to never holding her in my arms again.

After allowing us our moment of joy, Louis tactfully intervened, stressing that there were urgent matters to which both Latif and myself had to attend. At Inkjerbal, we were questioned by a group of Americans in smart suits for the first of many times. I was asked many questions and went over the same ground repeatedly. I became frustrated when the suggestion was made that I was not fleeing Saddam at all, but was in fact a 'spy' for the regime. My interrogators tried to trick me and I was asked a score of questions in which I saw no sense or relevance.

Finally, that first session ended and I was told I would be flown with Sophie and Latif to North America. We stopped first at London Heathrow, where we spent four hours in the transit area, before flying across the Atlantic Ocean to a city I will not name. Once there, we were picked up by an Iraqi couple, both now naturalised citizens of their new homeland, and taken to their house, a three hour drive from the airport. The couple were enormously sympathetic to Sophie and myself, having themselves arrived as exiles twenty years ago, when my own story began. Some weeks later we were moved to another 'safe' house.

Since my arrival, I have lived under an alias and for the purposes of this book, have adopted a more Westernised version of my name: Mikhael Ramadan. My relationship with Sophie has been difficult at times, although our love for each other has not diminished. She endured horrors in Iraq which have mentally scarred her, and she will never be quite the same person I met in the Kuwaiti hospital. She is, understandably, more withdrawn and introvert than she once was, and I cannot say how the future will work out. Nevertheless, we remain devoted to each and perhaps the strength we derive from our shared experience will help pull us through. Although, as a US citizen, she is free to come and go as she pleases, she chooses to stay by my side.

Latif was initially placed with another Iraqi couple thirty kilometres away. Later, in the interests of security, he too was transferred to another location, but we are still able to see each other occasionally. He soon became involved with the Iraqi opposition movements when we arrived here, though he only communicates with them via the internet, saying nothing about who he is and what he did when in Iraq. He believes the opposition in exile has been infiltrated at all levels by Saddam's agents and only Sophie and myself are aware of his background.

The activities of Saddam's overseas agencies are well documented in the Western media. After the Gulf War, much of Iraq's complex overseas intelligence network was broken down, but there clear indications that it is recovering its pre-war reputation. In January, shortly after my arrival here, I read that seven men and a woman, including an Iraqi diplomat, had been tortured and butch-ered in Amman at the home of an Iraqi businessman. One of the victims was believed to have connections with Hussein Kamil and the murders bore all the hallmarks of the Mukhabarat. In April, a Jordanian lawyer who was thought to have advised Hussein Kamil on handling his fortune, was murdered with his son when visiting his doctor. The doctor was killed also. There were several incidents, most notably in London, of exiled dissidents being poisoned with thallium, a rat poison, causing the victims to collapse in agony. Many died. Nowhere is completely safe from Saddam's reach.

I have seriously considered applying for political asylum here and have been urged to do so by the people I live with. My visa, for what it was worth, expired in June and I am now an illegal alien. I am not prepared to reveal my whereabouts, but I could legitimise my presence here by marrying Sophie. Unless I use my real name, the marriage would be meaningless and since I am loathe to reveal my presence here, marriage and legitimacy must wait.

Apart from my fear of Saddam's agents, I am far from confident that the US government would be sympathetic to my plight. There are presently six Iraqi dissidents in jail in Los Angeles facing deportation back to Iraq. Each of them has dedicated their lives to the overthrow of Saddam and will without question be executed if they return. One of the men is Dr Ali Yassin Mohammed Karim, a Kurdish physician who was once the private doctor of Ahmad al-Chalabi, head of the Iraqi National Congress, the most active of the opposition groups in exile.

Another, Safa al-Din al-Batat, was one of the leaders of the post-Gulf war Shi'a revolt in 1991. He was wounded in an assassination attempt on Saddam in 1994 and was poisoned by the Mukhabarat with thallium, but survived. The full facts are not in my possession, as I have no contact with the Iraqi National Congress, but as I understand it, the US Government has decided to deport the men without due process and with no grounds for appeal. The case against them cannot be scrutinised as the charges are classified. Suffice it to say that these men were far more active against Saddam than I ever was, so what chance would I have of being allowed to stay?

I did not initially intend to reveal the part Hashim played in my story, but I have recently heard he has fled Iraq and is in London. I would guess that, given his long association with the Mukhabarat, the British are treating him suspiciously and his fate seems very uncertain. I pray for him.

Abdullah Yunis has fled Iraq also, although he is still on the Arab peninsula with his wife, Amina. He desperately wants to meet up with me, and has indicated he is prepared to join me here. I hope that can soon be arranged. For this information regarding Hashim and Abdullah, I am indebted to Louis, whom I have spoken to twice since I came to this place. Despite his reticence on the subject, I always assumed he was working for the CIA, but subsequent events make this unlikely. When we were in Iraq, he sometimes referred to my being debriefed by American Intelligence agents if and when I ever got out. When I raised the subject on each of his two visits, he seemed reluctant to take it further. Louis is then a mystery. I do not know who employs him, or indeed if he is an independent agent selling his services to the highest bidder. Certainly, his is funded. I have still have the original $5,000 he gave me when we first met.

Because of the uncertainty about him and his motives, I am now glad I did not pass on what I learned from Saddam about his intentions towards the West. I have been reluctant to disclose it to anyone for fear of triggering an over-reaction by the UN, with God knows what consequences. Most nights I lay awake, trembling at the potential outcome if Saddam goes ahead with his vendetta against the democracies. It was fear of this that motivated me to tell my story and release it to the world. I feel I cannot trust governments or Iraqi opposition groups. I have no choice but, through the handful of friends I have, to let my memoirs be published so that the people of the world can make their own judgement.

I therefore return to my meeting with Saddam, almost the last occasion we were alone together. I was not allowed to sight the dossier he so boastfully quoted from. Nor do I remember the fine detail, only the broad sweep of what was itself a précis. Later that day though, I filled both sides of a sheet of notepaper with a private code. This document I kept thereafter in a hidden compartment in my wallet. It is from these notes that the final section of this book is extracted.

When Saddam opened the dossier with a lightly trembling hand, I had wondered again if I was looking at a man stricken with some insidious affliction. There were no other outward signs, yet some instinct told me that he was not well.

'I will not bore you with the technical data, my friend,' he said. 'This will be a layman's resumé.' He flipped past the first two pages and began reading from the third. The essence of the introduction was that, as a result of the United Nations Security Council's persistent restraints on its sovereignty and legitimate right to defend its borders, Iraq had initiated a programme, in collaboration with another state [not identified], to relocate its research facilities beyond its national boundaries.

A list of potential sites was currently under review. Once suitable sites had been selected the laboratories would be set up and the technical staff deployed. This part of the programme was scheduled for completion by mid-1998, and was referred to by Saddam as Point One.

Free of UN inspectors' interference, the development of the SV1417 strain of the West Nile virus was to be accelerated. In order to satisfy the potential requirements outlined in Section 'X' of the dossier [the reference was stated but I cannot recollect it], it is estimated that the research will be completed within two years, and stock-piling of the virus will require a further twelve months. This three-year term was referred to as Point Two.

Up to late 1997 the practical value of the virus SV1417 had been limited by Iraq's inability to influence the degree and extent of contamination. No control could be exercised over the natural physical conditions that deter-mine its direction and distance capability. It was also beyond the ability of our scientists to predict the longevity and full potential of the virus in optimum climatic condi-tions. According to Saddam, it has the capacity to destroy as much as 90% of all life in an urban environment, but until a few months ago the means did not exist to protect the Iraqi people and those of our allies.

New developments have removed these constraints. The almost accidental discovery of a fully efficient and economically viable antidote, means that protection from the virus can be guaranteed. Within the terms of Point Two, it was estimated that the antidote could be produced in sufficient quantity to protect the lives of thirty million people from the effects of the SV1417 virus. Full logistical details of distribution of the antidote are given in Section 'Y'.

Saddam went on to explain to me that the SV1417 was to be operationally tested on an urban development with a population of no less than 100,000 persons and no more than 250,000, within a third world environment, probably about two years from then, that is early in the year 2000.

'Has the target been selected?' I asked timorously, certain in my mind that he would withhold that informa-tion.

He looked smug. 'Certainly, but it is not for your innocent ears.'

Cleverly, responsibility for the act would be diverted away from Iraq by the formation of a bogus terrorist group, with no known political affiliation or national cause. Evidence would be left at the scene to implicate this make-believe organisation. More proof of the boundless cunning of Saddam Hussein.

Once sufficient stocks of the virus and antidote have been accumulated, Saddam's agents will be sent out to release the virus at specified locations throughout the world. A list of primary and secondary international targets and the estimated loss of life for each was included in an appendix to the document, which he did not read to me. This part of the process was designated Point Three. Before releasing the virus, an announcement will be made to the United Nations to the effect that Iraq possesses both the means to wipe out the populations of entire continents and the antidote against it. The announcement will be followed by a series of ultimata, to be known as Point Four.

Saddam broke off reading abruptly, to bestow his famous broad smile on me.

'I could go on,' he said, 'but I think that is enough to whet your appetite, and for you to appreciate the extent of the unlimited power I will wield once this weapon is ready. You know, my friend, power is not about having the ability to destroy, it is about the willingness to use it without qualm or discrimination.'

The threat that Saddam now presents to the entire world compels me to reveal that which I swore not to reveal. The decision to recount the near-twenty year period of my life in Saddam's service was made in the hope that my warning would be taken seriously. The danger is imminent and of unprecedented enormity. While there is time, it is to be hoped that the governments of the West will listen and act.

Index

Some Iraqis do not use their family or tribal surnames. Therefore, all arabs have been listed in the index by their first forename, e.g. Saddam Hussein

321